AI-Based Data Analytics

This book covers various topics related to marketing and business analytics. It explores how organizations can increase their profits by making better decisions in a timely manner through the use of data analytics. This book is meant for students, practitioners, industry professionals, researchers, and academics working in the field of commerce and marketing, big data analytics, and organizational decision-making. Highlights of the book include:

- The role of Explainable AI in improving customer experiences in e-commerce
- Sentiment analysis of social media
- Data analytics in business intelligence
- Federated learning for business intelligence
- AI-based planning of business management
- An AI-based business model innovation in new technologies
- An analysis of social media marketing and online impulse buying behaviour

AI-Based Data Analytics: Applications for Business Management has two primary focuses. The first is on analytics for decision-making and covers big data analytics for market intelligence, data analytics and consumer behavior, and the role of big data analytics in organizational decision-making. The book's second focus is on digital marketing and includes the prediction of marketing by consumer analytics, web analytics for digital marketing, smart retailing, and leveraging web analytics for optimizing digital marketing strategies.

AI-Based Data Analytics
Applications for Business Management

Edited by
Kiran Chaudhary and Mansaf Alam

CRC Press
Taylor & Francis Group
Boca Raton London New York

CRC Press is an imprint of the
Taylor & Francis Group, an **informa** business

AN AUERBACH BOOK

First edition published 2024
by CRC Press
2385 NW Executive Center Drive, Suite 320, Boca Raton FL 33431

and by CRC Press
4 Park Square, Milton Park, Abingdon, Oxon, OX14 4RN

CRC Press is an imprint of Taylor & Francis Group, LLC

ISBN: 978-1-032-41176-7 (hbk)
ISBN: 978-1-032-61407-6 (pbk)
ISBN: 978-1-032-61408-3 (ebk)

DOI: 10.1201/9781032614083

Typeset in Times
by KnowledgeWorks Global Ltd.

Contents

Preface

This book offers worldwide visibility and promotion of their novel ideas and insights on different aspects of the theme. Data analytics, business, and marketing are interdisciplinary fields about processes and systems to extract knowledge or insights from data.

This book is focused on Artificial Intelligence (AI), Data Analytics, Sentiment Analysis for social media, and various approaches to AI in Business Management. This is an emerging field that can increase the performance management domain to improve understanding of business and marketing dynamics that can lead to better strategic decision-making. In this book, we have also given a variety of marketing and business analytics strategies to solve market and organizational challenges. The use of AI in business and marketing analytics can help to create value by proper allocation of all available resources. By using various techniques and tools of Big data analytics, we can improve the performance of the business.

The objective of this book is to explore the concept and applications related to marketing and business management. Besides this, it shall also provide future research directions in this domain. This book is meant for students, practitioners, industry professionals, researchers, and faculty working in the field of commerce, marketing, computer science, data analytics with AI, and wide-ranging elucidation to organizational strategic decision-making. This book includes both aspects of AI-based marketing and business that are helpful for business management to prolong in the marketplace by creating value.

The book is organized into 14 chapters: Use of AI in E-Commerce, Sentiment Analysis of Social Media with AI, Unlocking the Power of Explainable AI to Improve Customer Experiences in E-Commerce, Business Intelligence, Sentiment Analysis of Social Media: Bibliometric Analysis, Exploring Hugging Face Transformer Library Impact on Sentiment Analysis: A Case Study, Data Analytics in Business Intelligence, Federated Learning for Business Intelligence: Predictive Maintenance in Industry 4.0, Role of IoT in Smart Cities: Proliferation and Challenges, AI-Based Planning of Business Management, AI-Based Business Model Innovation in New Technologies, Cloud Computing: Storage Management, Security, and Privacy, Social Media Marketing and Online Impulse Buying Behaviour: An Analysis through Website Quality as Moderator, and Effect of Blockchain Technology on the Future of E-Commerce in India.

Kiran Chaudhary
Shivaji College, University of Delhi, New Delhi

Mansaf Alam
Jamia Millia Islamia, New Delhi

Acknowledgements

First and foremost, we humbly begin this acknowledgement by expressing our deepest gratitude to God, the ultimate source of wisdom, inspiration, and guidance.

We would like to express my deepest gratitude and appreciation to all those who have contributed to the creation of this book. Without their support, guidance, and encouragement, this endeavour would not have been possible.

We would particularly like to express our gratitude to Jitesh Kumar, Senior General Manager, NTPC Ltd, for his constant encouragement. We would also like to thank Prof. Haroon Sajjad and Dr. Arshad Khan, Jamia Millia Islamia, New Delhi for their unconditional support.

We owe my heartfelt thanks especially to research scholars, Manzoor Ansari, Nabeela Hasan, and other research scholars, BDCC lab of Department of Computer Science, Jamia Millia Islamia, New Delhi, for their constant support and selfless effort throughout the journey of writing this book.

Lastly, we wish to acknowledge and appreciate the Taylor and Francis team, Shivaji College, University of Delhi and Jamia Millia Islamia for their continuous support throughout the entire process of publication. Our gratitude is extended to the readers, who gave us their trust, and we hope this work guides and inspires them.

Kiran Chaudhary
Shivaji College, University of Delhi
New Delhi

Mansaf Alam
Jamia Millia Islamia
New Delhi

List of Abbreviations

AI	Artificial intelligence
ANN	Artificial neural network
API	Application programming interface
AR	Augmented reality
BI	Business intelligence
CLV	Customer lifetime value
DDoS	Distributed denial of services
DL	Deep learning
DNN	Deep neural networks
DPC	Distinct product category
DSS	Decision support systems
DT	Decision tree
DW	Data warehouse
EIS	Executive information systems
ELA	Explainable logical networks
ENA	Explainable neural networks
EPU	Economic policy uncertainty
ERN	Explainable rule networks
ERP	Enterprise resource planning
ESL	Explainable supervised learning
EUL	Explainable unsupervised learning
FAW	Fusion analytics warehouse
FL	Federated language
FML	Federated machine learning
GAN	Generative adversarial networks
GPT	Generative pre-trained transformer
GUI	Graphical user interface
IIoT	Industrial Internet of Things
IoT	Internet of things
KPI	Key performance indicators
LIME	Local interpretable model-agnostic explanation
LSTM	Long short-term memory
ML	Machine learning networks
NLG	Natural language generation
NLP	Natural language processing
NLQ	Natural language query
OAC	Oracle analytics cloud
OAS	Oracle analytics server
OEE	Overall equipment effectiveness
OIB	Online impulse buying
OIBB	Online impulse buying behaviour
OLAP	Online analytic processing

PATE-GANS	Private Aggregation of Teacher Ensembles with Generative Adversarial
PCA	Principal component analysis
RFID	Radio frequency identification
RL	Reinforcement learning
SMM	Social media marketing
SMPC	Secure multi-party computation
SVD	Singular value decomposition
SVM	Support vector machine
TAS	Trend in amount spent
USP	Unique selling proposition
VR	Virtual reality
WQ	Website quality
WSIN	Word–Sentence Interaction Network
WSN	Wireless sensor network
XAI	Explainable AI

About the Editors

Dr. Kiran Chaudhary is working as an Associate Professor in the Department of Commerce, Shivaji College, University of Delhi. She has completed a Ph.D. in Marketing (Commerce) from Kurukshetra University, Kurukshetra, Haryana. Her area of research includes Big Data Analytics, Artificial Intelligence, Cyber Security, Marketing, Human Resource Management, Organizational Behaviour, Business, and Corporate law. She has published a book on Probability and Statistics. She has published several research articles in reputed International Journals and Proceedings of reputed International conferences published. She is an editor books entitled *Big Data Analytics: Applications in Business and Marketing* and *Big Data Analytics: Digital Marketing and Decision Making* by Taylor and Francis and *Developing Entrepreneurial Ecosystems in Academia* by IGI Global Publisher. She also organized a special session on Big Data Analytics and Artificial Intelligence in Business and Marketing in the International Conference on Data Analytics and Management-ICDAM-2021, which will be published by Springer. She delivered various National and International invited talks. She has chaired sessions at various international conferences. She recently received an International Patent (Australian) on An Artificial Intelligence-Based Smart Dustbin.

Prof. Mansaf Alam has been working as a Professor in the Department of Computer Science, Faculty of Natural Sciences, Jamia Millia Islamia, New Delhi; Young Faculty Research Fellow, DeitY, Govt. of India; and Editor-in-Chief, *Journal of Applied Information Science*. He has published several research articles in reputed International Journals and Proceedings at reputed International conferences published by IEEE, Springer, Elsevier Science, and ACM. His area of research includes Artificial Intelligence, Big Data Analytics, Machine Learning and Deep Learning, Cloud Computing, and Data Mining. He is a reviewer of various journals of international repute, like *Information Science*, published by Elsevier Science. He is also a member of the program committee of various reputed international conferences. He is on the Editorial Board of some reputed Intentional Journals in Computer Sciences. He has published three books: *Digital Logic Design by PHI, Concepts of Multimedia by Arihant,* and *Internet of Things: Concepts and Applications* by Springer and *Big Data Analytics: Applications in Business and Marketing* and *Big Data Analytics: Digital Marketing and Decision Making* by Taylor and Francis. He recently received an International Patent (Australian) on An Artificial Intelligence-Based Smart Dustbin.

Contributors

Lakshay Agarwal
UPES University
Dehradun, India

Syed Arshad Ali
Sharda University
Greater Noida, India

Manzoor Ansari
Jamia Millia Islamia
New Delhi, India

Nitin Arora
Indian Institute of Technology
Roorkee, India

Shivani Arora
Delhi University
Delhi, India

Manoj Bansal
Chaudhary Devi Lal University
Sirsa, India

Varun Barthwal
H.N.B. Garhwal University
Srinagar, India

Taran Singh Bharati
Jamia Millia Islamia
New Delhi, India

Prerana Chaha
UPES University
Dehradun, India

Richa Chaudhary
UPES University
Dehradun, India

Aashita Chhabra
Jamia Millia Islamia
New Delhi, India

Shilpi Chhabra
University of Delhi
Delhi, India

Charu Gupta
UPES University
Dehradun, India

Deepti Gupta
Institute of Innovation in Technology
    and Management
Delhi, India

Kingsley T. Igulu
Ignatius Ajuru University of Education
Port Harcourt, Nigeria

Naman Jain
UPES University
Dehradun, India

Palimote Justice
Kenule Beeson Saro-Wiwa Polytechnic
Bori, Nigeria

Supriya Kamna
University of Delhi
Delhi, India

Satinder Kumar
Punjabi University
Patiala, India

Saurabh Kumar
Sharda University
Greater Noida, India

Sushma Malik
Institute of Innovation in Technology
    and Management
Delhi, India

Meera Mehta
Delhi University
Delhi, India

Friday E. Onuodu
University of Port Harcourt
Port Harcourt, Nigeria

Ebenezer Osuigbo
Kenule Beeson Saro-Wiwa Polytechnic
Bori, Nigeria

Sandip Rakshit
The Business School
RMIT University
Ho Chi Minh City, Vietnam

Anamika Rana
Maharaja Surajmal Institute
Delhi, India

ManMohan Singh Rauthan
H.N.B. Garhwal University
Srinagar, India

Chhavi Sharma
University of Delhi
Delhi, India

Anupam Singh
University of Petroleum and Energy
    Studies
Dehradun, India

Niharika Singh
University of Petroleum and Energy
    Studies
Dehradun, India

Thipendra P. Singh
UPES University
Dehradun, India

Rajeshwari Sissodia
H.N.B. Garhwal University
Srinagar, India

Ary Soro Utami
Alumnus of UNISULLA
Semarang, Indonesia

Ashutosh Yadav
Hansraj College
University of Delhi
Delhi, India

1 Use of AI in E-Commerce

Rajeshwari Sissodia, ManMohan Singh Rauthan, and Varun Barthwal
Hemvati Nandan Bahuguna Garhwal
University, Srinagar, India

1.1 INTRODUCTION

Artificial intelligence (AI) is used in every industry, including education, business applications, manufacturers, product operating procedures, marketing, consumer behavior research, data recording–related sales, compared with competitors, natural language processing, and in all other areas. AI plays a key role in the worldwide competitive economy. Complex problems can be handled in a nanosecond by utilizing AI. Before selling items, every business owner engages the marketplace through offering a high-quality product and fulfilling the needs, wants, and desires of consumers. All actions are undertaken in accordance with consumer specifications. Because client satisfaction is the major objective of every business, when introducing a new product to the market, every entrepreneur observes consumer behavior. Regarding their product, customers employ a variety of strategies, procedures, and technology. E-commerce is essential. With the use of e-commerce, marketers can easily deliver products to consumers, and consumers may save time by purchasing items online. AI enables e-commerce companies to effortlessly capture the market, earn a profit, and promptly answer the requests, requirements, desires, and ambitions of customers [1–10]. The businessman combines AI and e-commerce to improve sales since AI merges human intelligence into computers and robots. The current era prioritizes electronic transactions and employs AI to provide consumers with ever-increasing convenience. AI supports the adoption of cost-effective and efficient production procedures and methods.

1.2 SIGNIFICANCE OF AI ON E-COMMERCE

The businessmen's usages of AI and e-commerce have helped them in providing client satisfaction. E-commerce has progressed based only on consumer's timely changes in trends, customs, designs, and styles; however, with the help of AI, inventive new concepts have been adopted to analyze consumers' buying behavior and, depending on consumers' demands, build items. Value and earnings are dependent on the selling of products and services through promotional instruments and the deployment of efficient advertising tactics for sales and marketing. A company uses AI and e-commerce to reach its intended customer through a variety of channels, including media, advertisement, and good marketing material.

AI has an effect on e-commerce since customers are always monarchs of the market. Online shopping is emphasized more due to the ease it affords the consumer. AI has also an advantage for an illiterate person who cannot write, as those who can utilize the speech search bar to make a purchase and fulfill their wishes and needs for new items according to their needs, wants, and desires and use a laptop or Android phone, making it simpler for customers to visit the store without wasting time and accomplish this through the use of e-commerce.

E-commerce also allows the advertiser to analyze customer purchasing patterns based on the sort of consumer needs and demand for a particular product that the manufacturer has recognized and manufactured. For marketers to effectively capture the market and compete, customers must also be satisfied. When consumers are hesitant to acquire a company's products, the media helps persuade them to do so through the use of digital marketing strategies and advertising. App development is a component of the marketing plan that enables consumers and prospects to purchase a specific product at a specified location. AI is a cost-effective approach for promoting consumers to buy a particular consumable item. A consumer will purchase a product based on their needs, desires, and wants. Not only is the product easily available for purchase but its pricing may also be compared to that of competing products. Now that the company has consumer feedback, it may seek to improve the quality of its products and provide details about the product and the kinds of testing it has undergone through advertising.

- **Recommendations engines:** AI meets the wants and requirements of every individual. As a result of producing the items that employees need and the final commodities that will be delivered to customers' windows, companies are making the goods. As a result, companies like Amazon, Snapdeal, and several others recruited too many individuals to sell their goods and attract more customers through the creation of new strategies and the convincing of consumers to acquire their particular products. Sometimes consumers are willing to purchase but lack sufficient time; AI supports these consumers. Their needs and desires have been entirely satisfied.
- **Virtual assistance:** It is used for creating a list of students who purchase the products and place orders for home delivery. AI is able to assess the purchasing behavior of consumers to purchase the specified goods and services.
- **Products:** These are useful for predicting prospects who convert readily to consumers. All reputable organizations use these tactics and methods to study consumer behavior.
- **Chatbots based on artificial intelligence:** No discussion of AI in e-commerce would be complete without mentioning chatbots. AI plays a significant role in e-commerce since consumers can readily collect knowledge about products and company history by visiting corporate websites or links. In addition to providing a quality product, chatbots may also give consumers comfort. Consequently, a company's goodwill is enhanced if its product is readily accepted by consumers.

1.3 USE OF AI

AI opens a new avenue for the growth of a business hub. In the present period, competition is excessive, and every businessperson strives to grab the market to maximize profits. Every consumer goods corporation that has successfully integrated AI technology into multiple business elements, marketing analytics forecasts and forecasting of purchaser activities and invention preferences, are made with the help of AI. AI is utilized for fraud detection, tailored advertising, marketing communications, and customer service, among other applications.

E-commerce is very helpful for both consumers and businesses. This is because both parties use e-commerce and AI to easily reach their own goals. For example, AI helps consumers save time and buy goods from the comfort of their own homes, while AI also helps businesses give consumers unique product features to improve their reputation and make it easier to compete. Moreover, conquer the entire market. Many organizations that conduct online commerce, such as Myntra and Snapdeal, face competitions that require them to employ double algorithms and appoint personnel on the job in order to evaluate the effectiveness of those who do not reach their goals easily. AI retains all associated records.

1.4 AI IS A FOUNDATION OF E-COMMERCE

AI is incredibly advantageous for all businesses since the customer is always king of the market. To meet the consumer's needs and expectations, businesses must understand the consumer's wants and needs, as well as why a consumer purchases a specific product. This will help expand the firm and persuade consumers to purchase the manufactured items. AI is constantly at work to facilitate the production process and capture market share for manufacturers, businesspeople, and consumers.

- **Search:** It is a vital component of web-based business and AI; therefore, it should be enhanced. Through the use of search, devices persuade the intended interest group to purchase a specific item. It's good to come up with new ideas and opportunities for customers because the company can make high-quality products and ventures and get into the market easily if it does so in response to what customers want and need.
- **Automated supply chains:** AI makes it possible to improve the supply of manufactured goods based on what consumers want. As a result, it is simple to maximize profit and decrease expenditures.
- **Prepare for the future:** AI is capable of predicting the future and producing high-quality goods to entice customers to acquire a certain organization's product. Their simulated intelligence aids in predicting the future, as consumers desire to produce high-quality goods and meet market demand. AI and retailers working together to meet customers' needs can convince customers to buy a product from a certain company.

1.5 AREA OF AI

Currently, AI plays a crucial role. Nearly every industry uses AI, including education, computer science, medical profession, job search, and human resource planning. The following subsections are used to discuss certain subject areas.

1.5.1 Computer Science

A developer of AI also contributes to the introduction and development of efficient methodologies and strategies for addressing specific computer science challenges. AI had created far too many optimal solutions to difficult problems.

1.5.2 Education

AI participation in the study shows that AI fully supports the education industry and may be used to help students using modern technology. AI's various features make homework easier for students. Students can ask any academic question with AI. Students benefit from modern technology. Today's kids may study more and accomplish tasks faster with AI. Due to AI, there are also persistent, basic, and challenging issues. If someone could crack the AI code, AI would transform schooling. Problems are solved by computers. Students' ability to answer basic questions improves with AI-augmented information. Thanks to AI-assisted presentation development, students are able to better understand and express their concerns with the slides. 3D alignment and graphic representation, which are essential to creating successful and memorable slides, can be assisted by AI. Teachers' lives can be improved by AI by reducing administrative work, removing student misunderstandings through interactive lectures, and sparking their interest in learning. In the classroom, teachers used projectors, laptops, notes, graphics, and images. Students and teachers benefit from AI. Teachers are adept at explaining topics to kids who don't comprehend. AI transfers data between educational institutions. AI can teach and answer inquiries about our doubts. Many professors dislike AI because it forces them out of their comfort zones. They aren't open to new ideas since they want to buy new things and use them at work.

1.5.3 Market

It is challenging for entrepreneurs to capture the market and convince buyers to invest in their ideas. Businesses strive to persuade customers to assist them with investment decisions in numerous ways. AI makes all financial decisions easier. Every day, advertisers perform several counts and store and record the information of each consumer; preserving client records is not an easy operation, but AI is incredibly advantageous for finance and marketing personnel who are responsible for managing client data. Using AI technology, an individual from the different parts of the country who speaks another language can communicate easily with people who speak another language. Essential to computer-based intelligence are AI frameworks that provide numerical input and output.

1.5.4 Finance

The manufacturer produces a variety of commodities and products in order to generate profits. When they manufactured the product to present their product, they employed an excessive number of market capture techniques. Initially, among other things, all manufacturers conduct market research and analyze consumer behavior. They generate goods and services according to the requirements, wants, and desires of consumers. All of the following tasks are accomplished with the aid of AI. The primary purpose is to ensure that everyone who establishes a firm profits. The client is the market's sovereign. Promoters exert a great deal of mental work to display the goods and persuade the customer to acquire it. As a result, promoters aid shoppers with the purchase of goods and services, as customers spend money on items and businesses. All concerns associated with buyer behavior, financial regularity, and the examination of why buyers spend money on a certain item and why customers make specific purchases may be readily separated by AI.

1.5.5   INDUSTRY

AI's most recent use is robots. In enterprises as well as the home, robots play a crucial role. Now, robots occupy the positions once occupied by humans; in other words, robots have replaced humans in the workforce. AI's unveiling of robots is significant. Like humans, robots are filled with emotions and do not engage in argumentation. Robots are a hazard to human beings. Without a doubt, robots are also effective or efficient—electronic men (robots) commit errors when people or programmers input incorrect data. Without weariness or depravity, robots perform excellent work.

1.5.6   HOSPITAL AND MEDICINE

In medical centers, AI plays a crucial role in obtaining X-rays of patients' bodies, collecting money from patients automatically, and determining their bone age with software. Through the use of AI, jobs may be performed and records can be conveniently maintained, as well as the inventory of drugs.

1.5.7   INTERPRETATION

AI can also evaluate the data in digital photos or graphic images and emphasize the most relevant details. AI aids physicians in listening to patients' heartbeats, as AI enhances the human body and medical fields comprehensively.

1.5.8   HUMAN RESOURCES

Human resource managers are adept in planning, E-HRM, applicant recruitment, and personnel shortfall and surplus analysis. In addition, obtaining contrasts between trademarks is unquestionably more difficult because it is far more difficult to find sets of comparable trademarks, and there is no standard definition of what constitutes a comparable group of deceptively similar trademarks. To further complicate this issue, we must also address what occurs when two trademarks have virtually identical data but distinct content. Examining the duplicate content of these trademarks will yield unfavorable results. We cannot ignore the text, as it may appear on the emblem or in conjunction with a figure that resembles another brand.

1.5.9 MARKETING

In all sectors and fields, synthetic intelligence is making headlines. Digital marketing is its living example. Currently, AI is a popular topic of discussion. AI has offered numerous opportunities for candidates pursuing careers in digital marketing. AI is a major breakthrough in the modern world. AI has made the lives of customers, businesspeople, and anybody else involved in technology significantly simpler. By utilizing AI and e-commerce, one can save time while purchasing online.

1.5.10 MEDIA AND E-COMMERCE

A number of AI applications are implemented on mediums such as movies, television programs, advertisement videos, and audio files. Voice search enables consumers to search for new things based on their requirements, wants, and desires without utilizing a laptop or other digital media while they conduct online shopping. We live in an unsettling society in which there is insufficient time to go to the market and purchase necessary goods. Coordinated, regulated, and extraordinary organizations will thrive, while the remainder will perish. Computer-based intelligence enables companies to be recognized for their role in following execution and proficiency throughout the system, as well as drivers of change. In addition to maintaining their organizations and budgets, they must also serve as change agents. They require insight to effectively consolidate innovation and the wit to redefine innovation from an ideal capital expense to an operating cost. A variety of technological advancements have made digitalization a viable target for account work.

1.5.11 MILITARY

Customers can customize their shopping experience with the help of recommendation engines, which make it easier to do business online. Based on the buyer's past browsing patterns and shopping preferences, an e-commerce website can make relevant, customized product suggestions. Since a B2B client's value is greater than that of a store's customer, the B2B client's value is higher than that of a store's customer. A topographical setting is an additional means of achieving this goal. Stores can display merchandise and promotions that are increasingly relevant to the buyer's location. Using AI, retailers may also recommend warranties, additional accessories, etc. while discussing customization.

1.5.12 NEWS, PUBLISHING, AND WRITING

For AI-based solutions to be successfully implemented, correspondence and collaboration amongst IP offices will likely be essential. According to the Director of WIPO's Division of Global Databases, present collaborations with national organizations provide WIPO with a variety of data that is gathered, organized, and cleaned for the development of AI tools. The Madrid System has been using machine translation to expedite the creation of interpreter-created documents for products and projects, thereby reducing the cost of disseminating interpretation. As the AI invention is open source, WIPO is able to modify it to match the requirements of the association.

1.5.13 CUSTOMER SERVICE

Eventually, AI will enhance the quality of decisions by enhancing the capacity of the office and the quality of indexed lists compiled by an official; the innovation permits the distinction of picture trademarks with astounding precision, locating every significant image in its database that contains a similarity, explanation, trademark, or geographical indication. It also makes the procedure quick and difficult. To save time and speed up the registration process, it would be beneficial to have the option to direct this step sequentially.

1.5.14 POWER VALUE

It would be irresponsible to assume that AI won't eventually displace IP-based occupations, given the rapidity of technological advancement. At the moment, innovation is making the job of IP offices easier, but perhaps more importantly, it is helping system users more and more.

This trend will likely continue as more organizations adopt innovation and openly engage in its activities. AI design is reliant on the quantity and quality of available data to a substantial degree. The degree to which IP offices arrange their efforts here will likely have far-reaching effects on the future of the firm. Regardless, the days of trademark examiners physically sifting through a vast number of applications are, if not over, at any rate on the wane.

1.5.15 SENSOR

Moreover, an AI-prepared company does not translate into a significant demand for innovative skills. The top three most sought-after skills among India's business pioneers are those that capture the market most successfully. Occasionally, customers prefer not to acquire particular products. Nonetheless, devices must be used to persuade clients during the critical time period.

1.5.16 TELECOMMUNICATION

You searched for a veterinarian in your area, and now your social stream is dominated by ads for pet supplies? That is the level of AI intensity. Through the use of AI, merchants are able to identify dynamic client behavior patterns and provide individualized shopping experiences. With the power of machine learning (ML), businesses may forecast client preferences even before the customer is aware of his or her needs. Considering the purchase of pet food when suddenly you are surrounded by adverts for pet food? It's not magic, then.

1.5.17 GAMES

The layout and quality of product images in an e-commerce store play a fundamental role in generating sales. Over time, designers have adopted responsive architecture to adapt websites to various screen resolutions. Nonetheless, with the use of ML, designers are attempting to personalize the website for specific users. Imagine an ordered and displayed store! With AI, fashion e-commerce photographers are also moving away from traditionally expensive picture shoots and relying on AI to solve the apparel photography problem. Picture modifying applications, for instance, use AI to create finished images in minutes with minimal human intervention.

1.5.18 TRANSPORTATION

With the aid of cutting-edge evolutionary algorithms (EA), merchants are able to predict content marketing results by evaluating different arrangements. As a result of dynamic learning, more arrangements are developed and tested based on the success of previous meetings. Some of the most important places that can be reshaped well are brand information, site plan and design, and the proposal engine.

With advancements in AI and improved technology, the online business experience for both buyers and sellers will drastically change. The investigation focuses on e-retailers' preparedness to capitalize on this fortunate opportunity.

1.6 USE OF AI AND E-COMMERCE

Customers prefer online business supplies over neighborhood stores and large gun shops for the most important reason of convenience. While power mirrors indicate that B2B and B2C web-based businesses operate identically, there is an infinite difference in customer behavior. In contrast to a B2B brand, a customer interaction with a B2C brand is more immediate. A B2B buyer will not engage in a buying frenzy, unlike his B2C counterpart, and so on. Due to these distinctions, B2B web-based businesses encounter challenges in the following areas:

1. offering great customer service
2. managing cash flow and inventories
3. maintaining customer engagement
4. delivering consumables that have been customized and priced properly

In light of these obstacles, B2B online business requirements must increase to the point where web-based business companies will be able to appropriately meet the rising demand. Regarding the advancements in AI's open source, they do not appear to be problematic. This chapter will examine how AI and ML are enhancing B2B web-based commerce.

1.6.1 CUSTOMER SEGMENTATION

In the era of statistics, every relationship has stabilized the majority of its geographic, demographic, and behavioral measurements and metrics. Additionally, they have extensive access to company-specific data. Despite this, the company is unable to capitalize on these realities as it is stagnant. Your buyer personas constitute the foundation for your sales and marketing strategy. Using AI, you can sift through these pieces of data to enhance your buyer personas and better segment your customers. This will allow you to adjust your plans and enhance the consumer experience accordingly.

1.6.2 CHATBOX

Chatbox get smarter with each command because they can learn how to move. Significant advantage of fulfillment user can examine past chat logs to determine the most frequently asked questions and concerns expressed by guests and then build your content around these topics. Since content is a vital component of any B2B activity, ensure that you are pleased with the development of transactions.

1.6.3 ENHANCEMENTS TO CONTENT CREATION

You can examine historical chat logs to determine the most frequently asked questions and concerns raised by guests and then create content around those topics. Since content is an important part of any B2B activity, the growth of deals should make you happy.

1.6.4 ENHANCED PERSONALIZED CAPABILITIES

Through its straightforward Internet business arrangements, proposal motors is able to personalize the shopping experience for its customers. Based on the purchaser's past perusing patterns and shopping distinctions, the web-based business site can present customized product recommendations that are pertinent to the purchaser's preferences; another method by which customization facilitates dynamic evaluation. The value of a B2B customer is larger than that of a B2C customer as a result of the higher average order size; retailers can implement dynamic pricing to close the transaction. A geological setting is another approach for doing this. Stores can display products and promotions that are more relevant to the location of the customer. While we're on the subject of personalization, suppliers can also recommend warranties, supplementary accessories, etc., using AI.

1.6.5 SEARCH

With the advent of AI and ML, buyers will no longer need to rely on content-based detection for standard web-based company searches. As with content-to-discourse, facial attractiveness can speed the purchasing process. You can use advanced collaborators to evaluate the product's usefulness and submit a request. In terms of innovation requirements, there is photographic evidence of a larger-than-average improvement. Need to acquire an item but have no idea about its brand name or current condition? Simply click an image to import it into the application. The AI computation will determine your reliability by returning the most material information.

1.7 AI IS TRANSFORMING E-COMMERCE

Every businessperson increasingly captures the market by providing high-quality goods and identifying consumer needs, wants, and desires prior to selling the goods. The market is ruled by the purchaser. When a representative introduces a new product to the market to introduce it to purchasers, they should utilize various methods, techniques, and innovations. Web-based commerce plays a crucial role. Due to the fact that, with the aid of e-commerce, sellers efficiently delivered the product to the hands of customers, and shoppers saved time by paying for the product online, AI and e-commerce are generally utilized by businesspeople to increase sales, as AI incorporates an individual's knowledge into machines and PC frameworks. Customers invent new methods for assembling high-quality products. Agents use both AI and electronic commerce to positively impact the corporate environment. Currently, AI and e-commerce are complementary to one another. An Internet company has no presence with customers; customers' requirements and desires change over time, but with the aid of AI, inventive new strategies can be developed to recognize customers' purchasing behavior and products may be manufactured in accordance with their requests. Each firm must increase their profit, with profit reliant on product sales, and product sales dependent on the most effective marketing strategy to capture the market—the marketing strategy component of e-commerce. AI and e-commerce are leveraged by a business to reach its target market through various channels, such as business-to-business and business-to-customer. Many business leaders have placed a great deal of faith in AI to progress their companies, which has enhanced their organizations' benevolence.

1.7.1 PERSONAL SHOPPING TO COMMON CONSUMER

Organizations are willing to invest in human capital, but they want clear objectives. In order to run a successful business, it is necessary to possess both manual and technical skills. The greatest aptitude gaps are separated by relational abilities. Each organization must retain loyal customers in the event that it provides reliable and high-quality products, resulting in client-free informal exposure to the organization's product.

1.7.2 BUYER FACILITATE

As of now, there are a small number of online businesses that use chatbots for customer service, but this number is growing. AI is rapidly enhancing chatbots' ability to answer a variety of inquiries, as well as provide product recommendations and surveys. A personal virtual beautician for your appearance and a financial master for your financial transactions are examples of the AI trend in client care.

1.7.3 FORMATION AND REPRESENTATION EDITING

The layout and quality of product images in an e-commerce store play a fundamental role in generating sales. Throughout the years, architects have embraced adaptable designs to adapt websites to various screen resolutions. Nonetheless, with the use of ML, planners are attempting to tailor the website to individual customers. Imagine a store that was planned and presented to you. With AI, fashion e-retailers are moving away from pricey photoshoots and increasingly relying on AI to handle the outfit photography issue. Image editing services use AI to create finished images in minutes with minimal human intervention.

1.7.4 LOCATE SATISFIED AND LAYOUT

With the help of cutting-edge EA, shops can predict the results of content advertising by looking at possible deals. Based on the success of previous gatherings, more arrangements are spontaneously developed and tested with dynamic learning. EAs can change a lot of important things, like how the brand communicates, how the website is built, and how suggestions are made. With advancements in AI and improved technology, the online business experience for both clients and merchants will drastically alter. The investigation focuses on the eagerness of e-retailers to capitalize on this fortunate opportunity.

1.8 TRENDS IN E-COMMERCE AND AI

With the advent of AI and ML, users will no longer be required to conduct content-driven e-commerce searches. A facial appearance, such as text-to-speech, could speed up the buying procedure. You can utilize computerized colleagues to determine the usability of the goods and to place a purchase. Regarding technological criteria, image recognition is an unnecessary addition to this subject. Want to buy a product but are unaware of its manufacturer or brand? Simply clicking the image will cause it to be uploaded to the application. The AI computation will accomplish the task for you by returning the best suitable products.

1.8.1 IMPROVING PRODUCT AND PRICING

Individualization enhances dynamic estimation in an additional manner. Because the average order value for B2B clients is higher than that of B2C consumers, retailers can employ aggressive pricing methods to generate sales. Stores can display products and promotions that are more relevant to the customer's location. Using AI, dealers can prescribe warranties, additional accessories, etc. when customizing is being discussed.

1.8.2 PRICING OPTIMIZATION

In the era of statistics, each relationship has stabilized nearly every geographical, demographic, and behavioral measurement and metric. In addition, they have extensive access to their company's data. Despite this, the organization is stagnant and unable of capitalizing on these facts—your buyer personas serve as the basis for your sales and marketing strategy. Using AI, you can crawl through these data to improve your buyer personas and segment your customers more precisely.

1.8.3 TAG AND RECOGNITION OF IMAGES

The advancement of a commercial focal point is furthered by simulated intelligence. Each foundation in the current era enjoys a growing number of benefits in comparison to its competitors. A buyer-product alliance exists between each firm that has successfully adopted AI technology into multiple facets of its operations. With the aid of AI, marketing evaluation is measured, and AI also aids in anticipating buyer behavior and predicting product recommendations.

1.8.4 Website Personalization

AI will dramatically boost the rate of growth for India's corporate organizations and firm founders. These findings are the result of an inquiry conducted by Microsoft. Occasionally, customers would prefer not to purchase such items; however, this is a consequence of using photos to search for products. AI requires both human-created skill and intelligence in order to develop the mechanisms essential for societal transformation. Their strategy is centered on computer-based intelligence, which develops a culture of learning agility. This breakthrough innovation requires ongoing investment across time.

1.9   CONCLUSION

The agent combines AI and electronic commerce to increase sales, since AI incorporates human knowledge for use by robots and systems. Through e-commerce, retailers, wholesalers, and representatives are already utilizing AI to better comprehend their customers and develop innovative methods for assembling high-quality products. Representatives use both AI and e-business to have a beneficial impact on the corporate sector; recently, AI and e-business have begun to complement one another. The web-based firm lacks a physical presence with its clients, and buyers' needs and desires fluctuate from time to time; however, with the aid of AI, inventive new strategies have been developed to recognize buyers' purchasing behavior and tailor products to their demands.

People possess foundational knowledge, intuition, and flexibility that machines cannot replicate. These obstacles for AI interpretation in Internet business would not be faced by human translators.

REFERENCES

1. Abu, S. B. A. (2005). "A Corpus-Based Approach to Generalizing a Chabot System," *ELIZA-Wikipedia, the Free Encyclopedia*. School of Computing, University of Leeds, Leeds [Online]. Available: http://en.wikipedia.org/wiki/ELIZA (accessed on 1 December 2020).
2. Amit, K. S., & Manvendra, J. (2018). *Engineering Applications of Artificial Intelligence: A Bibliometric Analysis of 30 Years (1988–2018)*. https://doi.org/10.1016/j.engappai.2019.06.010
3. Chaudhury, A., & Jean-Pierre, K. (2002). *E-Business and E-Commerce Infrastructure*. McGraw-Hill. ISBN: 978-0-07-247875.
4. Graler, A. (2009). "Development and Growth of the Country: A Review about Artificial Intelligence Geography Compass," *Sociology Compass*, 2(3), 771.
5. Human, P., & Jung, M. (2013). *In-Depth Benchmark of 12 E-Commerce Solutions (PDF)*. NBSSystem, https://is.gd/e_commerce (accessed on 8 March 2020).

6. Jeremy, B. (2019). *Embedding Projection for Targeted Cross-Lingual Sentiment: Model Comparisons and a Real-World Study.*

7. Kessler, M. (2003). "More Shoppers Proceed to Checkout Online. USA. Today Self-Healing Structural Composite Materials," *Composite Part A: Applied Science and Manufacturing, 34*(8), 743–753.

8. Loudon, K. C., & Guerin, T. C. (2014). *E-Commerce, Business, Technology, Society* (10th edn.). Pearson. ISBN: 978-013-302444-9.

9. Mayhem, R., Siham, Y., Mounia, M., & Hajar, M. (December 2019). "An Intelligent Swarm-Based Optimization Technique for Oscillatory Stability Assessment in Power System," *IAES International Journal of Artificial Intelligence (IJ-AI), 8*(4), 342–351. ISSN: 2252–8938.

10. Nissanoff, D. (2016). *Future Shop* (Hardcover edn., p. 24). The Pencert Press. ISBN: 908-1-65420-077-9.

2 Sentiment Analysis of Social Media with AI

Ashutosh Yadav[1]
and Shilpi Chhabra[2]
[1]Hansraj College, University of Delhi,
Delhi, India
[2]Faculty of Management Studies,
University of Delhi, Delhi, India

2.1 INTRODUCTION

The widespread usage of online social networks has created several chances to spark interest in a variety of topics from both a user's individual and a group standpoint. The connections that users make among themselves help to develop a virtual community, a forum for conversation that gives users the chance to engage with a variety of online communities, express themselves, and influence others. With the increased individual presence on social media, it has become the most preferred platform to vent out their experiences (negative/positive) about a product/ service or existing debate going around in an economy or even a policy decision being made currently, be it political or economy-related. With the feeling that individual voices do matter, individuals have this constant urge to share their feedback, both positive and/or negative. With this increased expression on social media platforms, there has arisen a unique opportunity for the stakeholders on the other side of the table to use this to their advantage. Largely, the markets are driven by public sentiments; organisations and policy makers could employ artificial intelligence (AI) to analyse these sentiments and take decisions accordingly. Sentiment analysis, in this context, is a method that makes use of natural language processing (NLP) to extract, convert, and analyse thoughts from a text and categorise them as positive, negative, or natural sentiment depending on the intended emotional tone in each word.

Analysis of such sentiments over social media by business houses, corporates, government agencies, ad agencies, etc. provides them with a unique pathway to understand the psychology, preferences, decision taking dynamics, etc. and take the corrective course of action, if required. The development in the field of AI has made it possible for such sentiments to be analysed both qualitatively and quantitatively. In today's world, it would be irrational for policy makers and businesses to disseminate ideas/information and products without understanding the needs of the beneficiaries.

As we will learn later in the chapter, how this field of work has acquired a seminal place in business, finance, and policy making alike, such that there are separate in-house divisions as well as outsourcing agencies social media data analytics.

DOI: 10.1201/9781032614083-2

2.2   USE OF ALGORITHMS IN ARTIFICIAL INTELLIGENCE TO CONDUCT SENTIMENT ANALYSIS FOR SOCIAL MEDIA PLATFORMS

Using AI algorithms, sentiment analysis can be done in a variety of ways. The algorithm is trained on a sizable dataset of labelled text data, with the labels representing the attitude of the text, as one method uses ***supervised learning***. The computer may then utilise this training data to forecast how new, unexplored text data would feel.

In supervised learning, a machine learning (ML) model is trained on a labelled dataset, which consists of input data and corresponding correct output labels. The model uses this training data to learn to make predictions on new, unseen data. By employing a labelled dataset of social media posts and their related sentiment labels (such as positive, negative, or neutral), supervised learning can be utilised for sentiment analysis in social media. The sentiment of fresh social media posts can then be categorised using the model.

The procedures below must be taken in order to do supervised learning for sentiment analysis in social media:

1. Gather a sizable dataset of text examples from social media along with the labels that go with them. The text can be labelled manually by hiring human annotators, automatically by utilising pre-existing datasets, or by combining both of these approaches.
2. Pre-process the text data by removing stop words, tokenising, and stemming, among other operations.
3. Divide the dataset into a test set and a training set. The model is trained using the training set, and its effectiveness is assessed using the test set.
4. Use the training set to train a supervised learning model. Support vector machines (SVMs), decision trees, and deep learning models are a few examples of supervised learning models that can be utilised for sentiment analysis.
5. Assess the model's effectiveness on the test set. Metrics like precision, recall, and accuracy can be calculated in order to accomplish this.
6. To improve the model's performance, tweak it by changing its hyperparameters or by applying strategies like feature selection or dimensionality reduction.
7. Use the model to classify the sentiment of fresh text samples as they are received.

For supervised learning in sentiment analysis, a variety of ML algorithms can be applied, including:

1. Linear regression: This method predicts continuous values (e.g., the sentiment of a post on a scale from -1 to 1).
2. Logistic regression: It is a method for forecasting outcomes that are binary (e.g., positive or negative sentiment).
3. Support vector machines (SVMs): This linear classifier algorithm can be applied to jobs requiring classification of either binary or multi-class data.

4. Decision trees: For both classification and regression problems, this technique builds a tree-like model of decisions and their potential outcomes.
5. Deep learning models: These models, which are neural network-based, can be used to a variety of tasks, including sentiment analysis.

Supervised learning functions most effectively when a sizable, varied, and representative dataset is available for training. Since the effectiveness of the model can be greatly impacted by the labels' quality, it is crucial to carefully evaluate how to label the text data when performing sentiment analysis.

Unsupervised learning is a different strategy where no labelled training data are given to the system. Instead, it must independently identify the underlying trends and connections in the data. Using clustering techniques, which combine related data points, is one approach to achieve this. The programme can then estimate the sentiment of fresh text data using these clusters.

There are several techniques to apply unsupervised learning for sentiment analysis in social media:

1. Clustering: Text samples that are similar in some way, such as by topic or sentiment, can be grouped using clustering techniques. You could, for instance, employ a clustering algorithm to classify text samples from social media into groups based on how similar their word combinations are. The main emotion of the text samples inside each cluster might then be used to name the clusters. The text samples can be manually labelled as positive, negative, or neutral once they have been classified into clusters depending on their content. A supervised learning model can then be trained with these labels to categorise the sentiment of fresh text samples.
2. Word embedding: Word embedding is a method that converts words into a two-dimensional space while preserving their relationships. This strategy reduces the dimension of the text data using dimensionality reduction methods like singular value decomposition (SVD) or principal component analysis (PCA) or factor analysis. Words that are similar in meaning or context, for instance, may be mapped to nearby locations in the embedding space. By training a classifier on a dataset of labelled text samples and utilising the embeddings as features, you may utilise word embeddings to categorise the sentiment of text samples. The data can then be visualised using tools like scatter plots and t-SNE plots to investigate its structure and spot trends that might represent various emotions.
3. Deep learning: It's vital to remember that unsupervised learning needs human labelling of the data, which can take more time and resources than supervised learning. To develop usable representations of text input, deep learning models, such as convolutional neural networks and recurrent neural networks, can be trained unsupervised. For instance, you could utilise a sizable dataset of text samples from social media to train a deep learning model and then use the learned representations as features for a subsequent classification job. Dependant on the quality of the clustering or dimensionality reduction technique and the user's capacity to spot significant patterns

in the data, the quality of the results acquired through unsupervised learning can also be highly variable.

Unsupervised learning, which relies on the model's capacity to identify patterns and correlations in the data without the aid of labelled training samples, can be trickier than supervised learning. Unsupervised learning techniques may therefore be more sensitive to the calibre and organisation of the incoming data. Without any labelled examples to serve as the model's training data, sentiment analysis of text samples might be challenging.

To summarise, the objective of sentiment analysis, regardless of the method utilised, is to correctly categorise the sentiment of text data as positive, negative, or neutral. Social media platforms may find this helpful in determining the general tone of the talks taking place on their platform and locating any potential red flags.

2.3 APPROACH OF SENTIMENT ANALYSIS/ HOW DOES SENTIMENT ANALYSIS WORK

There are three approaches/algorithms of sentiment analysis: first one is rule-based, the second approach is known as automated sentiment analysis, and the third approach is the hybrid method. All of these approaches use NLP or any other machine-based algorithm to identify the sentiment (angry, happy, and sad) of the consumers through text. In the following sub-sections, we will be discussing each of these approaches in detail.

2.3.1 RULE-BASED SENTIMENT ANALYSIS

Rule-based sentiment analysis algorithms are the easiest, though they do not always capture the complexities of different words. If any social networking site is expecting basic and not advanced analysis, then rule-based sentiment analysis could be adopted for capturing customers' sentiments. In this method, based on pre-determined rules, the system automatically polarises data into different sentiment baskets. To carry out sentiment analysis based on pre-defined rules, NLP is used to identify and classify words. NLP techniques, such as lexicons, stemming, tokenisation, and parsing, are used to conduct sentiment analysis on a set of manually created rules.

To illustrate how a rule-based sentiment analysis works let's understand through an example. A different set of words is associated with different sentiments, following that the sentence is then analysed. In that particular sentence analysed, polarised words used are counted and classified into different sentiment baskets (such as positive, negative, or neutral) and then the highest score attained by any particular sentiment basket is captured. To score and classify words into different baskets, words such as annoyed, pathetic, and slow are negative words, while words such as awesome, good, and pleasant are positive words. Following are the steps in conducting rule-based sentiment analysis:

1. Lexicon: A list of positive and negative words is created to describe sentiments.
2. Tokenisation: This step involves converting text into a language that can be understood and analysed by a machine. Tokenisation further breaks sentences

into different words or small parts or tokens. Let us assume that a social media website user gave feedback that 'the worst experience'; this sentence would be broken into tokens, such as the, worst, and experience. Further common words, such as a, an, the, of, and in, have very little relevance in sentiment analysis; hence, machines would keep them from the analysis.

3. The machine then counts the number of positive words, negative words, and neutral words in a sentence.

4. Finally, the overall score of the sentiments is counted and based on the score attained a sentence/customer's review is classified as a positive, negative, or neutral sentiment. The final score ranges between −100 and 100, with −100 being negative sentiment, 0 being and 100 score means that the customer has a positive sentiment based on a rule.

The disadvantage of rule-based algorithms is that they do not take 'context' into account, which results in some outcomes being produced with insufficient precision or flexibility. However, it can determine the messages' tonality, which is helpful for customer service. Linguistic problems might also arise with rule-based methods. Slang is fluid and can make it difficult to match words to positive or negative emotions.

2.3.2 AUTOMATED/AUTOMATIC SENTIMENT ANALYSIS

ML is mostly used in sentiment analysis to enhance and automate the low-level text analytics tasks. Data scientists can, for instance, use a vast amount of text documents with examples that have already been pre-tagged to train an ML model to recognise nouns. The model will learn what nouns 'look like' using ML approaches, such as neural networks and deep learning.

Deep text analysis using automatic sentiment analysis yields valuable information. Automatic sentiment analysis employs ML to comprehend the structure of communication rather than basing its work on criteria that are pre-defined (such as rule-based). This automated method makes use of supervised ML classification algorithms to increase precision and accuracy while processing data quickly according to a variety of criteria. ML techniques are used in sentiment analysis to examine data. ML algorithms to classify texts used in automatic sentiment analysis include using linear regression analysis, naïve Bayes, logistics regression, neural network derivatives, SVMs, and transformer models among others. Sentiment can be challenging because it appears to be a common extraction of specific insight. Nevertheless, it takes a lot of effort to capture the feeling accurately.

ML methods are used for automated sentiment analysis. In this situation, an ML system is trained to categorise sentiment based on the words and their placement. The calibre of the algorithm and training dataset determines how well this method works. Following are the steps in the automatic sentiment analysis approach:

1. Vectorisation: For a machine to understand and comprehend the text, the text is converted into numbers with the help of vectorisation. The numeric representations of text known as 'feature' are prepared by teaching algorithms to associate words from large texts. To improve the accuracy of sentiment analysis, words having similar meanings are given the same numeric values.

2. Training: The algorithm is fed a training set with sentiment labels in this step. The model then develops the ability to match input data with the best possible label. This input data can, for instance, consist of pairs of features (or text representations represented numerically) and the accompanying positive, negative, or neutral label.
3. Prediction: In this last step, the model is updated with fresh text. Using the model developed from the training data, the model then predicts labels (also known as classes or tags) for this unobserved data. Thus, the sentiment of the data can be classified as either good, negative, or neutral. In rule-based sentiment analysis, a pre-defined lexicon is no longer necessary because of this. The final stage is where ML sentiment analysis outperforms rule-based methods the most.

2.3.3 HYBRID

The combination of both rule-based and automatic approaches is known as a hybrid approach. The advantage of this approach is that it is more conclusive and combines elements of both approaches yielding more accurate results.

In general, text must initially be pre-processed in order for sentiment analysis algorithms to function, and this often entails actions like tokenisation, stemming, and stop word removal. After being processed, the text is fed to a classifier, which gives it a sentiment label (such as positive, negative, or neutral).

It's critical to remember that sentiment analysis is not a perfect science and that its accuracy might be impacted by things like the text's tone, context, and authorial subjectivity. Therefore, it is crucial to thoroughly assess the precision of any sentiment analysis method and to make the best use of it.

2.4 TYPES OF SENTIMENT ANALYSIS

The following section discusses the various types of sentiment analysis as summarised in Figure 2.1. All of these assessments base their conclusions and forecasts on data-driven ML and AI tools.

2.4.1 FINE-GRAINED SENTIMENT ANALYSIS

The polarity of public opinion is interpreted via fine-grained sentiment analysis. This analysis can be as straightforward as a binary like (positive) or dislike scale (negative) distinction, or it can be more intricate with finer details like a Likert scale assessing levels of strong agreement to strong disagreement with regard to behavioural concerns. Mostly, a fine-grained sentiment analysis uses five discrete classes to depict consumers' sentiments (Rao, 2021). The five discrete responses measure consumers' responses towards a particular product or a service. For instance, a social media website wants to observe whether the user feels the website has a user-friendly interface. In cases like these, consumers' responses can be captured through fine-grained sentiment analysis wherein their opinion can range from, strongly disagree, disagree, neutral, agree, and strongly agree as shown in Figure 2.2.

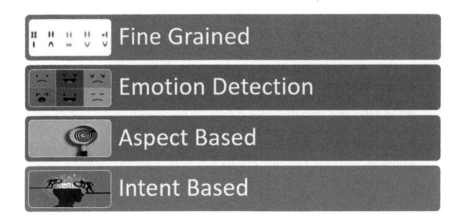

FIGURE 2.1   Types of sentiment analysis. (Author's representation.)

Likert Scale	Strongly Disagree	Disagree	Neutral	Agree	Strongly Agree
Website X is user friendly	X	X	X	✓	X
It is easier to upload pictures on Instagram than uploading on Facebook	X	✓	X	X	X

FIGURE 2.2   Five-point Likert scale capturing consumer's responses. (Author's depiction.)

There are few constraints associated with fine-grained analysis, though they are appropriate for capturing binary sentiments such as positive or negative. Consumers' sentiments on social media websites such as from tweets, product reviews from websites, and customer feedbacks given can be captured through this. When doing information extraction by comparing expressions, a fine-grained analysis can provide more precise findings to an automated system that gives prioritisation to resolving customer concerns. For example, 'It is easier to upload pictures on Instagram than uploading on Facebook'. Additionally, binary sentiment classifiers may be misled by contradictory statements such as 'The website X does not have a user-friendly interface, but still the website X has a huge consumer base' which might result in inaccurate class predictions.

2.4.2 EMOTION DETECTION

Based on language and ML algorithms, emotion-based sentiment analysis can identify certain emotional states that are present in customers' feedback and reviews. The findings reveal the reasons behind customers' opinions of various products or services. Also known as emotion recognition, it seeks to recognise the feelings conveyed in texts, such as happiness, excitement, sadness, surprise, rage, and grief. Emotional detection also permits the six-scale (anger, disgust, fear, happiness, sadness, surprise) on both psychology theories and emotion models, in addition to recognising the so-called primary psychological conditions, i.e., happy, sadness, and anger. Dimensional and categorical emotional models and theories are the two basic groups into which they fall. The valence, arousal, and dominance elements of dimensional emotion models are used to depict emotions. Valence refers to polarity, arousal to the excitement of a feeling, and dominance to the control of an emotion (What Is Sentiment Analysis?, n.d.).

Emotional detection helps in gauging consumers' perceptions and sentiments concerning different products and services. The context-dependence of emotions in writing makes identifying them one of the most difficult tasks. Even without utilising the word 'anger' or any of its counterparts, a sentence can contain elements of anger.

2.4.3 Aspect-Based Sentiment Analysis

Aspect-based sentiment analysis delves much deeper as compared to the aforementioned two types of sentiment analysis. The focal point of the analysis is on a particular aspect or feature of a product or service. Aspect-based analysis covers aspects, such as 'how do consumers perceive the introduction of reels feature in Instagram'. This type of analysis helps in knowing the consumer's perception of new features and it further highlights the features liked or disliked by consumers. As aspect-based ML analysis can identify whether a new service or product aspect has been liked by consumers, disliked by them, or they are indifferent.

This type of analysis helps in real-time monitoring of consumers' feedback and acceptability. Issues that customers are reporting on social media or in reviews can be found right away by businesses. This can shorten response times and enhance the clients' customer service. Social media platforms which are using aspect-based sentiment analysis through AI can identify areas of improvement by gauging the consumer's sentiments for a particular aspect of a product or service.

2.4.4 Intent Analysis

As the name suggests, intent analysis captures the specific intention behind customers' feedback, review, complaints, or suggestions. This type of analysis captures whether the customer's message is of a query form, feedback type, review comment, recommendation, or a praise. Intent analysis is the most comprehensive form which captures the intention of the customer through NLP. It is a more advanced computational method of capturing user-generated text to capture people's preferences, aspirations, and goals. For example, instead of saying I want a new laptop, a consumer writes my laptop is getting very slow, and new laptops have higher RAM; capturing intentions behind consumers' comments is what intent analysis does. Intent analysis can help websites target customers with requisite advertisements.

2.5 PROS AND CONS OF SENTIMENT ANALYSIS FOR SOCIAL MEDIA USING AI

The following are benefits of employing AI for sentiment analysis on social media:

- Efficiency: AI-based systems are rapid and accurate in processing massive amounts of social media data, which is helpful for spotting trends and patterns in real-time.
- Objectivity: Since AI systems do not factor in their own emotions and opinions throughout the study, they may be less prone to bias than human analysts.
- Consistency: AI systems can produce reliable results since they are not affected by human weaknesses like weariness or other things that can lower the quality of the analysis.

The following are some possible drawbacks of utilising AI for sentiment analysis on social media:

- Complexity: The design and implementation of an AI-based sentiment analysis system can be challenging and expensive.
- Accuracy: While AI systems have the potential to be very accurate, they are not infallible and occasionally give incorrect findings. This can be particularly tough when it comes to social media because the casual and ad hoc character of the language might make it challenging for the algorithm to accurately recognise the sentiment communicated.
- Ethical issues: The use of AI for social media sentiment analysis presents ethical issues, including the possibility of misuse and the effect on privacy. When creating and utilising AI systems for sentiment analysis, it is crucial to properly take these concerns into account.

2.6 SOFTWARE USED FOR CONDUCTING SENTIMENT ANALYSIS FOR SOCIAL MEDIA USING AI

AI-based sentiment analysis on social media data can be done utilising a variety of software programmes and platforms. Several instances include:

1. The Watson Tone Analyzer and the Watson Natural Language Understanding service are just two of the sentiment analysis tools and services provided by *IBM Watson*, a cloud-based AI platform.
2. Sentiment analysis tools and services are available through *Google Cloud Natural Language*, a cloud-based AI platform that also includes the sentiment analysis API.
3. *Microsoft Azure*: A variety of tools and services for sentiment analysis are available through Microsoft Azure, a cloud-based AI platform. These include the Text Analytics API and the sentiment analysis module of the Azure Machine Learning service.

4. *SAP Leonardo*: The SAP Leonardo Machine Learning Foundation service is just one of the sentiment analysis tools and services available through the cloud-based AI platform SAP Leonardo.
5. Sentiment analysis capabilities are provided by the social media analytics application *Hootsuite Insights*.
6. *Brand24* is a tool for monitoring social media that includes sentiment analysis features.
7. *Talkwalker* is a sentiment analysis-capable social media analytics and monitoring tool.
8. A sentiment analysis feature is available in *Brandwatch*, a social media analytics and monitoring tool.
9. *NetBase* is a sentiment analysis-capable social media analytics and monitoring application.
10. *Mention* is a social media analytics and monitoring tool with capabilities for sentiment analysis.

These are but a few examples of the numerous platforms and software solutions that may be used to perform sentiment analysis on social media data. You may want to think about comparing a number of possibilities to get the tool that best suits your demands depending on your unique requirements and desires.

2.7 APPLICATIONS OF SENTIMENT ANALYSIS OF SOCIAL MEDIA FOR BUSINESS, ECONOMICS, AND FINANCE

Sentiment analysis has become crucial in today's consumer-centric environment. The importance can be highlighted with its usage in helping firms understand consumers' attitudes towards their brands. Organisations can make wise choices by automatically categorising the emotions that underlie social media interactions and reviews. Automatically analysing social media posts, sentiment analysis identifies key assertions or opinions and categorises them based on their emotional attitude. Its importance can be highlighted by envisaging the applications that it has across various domains discussed in this section:

2.7.1 BUSINESS

As per Statistica, over 4.26 billion individuals used social media in 2021, with that figure expected to reach approximately 6 billion by 2027. The number of social media users is growing every day. It is loaded with unprocessed raw data, but thanks to advances in technology, particularly in ML and AI, the data can now be processed and turned into information that is valuable to most business organisations.

Sentiment analysis gives company owners advantages by allowing them to determine how well liked their products or services are by customers (Dhaoui et al., 2017; Rahman et al., 2019) as well as by gauging how well their brand communicates with the customer base on social media (Poecze et al., 2018) and how well their brand is performing overall (Suman et al., 2017).

For businesses to stand out in the market, it is essential to comprehend customer feedback on social media, interact with customers about their negative experiences, and take the appropriate action. In order to create goods and services that are suited to their consumers' demands, companies can analyse client input, such as comments made in survey replies and discussions on social media. According to a recent study by McKinsey, customers can spend up to 40% more when businesses respond to their social media requests. Therefore, it is essential for firms to analyse customer reviews on social media to comprehend their sentiments.

A company can learn more about the deeper context behind a tweet, status update, blog post, comment, or reply by performing social media sentiment analysis. Social media sentiment analysis enables businesses to examine the emotions their audience is producing and to identify their pain areas. According to Isah et al. (2014), sentiment analysis can help businesses and organisations take the proper steps to improve their goods or services and business strategy. Product analysis is aided by sentiment analysis. In the use of sentiment analysis, client feedback is of the highest importance since it may help businesses and organisations take the proper action to enhance their goods or services and business strategy. Isah et al. (2014) using sentiment analysis, summarised views and experiences of drug and cosmetic products among social media users.

Additionally, it is now simpler to assess consumer, market trends and industry characteristics. A business can take more steps to satisfy the customers' needs if it has more knowledge about the market. Therefore, studying customer sentiment on social media would provide business with new information and suggestions for creating successful strategies. Numerous sentiment analysis technologies are available to aid in enhancing business and marketing strategies. Akter and Aziz (2016) examined patterns and traits of people's eating behaviours that the business organisation may employ when formulating their product and marketing strategy using sentiment analysis. Further, it allows for the identification of areas that require improvement as well. According to Martin-Domingo et al. (2019), sentiment analysis makes it possible to identify airport service quality issues and to implement appropriate corrective action, like paying attention to social media comments from travellers. Besides, sentiment analysis allows the firms to evaluate how well are they fairing against their competitors (Drus and Khalid, 2019).

Social media is used to connect people, exchange information, and express personal opinions, but increasingly businesses are utilising it to interact with customers and learn more about how to enhance their products and services.

2.7.2   Economics

The development of econometric methods to convert qualitative sentiment data into quantitative sentiment variables has been prompted by the emergence of vast volumes of textual, audio, and visual data. These quantitative sentiment variables can then be used to analyse the association between sentiments and other variables of economic interests.

Malandri et al. (2018) and Xing et al. (2019) stated that sentiment analysis of social media can significantly improve forecasting models. Chang et al. (2016) further highlight that these more accurate forecasts can serve as the premise for more informed economic decisions. One perfect example that can be cited here is the gauging of consumer confidence in economy which has been described by Casey and Owen (2012) as the consumers' expectations about the future state of the economy. Another example worth mentioning is the renowned Economic Policy Uncertainty (EPU) Index given by Baker et al. (2016). This index has been further used by numerous studies to see the co-movements and other associations with economic variables for instance exchange rate volatility (as in Arouri et al., 2016; Gilal, 2019; and Liming et al., 2020 among others). Lukauskas et al. (2022) attempted to evaluate the correlation between the economic activity indicators and social media sentiments.

A dynamic stochastic general equilibrium (DSGE) model is developed by Barsky and Sims (2012) that takes into account both the informational and the animal spirits perspectives on confidence. The majority of the empirical data they discover supports the idea that changes in confidence are a reflection of information about future economic prospects. One plausible explanation is that often, economic sentiments act as self-fulfilling prophesy (Petropoulos Petalas et al., 2017). Actual negative growth may be a direct result of consumer or industry pessimism about economic growth (Algaba et al., 2020).

The popularity of social networking sites has led to the emergence of several areas that focus on dissecting social networks and their contents in order to gather crucial data (Wankhade et al., 2022). Another area where sentiment analysis can be applied is to gauge policy response from the target population. This would yield multitude of benefits to the government authorities/policy makers to exactly know what areas it needs to focus on for clarifying the potential pros of the policy being decided upon.

2.7.3 FINANCE

Big data's impact on the emergence of financial texts has presented challenges for most firms and increased need for analysis tools. Due to the expansion of postings on the Internet and the rising desire for market transparency, financial texts are now more widely available. These text streams are typically more difficult to manage than numeric data streams. Despite their natural lack of order, text streams reflect collective expressions that are valuable in making any financial decision. Financial social media connects individuals, businesses, and organisations so they can exchange ideas, information, knowledge, and viewpoints with respect to the decisions being taken in the financial space. The information shared on the social media might serve as an important tool in the form of unstructured data (Big Data) that can be incorporated into the decision-making process. It is not entirely novel to think about using text analysis to study the financial markets, and impact of sentiments on financial markets is well established too. Sentiment analysis offers solution to making sense of unstructured textual material, which can be difficult but also vital. Given the volatile nature of financial markets, examining important issues connected to the surge in interest in unstructured data insight extraction and how to identify whether such insight offers any cues about the direction of financial market patterns is of utmost importance.

The two main approaches to application of sentiment analysis in finance proposed by the AI-enabled solution providers include one, development of search engines which can sift through massive amount of social media content including news, blogs, tweets, etc., and categorise the relevant information from industry standpoint. And the second entails utilising already-existing data repositories and corporate papers to interpret, classify, and create succinct reports from unprocessed data that express positive, unfavourable, or impartial attitudes.

Chan and Chong (2017) examined a financial text stream with 12 million words that aligned with a stock market index. Strong evidence of a long persistence in the mood time series produced by the proposed engine by the study can be seen in the results and their statistical significance. Furthermore, despite the fact that such feelings and market indices are typically thought to be completely uncorrelated, their methodology provided evidence that these sentiments can be useful for understanding the changes in a stock market index. Yang and Mo (2016) discussed about different methods for creating investing strategies employing market feedback strength, surprises, and sentiment analysis. The study also showed that based on the assumption that extreme investor sentiment shifts tend to have long-lasting effects on market movement, abnormal news sentiment can be used as a predictive proxy for financial market returns and volatility. The findings also demonstrated that sentiment-based strategies outperform other benchmark strategies in terms of risk-adjusted returns. Sohangir et al. (2018) examined source materials and applied NLP techniques, such as long short-term memory, doc2vec, and CNN, to determine the stock market opinions posted in StockTwits. Katayama and Tsuda (2020) analysed the sentiment of Japanese news and attempts to apply it to investment strategies in individual stocks. Schumaker and Chen (2009) using textual representations analysed if individual stock prices could be predicted with a certain time lag from release of an article. Tetlock (2007), Katayama et al. (2019), Okimoto and Hirasawa (2014), Heston and Sinha (2017), Allen et al. (2019), Valencia et al. (2019), and Yadav et al. (2020) are a few studies which used social media sentiment analysis to demonstrate use of sentimental analysis in predicting stock market performances. Qian et al. (2022) evaluated public tweets on NFTs (Non-fungible Tokens) and postulate that, unlike stock markets, NFT markets are more influenced by general opinion, expectations, consumers' perceptions, and the creators' goodwill.

The use of sentiment analysis of social media is processed in the asset management domain too. Mayew and Mohan (2012) evaluated the voice of a company's representative at an earnings conference to use it for forecasting earnings. Similarly, Tetlock et al. (2008) used sentiment analysis to measure firms' fundamentals. Zhong and Ren (2022) reported that through sentiment analysis, subjective expressions presented in financial report text offer valuable additional information that can help predict the company's future performance, influencing investors' perceptions of the company's prospects.

Financial social media brings people, companies, and organisations together so that they can generate ideas and share information with others. It is this media that provides a huge amount of unstructured data (Big Data) that can be integrated into the decision-making process. Such a data can be considered a great source of real-time estimation because of its high frequency of creation and low-cost acquisition.

2.8 CAUTION, LIMITATIONS, AND CHALLENGES OF SENTIMENT ANALYSIS OF SOCIAL MEDIA

Sentiment analysis has become increasingly popular in recent years as a tool for understanding the sentiments of consumers, particularly in the context of social media. However, there are several challenges that need to be addressed in order to effectively perform sentiment analysis on social media data. When employing AI to undertake sentiment analysis for social media, due care should be undertaken with respect to the following:

1. **Diverse data:** Ensuring that the data being used to train your sentiment analysis model is diverse and reflective of the population you are attempting to examine. The model's predictions will be inaccurate or not up to the expectations if the data is skewed.
2. **Variety of data source:** When training your model, a variety of data sources should be used. This will lessen the possibility of overfitting and further strengthen the model.
3. **Combination of supervised and unsupervised learning methods:** To train your model, it is advisable to combine supervised and unsupervised learning methods. This will ensure that the model can generalise to new data and help it perform better.
4. **Domain-specific embeddings:** To enhance the performance of the model, think about utilising domain-specific word embeddings or other domain-specific features.
5. **Frequent assessments:** To make sure the model is producing accurate results, it is imperative to frequently assess its performance and tweak it as necessary.
6. **Checking accuracy:** Ensure that you correctly analyse and communicate the sentiment analysis's findings. The predictions of the model should not be considered to be the last word and should be used to support human analysis rather than to replace it.

Two main approaches for conducting sentiment analysis are rule-based and automatic using ML and NLP. The abundance of *noise* in social media data is a significant obstacle. Short, informal communications that may contain typos, abbreviations, and slang are frequently shared on social networking networks. As a result, it may be challenging for an ML model to comprehend the sentiment effectively because it is unfamiliar with these unusual linguistic patterns. The volume of noise on social media is a major barrier. On social media networks, quick, informal messages that could be slang, abbreviated, or contain errors are commonly shared. As a result, it could be difficult for an ML model to comprehend the sentiment being expressed.

The use of *irony and sarcasm* on social media is another difficulty. Irony and sarcasm are frequently used by users to convey the opposite of their genuine feelings, and it can be challenging for an ML model to pick this up. As a result, the mood being conveyed may not be correctly classified, which could affect perceptions of the general sentiment on a particular topic. Humour, irony, and sarcasm are few genres which are still difficult to capture through sentiment analysis. In humour, irony, and sarcasm, a lot of positive words are used, but in a pun. A machine would pick those words positively, and not capture the true feelings of a person (Gupta et al., 2021). Words in idioms and phrases can confuse the ML algorithm. For instance, feedback by a consumer for a social website that, 'The website has emerged against all odds' or 'Blow your own trumpet' might not be interpreted by the machine in the way a human would.

The existence of *subjectivity* in language poses a third difficulty. Depending on their individual experiences and viewpoints, various people can give the same words or phrases with different interpretations. Due to this subjectivity, an ML model may find it challenging to correctly categorise the sentiment being communicated because it may not be able to effectively capture the subtleties of human emotion and comprehension.

The difficulty of *managing numerous languages* on social media is the final challenge. People from all over the world use social media platforms, and it is usual for users to express their opinions in languages other than English. Because of this, it may be challenging for an ML model that was trained on English data to correctly categorise the sentiment being communicated in another language.

The usage of irony and sarcasm, the subjectivity of language, the existence of noise, the necessity to handle many languages, and other issues make sentiment analysis on social media data difficult overall. However, these obstacles can be successfully surmounted and useful insights into customer mood on social media can be obtained by using the appropriate methods and strategies.

REFERENCES

Akter, Sanjida, and Muhammad Tareq Aziz. 2016. "Sentiment Analysis on Facebook Group Using Lexicon Based Approach." *2016 3rd International Conference on Electrical Engineering and Information Communication Technology (ICEEICT)*, September. https://doi.org/10.1109/ceeict.2016.7873080

Algaba, Andres, David Ardia, Keven Bluteau, Samuel Borms, and Kris Boudt. 2020. "Econometrics Meets Sentiment: An Overview of Methodology and Applications." *Journal of Economic Surveys* 34 (3): 512–47. https://doi.org/10.1111/joes.12370

Allen, David E., Michael McAleer, and Abhay K. Singh. 2019. "Daily Market News Sentiment and Stock Prices." *Applied Economics* 51 (30): 3212–35. https://doi.org/10.1080/00036 846.2018.1564115

Arouri, M. E. H., C. Estay, C. Rault, and D. Roubaud. (2016). "Economic Policy Uncertainty and Stock Markets: Long-Run Evidence from the US." *Finance Research Letters, 18*, 136–41. https://doi.org/10.1016/j.frl.2016.04.011

Baker, S. E., N. Bloom, and S. J. Davis. (2016). "Measuring Economic Policy Uncertainty*." *Quarterly Journal of Economics, 131*(4), 1593–1636. https://doi.org/10.1093/qje/qjw024

Barsky, Robert, and Eric R. Sims. 2012. "Information, Animal Spirits, and the Meaning of Innovations in Consumer Confidence." *The American Economic Review, 102*(4), 1343–77. https://doi.org/10.1257/aer.102.4.1343

Casey, Gregory P., and Ann L. Owen. 2012. "Good News, Bad News, and Consumer Confidence." *Social Science Quarterly* 94 (1): 292–315. https://doi.org/10.1111/j.1540-6237.2012.00900.x

Chan, Samuel W. K., and Mickey W. C. Chong. 2017. "Sentiment Analysis in Financial Texts." *Decision Support Systems* 94 (February): 53–64. https://doi.org/10.1016/j.dss.2016.10.006

Chang, Ching-Yun, Yue Zhang, Zhiyang Teng, Zahn Bozanic, and Bin Ke. 2016. Measuring the Information Content of Financial News. *Proceedings of COLING 2016, The 26th International Conference on Computational Linguistics: Technical Papers.* The COLING 2016 Organizing Committee. https://aclanthology.org/C16-1303

Chen, Liming, Ziqing Du, and Hu Zhihao. 2020. "Impact of Economic Policy Uncertainty on Exchange Rate Volatility of China." *Finance Research Letters*, 32 (January), 101266. https://doi.org/10.1016/j.frl.2019.08.014

Dhaoui, Chedia, Cynthia M. Webster, and Lay Peng Tan. 2017. "Social Media Sentiment Analysis: Lexicon Versus Machine Learning." *Journal of Consumer Marketing* 34 (6): 480–88. https://doi.org/10.1108/jcm-03-2017-2141

Drus, Zulfadzli, and Haliyana Khalid. 2019. "Sentiment Analysis in Social Media and Its Application: Systematic Literature Review." *Procedia Computer Science* 161: 707–14. https://doi.org/10.1016/j.procs.2019.11.174

Gilal, M. (2019). "Economic Policy Uncertainty and Stock Market Returns in Indonesia." *ResearchGate*. https://doi.org/10.13140/RG.2.2.10905.88168

Gupta, Prasoon, Sanjay Kumar, R. R. Suman, and Vinay Kumar. 2021. "Sentiment Analysis of Lockdown in India During COVID-19: A Case Study on Twitter." *IEEE Transactions on Computational Social Systems* 8 (4): 992–1002. https://doi.org/10.1109/tcss.2020.3042446

Heston, Steven L., and Nitish Ranjan Sinha. 2017. "News vs. Sentiment: Predicting Stock Returns from News Stories." *Financial Analysts Journal* 73 (3): 67–83. https://doi.org/10.2469/faj.v73.n3.3

Isah, Haruna, Paul Trundle, and Daniel Neagu. 2014. "Social Media Analysis for Product Safety Using Text Mining and Sentiment analysis." *2014 14th UK Workshop on Computational Intelligence (UKCI)*, September. https://doi.org/10.1109/ukci.2014.6930158

Katayama, Daisuke, Yasunobu Kino, and Kazuhiko Tsuda. 2019. "A Method of Sentiment Polarity Identification in Financial News Using Deep Learning." *Procedia Computer Science* 159: 1287–94. https://doi.org/10.1016/j.procs.2019.09.298

Katayama, Daisuke, and Kazuhiko Tsuda. 2020. "A Method of Using News Sentiment for Stock Investment Strategy." *Procedia Computer Science* 176: 1971–80. https://doi.org/10.1016/j.procs.2020.09.333

Lukauskas, Mantas, Vaida Pilinkienė, Jurgita Bruneckienė, Alina Stundžienė, Andrius Grybauskas, and Tomas Ruzgas. 2022. "Economic Activity Forecasting Based on the Sentiment Analysis of News." *Mathematics* 10 (19): 3461. https://doi.org/10.3390/math10193461

Malandri, Lorenzo, Frank Z. Xing, Carlotta Orsenigo, Carlo Vercellis, and Erik Cambria. 2018. "Public Mood–Driven Asset Allocation: The Importance of Financial Sentiment in Portfolio Management." *Cognitive Computation* 10 (6): 1167–76. https://doi.org/10.1007/s12559-018-9609-2

Martin-Domingo, Luis, Juan Carlos Martín, and Glen Mandsberg. 2019. "Social Media as a Resource for Sentiment Analysis of Airport Service Quality (ASQ)." *Journal of Air Transport Management* 78 (July): 106–15. https://doi.org/10.1016/j.jairtraman.2019.01.004

Okimoto, Tatsuyoshi, and Eiji Hirasawa. 2014. "Stock Market Predictability Using News Indexes." *Security Analysis Journal*, 52(4): 67–75.

Petalas, Diamantis Petropoulos, Hein Van Schie, and Paul Hendriks Vettehen. 2017. "Forecasted Economic Change and the Self-Fulfilling Prophecy in Economic Decision-Making." *PLOS ONE*, 12(3), e0174353. https://doi.org/10.1371/journal.pone.0174353

Poecze, Flora, Claus Ebster, and Christine Strauss. 2018. "Social Media Metrics and Sentiment Analysis to Evaluate the Effectiveness of Social Media Posts." *Procedia Computer Science* 130: 660–66. https://doi.org/10.1016/j.procs.2018.04.117

Qian, Cheng, Nitya Mathur, Nor Hidayati Zakaria, Rameshwar Arora, Vishal Gupta, and Mazlan Ali. 2022. "Understanding Public Opinions on Social Media for Financial Sentiment Analysis Using AI-Based Techniques." *Information Processing and Management*, 59 (6), 103098. https://doi.org/10.1016/j.ipm.2022.103098

Rahman, Sahar a. El, Feddah Alhumaidi AlOtaibi, and Wejdan Abdullah AlShehri. 2019. "Sentiment Analysis of Twitter Data." *2019 International Conference on Computer and Information Sciences (ICCIS)*, April. https://doi.org/10.1109/iccisci.2019.8716464

Rao, Prashanth. 2021. "Fine-Grained Sentiment analysis in Python (Part 1) – Towards Data Science." Medium. December 11, 2021. https://towardsdatascience.com/fine-grained-sentiment-analysis-in-python-part-1-2697bb111ed4

Schumaker, Robert P., and Hsinchun Chen. 2009. "Textual Analysis of Stock Market Prediction Using Breaking Financial News." *ACM Transactions on Information Systems* 27 (2): 1–19. https://doi.org/10.1145/1462198.1462204

Sohangir, Sahar, Dingding Wang, Anna Pomeranets, and Taghi M. Khoshgoftaar. 2018. "Big Data: Deep Learning for Financial Sentiment Analysis." *Journal of Big Data* 5 (1). https://doi.org/10.1186/s40537-017-0111-6

Suman, Nishant, P. K. Gupta, and Pankaj Sharma. 2017. "Analysis of Stock Price Flow Based on Social Media Sentiments." *2017 International Conference on Next Generation Computing and Information Systems (ICNGCIS)*, December. https://doi.org/10.1109/icngcis.2017.34

Tetlock, Paul C. 2007. "Giving Content to Investor Sentiment: The Role of Media in the Stock Market." *The Journal of Finance* 62 (3): 1139–68. https://doi.org/10.1111/j.1540-6261.2007.01232.x

Tetlock, Paul C., and Maytal Saar-Tsechansky, and Sofus Macskassy. 2008. "More Than Words: Quantifying Language to Measure Firms' Fundamentals." *The Journal of Finance* 63 (3): 1437–67. https://doi.org/10.1111/j.1540-6261.2008.01362.x

Valencia, Franco, Alfonso Gómez-Espinosa, and Benjamín Valdés-Aguirre. 2019. "Price Movement Prediction of Cryptocurrencies Using Sentiment Analysis and Machine Learning." *Entropy* 21 (6): 589. https://doi.org/10.3390/e21060589

Wankhade, Mayur, Annavarapu Chandra Sekhara Rao, and Chaitanya Kulkarni. 2022. "A Survey on Sentiment Analysis Methods, Applications, and Challenges." *Artificial Intelligence Review* 55 (7): 5731–80. https://doi.org/10.1007/s10462-022-10144-1

"What Is Sentiment Analysis?" n.d. TIBCO Software. https://www.tibco.com/reference-center/what-is-sentiment-analysis. (accessed on December 24, 2022).

Xing, Frank Z., Erik Cambria, and Yue Zhang. 2019. "Sentiment-Aware Volatility Forecasting." *Knowledge-Based Systems* 176 (July): 68–76. https://doi.org/10.1016/j.knosys.2019.03.029

Yadav, Anita, C. K. Jha, Aditi Sharan, and Vikrant Vaish. 2020. "Sentiment Analysis of Financial News Using Unsupervised Approach." *Procedia Computer Science* 167: 589–98. https://doi.org/10.1016/j.procs.2020.03.325

Yang, Steve Y., and Sheung Yin Kevin Mo. 2016. "Social Media and News Sentiment Analysis for Advanced Investment Strategies." In *Studies in Computational Intelligence*. https://doi.org/10.1007/978-3-319-30319-2_11

Zhong, Ni, and JunBao Ren. 2022. "Using Sentiment Analysis to Study the Relationship between Subjective Expression in Financial Reports and Company Performance." *Frontiers in Psychology* 13 (July).

3 Unlocking the Power of Explainable AI to Improve Customer Experiences in E-Commerce

Manzoor Ansari[1], Syed Arshad Ali[2], Mansaf Alam[1], Kiran Chaudhary[3], and Sandeep Rakshit[4]

[1]Department of Computer Science, Jamia Millia Islamia, New Delhi, India

[2]Department of Computer Science & Applications, School of Engineering & Technology, Sharda University, Greater Noida, India

[3]Department of Commerce, Shivaji College, University of Delhi, Delhi, India

[4]The Business School, RMIT University, Ho Chi Minh City, Vietnam

3.1 INTRODUCTION

The proliferation of internet-enabled devices and the growing reliance on e-commerce have changed how customers interact with businesses. As customers increasingly rely on technology for their purchasing decisions, businesses must ensure that their customers have a positive and seamless experience. To achieve this, businesses are increasingly exploring the potential of eXplainable Artificial Intelligence (XAI) to improve customer experiences in e-commerce. The ever-growing complexity of AI technologies has enabled businesses to take advantage of its immense potential to improve customer experiences in e-commerce. However, the lack of explainability and transparency of AI models, often referred to as "black box" models, has fully limited e-commerce businesses' ability to leverage AI's potential [1]. As a result, customers are often left in the dark regarding the decisions made by AI models and may not understand how AI algorithms are influencing their shopping experience. This is where XAI comes into play. XAI provides a way to bridge the gap between AI models and customers by explaining the models' decisions, allowing customers to understand why certain decisions were made [2]. Additionally, XAI models can help businesses manage customer expectations better and build trust, as customers will know exactly how AI affects their shopping experience. With the help of XAI, e-commerce businesses can gain deeper insights into customer behavior, optimize their AI models for improved customer experiences, and engage customers in a more meaningful way [3].

DOI: 10.1201/9781032614083-3

31

This study aims to understand how XAI can be applied in the e-commerce context to improve customer experiences. This research chapter explores the potential of XAI to improve customer experiences in e-commerce:

- To understand the current state of XAI and how it can be applied to the e-commerce context.
- To explore the potential of XAI to improve customer experiences in e-commerce.
- To examine the ability of XAI to explain product recommendations, personalize customer experiences, and provide intelligent customer service.
- To examine how XAI can enable customers to understand the decision-making process of automated systems.
- To assess the potential benefits and challenges of XAI in e-commerce contexts.
- To identify emerging opportunities for the application of XAI in e-commerce.
- To suggest best practices and strategies for leveraging XAI to optimize customer experiences in e-commerce.

3.1.1 BACKGROUND OF EXPLAINABLE AI (XAI)

XAI is an AI branch that focuses on making AI systems more transparent and interpretable. XAI seeks to make AI systems more understandable to humans by providing explanations for decisions and predictions that the AI system makes [4]. This is done by building explainability features into the AI system, such as providing visualizations, generating explanations, and using techniques such as Feature Attribution or Feature Selection [5]. One of the first XAI models was developed by Google in the early 2000s. It was called "Deep Blue" and was able to solve problems that were too difficult for humans to understand [6]. Since then, other companies have developed XAI models. One of the most popular models is called "Rainbow". It can explain how algorithms work and can be used to make AI more understandable for humans [7]. XAI is important because it can make AI more accessible to people, and it can make it easier for people to use AI for their purposes. XAI is important to help humans understand how an AI system works and to help humans trust AI systems. XAI has become increasingly important as AI systems are used more and more in everyday applications such as e-commerce [8], business management [9–11], medical diagnosis [12], social media consumer behavior [13], voice-based assistant [14], environment monitoring [15, 16], resource management [17], and autonomous driving [18]. XAI is also important for regulatory and compliance reasons, as regulators increasingly demand explainability from AI systems. XAI is an emerging field that is expected to grow in importance in the coming years.

3.1.2 CATEGORIES OF XAI

A few different types of XAI systems have been developed so far. The first type is called explainable neural networks (ENAs), a machine learning (ML) algorithm that can explain the results of an ML algorithm in a way that is easily understandable for humans [19]. ENAs are used to explain the performance of various ML algorithms. Another type of XAI system is called Explainable Logic Networks (ELNs), an ML algorithm that can generate human-readable explanations for its decision-making process. ELNs use symbolic logic and rule-based systems to provide transparency into why a particular decision was made, making them particularly valuable in domains where interpretability and accountability are critical, such as healthcare, finance, and autonomous vehicles [20]. The third type of XAI system is called Explainable Rule Networks (ERNs), a novel approach that combines the power of neural networks with the transparency of rule-based systems. In this method, we begin by creating several operator modules and train them to function as specific relational operators through a self-supervised learning process [21].

The fourth type of XAI system is called explainable supervised learning (ESL), focusing on making the decision processes of supervised machine learning algorithms transparent and understandable, particularly valuable in fields requiring interpretability [22]. The fifth type of XAI system is called explainable unsupervised learning (EUL), aiming to provide clarity and transparency in the decision processes of unsupervised machine learning algorithms. This is especially useful in situations where understanding the patterns and relationships discovered by unsupervised learning models is crucial for decision-making or interpretation [23]. Each of these XAI systems possesses distinct advantages and limitations, underscoring their significance in the pursuit of transparency and comprehensibility in AI. It is imperative to meticulously assess these trade-offs when selecting the most appropriate XAI framework for a particular application. This judicious evaluation allows us to leverage their strengths while mitigating their shortcomings, thereby propelling the advancement and adoption of AI technology in a more informed manner.

3.1.3 Mathematical Representation of XAI in E-Commerce

XAI for e-commerce can be expressed mathematically as

$$\Upsilon_{XAI} = (x_{user} + x_{e\text{-commerce\_data}}) * x_{AI\_algorithms} * x_{explainability} * x_{feedback\_loop}$$

where:

x_{user} is user preferences, behavior, and activities.

$x_{e\text{-commerce\_data}}$ is market trends, product catalog, customer data, etc.

$x_{AI\_algorithms}$ is ML and Deep Learning (DL).

$x_{explainability}$ is human interpretable explanation of AI decisions and recommendations.

$x_{feedback\_loop}$ is user feedback and evaluation of AI decisions and recommendations.

This equation shows how XAI for e-commerce leverages user and data input to produce AI algorithms and explainable decisions to improve customer experiences in e-commerce. The feedback loop is an important factor in the equation, as it can help the AI algorithms to improve over time based on user feedback. Therefore, unlocking the power of XAI to improve customer experiences in e-commerce requires a combination of user data, e-commerce data, AI algorithms, explainability, and feedback loops.

3.2 CONCEPTS RELATED TO XAI METHODS

Overview of the different concepts on developing methodologies for XAI adapted from the studies by Vilone and Longo [24]. In Figure 3.1, we summarize the main concepts behind XAI application development.

- **Explanation-based methodologies:** Explanation-based methodologies are used to develop XAI systems that generate explanations from an existing model. This approach relies on extracting interpretable features and concepts from the underlying model and presenting them in a way humans can understand. Explanation-based methods often employ feature extraction, clustering, feature selection, and data visualization techniques to generate explanations.
- **Model-agnostic methodologies:** Model-agnostic methods are designed to be used with any model, regardless of its type or complexity. These methods are designed to explain the behavior of a model without the need to understand the underlying model itself. Common techniques employed by model-agnostic methods include sensitivity analysis, local interpretable model-agnostic explanation (LIME), and Shapley values.
- **User-centered methodologies:** User-centered methodologies focus on developing XAI systems tailored to the user's needs. This approach focuses on understanding how humans think and interact with the system to develop an XAI system that is intuitive and understandable by the user. Common techniques employed by user-centered methods include natural language processing (NLP), interactive visualization, and user evaluation.
- **Interactive methodologies:** Interactive methodologies allow users to interact with the XAI system to gain insights into its workings. This approach

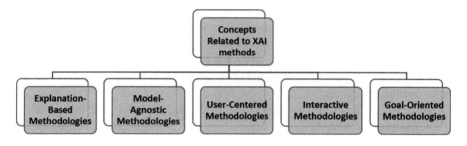

FIGURE 3.1 XAI concepts.

leverages interactive visualization, data exploration, and user feedback to
enable users to explore and understand the model's behavior.

- **Goal-oriented methodologies:** Goal-oriented methodologies are used to
  develop XAI systems focused on achieving a particular goal or outcome.
  This approach uses reinforcement learning (RL), goal-oriented optimization, and decision trees (DT) to optimize the system for a specific purpose.

The following section provides an overview of the current state of XAI and its
implementation in e-commerce. It compares different XAI methods and examines
how XAI can be used to improve customer experiences. It also presents a working
model of XAI for e-commerce, the benefits of XAI for customers and e-commerce
businesses, and the challenges to successfully adopting XAI. Potential solutions to
overcome these challenges are also discussed. Finally, it considers the future potential of XAI in e-commerce and the implications for businesses and customers. This
research is important because it can help businesses leverage XAI to create intuitive, personalized, and engaging customer experiences. Additionally, understanding
XAI's current state and potential in e-commerce can enable businesses to develop
strategies to utilize XAI effectively and remain competitive in the ever-evolving digital landscape. Ultimately, this research aims to provide businesses with insights into
the opportunities and challenges associated with XAI in e-commerce and guidance
on how to maximize its potential.

3.3   RELATED WORKS

This section reviews the literature on the use of XAI for e-commerce customer experience. We discuss recent research, including the use of explainable AI for product
recommendation, customer segmentation, and personalization. We also consider the
implications of XAI for customer trust and engagement and its potential to improve
customer satisfaction. Finally, we discuss the challenges and opportunities posed by
XAI for e-commerce customer experience.

In this study [25], the authors examine ML models for online purchases, intro-
spection on what is required for a successful online purchase, and the generation of
hypotheses regarding what contributes to a successful online purchase. Researchers
in this study [26] discuss the application of ML and AI in e-commerce, corporate
management, and finance. Data complexity and diversity are managed by ML models
in the e-commerce industry, and AI is especially appealing to finance managers. In
this study [27], the authors have developed an ML model that can predict checkout
abandonment rates for online merchants. The model can predict abandonment rates
for both in-app and out-of-app transactions. The authors have also allowed the
merchants to explore the reasons for each single prediction output. This will ensure
that online merchants can make sound decision-making and effective stock management. In this study [28], the multi-output deep neural network (DNN) model outperforms the single-output DNN model, multi-output DT, and multi-output Random
Forests (RF) across all assessment measures, proving that the multi-output DNN
model is more suitable for multi-category e-commerce retailers' usage.

Furthermore, Shapley values derived through the explainable AI method are used to interpret the decisions of the DNN. This practice demonstrates that inputs contribute more to the outcomes (a significant novelty in interpreting the DNN model for the customer lifetime value [CLV]). The study [29] found that customers' churn is determined by their payment value, number of items bought, and shipping cost. It also found that customers' categories of products bought, and the demographic environment of the customer determine their propensity to churn. Lastly, the study found that customers' purchase summaries and customer location have no impact on their propensity to churn. A comparative study of related work is presented in Table 3.1.

3.4 CURRENT STATE OF XAI IN E-COMMERCE

The use of XAI in e-commerce is still in its early stages. However, it is becoming increasingly popular due to its potential to provide better customer service, customer experience, and decision-making [30]. By using predictive analytics and ML, XAI enables e-commerce companies to provide more personalized and automated customer service.

XAI can help customers better understand the products and services offered by e-commerce companies. For example, XAI can explain why a product recommendation was made, or a particular price was suggested [31]. XAI can also be useful for understanding customer behavior, helping to identify customer segments, and providing personalized product recommendations. In addition, XAI can improve the accuracy of automated decision-making processes, such as fraud detection, credit scoring, and inventory management.

Finally, XAI can be used to improve the efficiency of operations, such as marketing campaigns, customer service, and order fulfillment.

Overall, XAI has the potential to revolutionize the e-commerce industry by providing a more personalized and automated experience for customers. However, more research and development are needed before XAI can fully integrate into e-commerce companies.

According to Table 3.2, the current state of XAI is characterized by the use of NLP, ML, DL, and RL for various use cases. These technologies offer advantages, such as quickly and accurately processing customer inquiries, predicting customer churn, optimizing product search, personalizing product recommendations, and optimizing marketing campaigns. However, these technologies also pose certain disadvantages, requiring significant training and tuning to achieve accuracy.

3.5 PROCESS OF IMPLEMENTING XAI IN E-COMMERCE

This section aims to outline a step-by-step process for implementing XAI in an e-commerce setting to improve customer experiences. The XAI system comprises four key components: (1) data collection and analysis, (2) algorithm selection,

TABLE 3.1
Comparative Study of Different XAI Methodologies in E-Commerce

References	Main Objective	Methodology	Outcome	Challenges	Opportunities
Khrais [25]	In e-commerce, AI is primarily focused on ethical soundness.	Word cloud, Voyance, and concordance analysis	Insights into decision-making, data, and variables.	• Explain AI systems in e-commerce • Find solutions to the "black box" issue	To establish customer relationships, and to examine solutions to the "black box" problem.
Pallathadka et al. [26]	Applications of machine learning and artificial intelligence in e-commerce, financial, and food sectors.	Machine learning, artificial intelligence	Enhance customer experience, supply chain management and operational efficiency.	• Standardized quality control methods • Reliable quality control methods • Consistent quality control measures	The development of advanced machine learning models for the food industry.
Rifat et al. [27]	Developing a machine learning system to assist merchants to minimize the rate of checkout abandonment.	Machine learning	ML algorithm to decrease checkout abandonment rates and provide insight into reasons for business growth predictions.	• High conversion rates • ML systems and models to predict checkout activity • Understanding predicted results	To help in business growth and effective stock management, we developed a robust ML model that predicts checkout abandonment.
Yilmaz et al. [28]	This study aimed to determine which customers will generate the highest revenue in the future based on distinct product category (DPC) and trend in amount spent (TAS).	Deep neural networks, customer lifetime value (CLV) distinct product categories (DPC), single-output, multi-output Decision Trees (DT), and multi-output Random Forests (RF)	The results indicate that the multi-output DNN model outperforms other models.	• Lack of multi-category breakdown • Poor understanding of one-time purchasers • Lack of comparison of segmentation techniques	Investigate CLV and other attributes in customer strategies, seek new features for forecasting, predict category-based CLV metrics, and cross-sell product categories.
Matuszelański and Kopczewska [29]	This study aimed to develop and test a comprehensive churn model for e-commerce using data from the Brazilian Olist company.	Latent Dirichlet Allocation, Dirichlet Multinomial Mixture, and Gibbs sampling	Customers' propensity to churn can be affected by payment value, number of items bought, shipping cost, product categories, demographics, and location.	• Lack of comparative studies • The need for post-COVID comparisons • Limited geographic area	Build a churn model for Olist e-commerce using ML and spatial analysis.

TABLE 3.2

Overview of Technologies and Their Use Cases, Advantages, and Disadvantages

Technology	Use Cases	Advantages	Disadvantages
Natural Language Processing (NLP) [32]	Automatically categorizing customer inquiries, personalizing product recommendations, providing automated customer support	NLP can quickly and accurately process customer inquiries and provide personalized product recommendations. It can also reduce customer support costs by automating customer support.	NLP can be slow to process large amounts of data and may require significant training and tuning to achieve accuracy.
Machine Learning (ML) [33, 34]	Automatically detecting fraud, predicting customer churn, and optimizing product search	ML can quickly and accurately detect suspicious activity, predict customer churn, and optimize product searches. It can also help identify customer segments and optimize marketing campaigns.	ML can be difficult to implement and require significant training and tuning to achieve accuracy.
Deep Learning (DL) [35]	Automatically detecting product defects, identifying customer segments, and recognizing customer's faces	DL can quickly and accurately detect product defects, identify customer segments, and recognize customers' faces. It can also help optimize product search and marketing campaigns.	DL can be computationally intensive and may require significant training and tuning to achieve accuracy.
Reinforcement Learning (RL) [36]	Automatically optimizing the customer journey, personalizing product recommendations, and optimizing marketing campaigns	RL can quickly and accurately optimize the customer journey, personalize product recommendations, and optimize marketing campaigns. It can also help identify customer segments and optimize marketing campaigns.	RL can be difficult to implement and require significant training and tuning to achieve accuracy.

(3) explainability techniques, and (4) customer feedback. Figure 3.2 illustrates the process of XAI used in e-commerce.

- **Data collection and analysis:** First and foremost, it is important to gather the right data to analyze customer interactions, behaviors, and preferences. This data can come from various sources, such as customer surveys, website

FIGURE 3.2   Process for XAI in e-commerce.

analytics, and customer support calls, and should be utilized to build a comprehensive view of the customer's needs and wants. Additionally, this data
can identify patterns and trends in customer behavior, allowing for more
accurate predictions of customer preferences.

- **Algorithm selection:** After the data has been collected, the next step is
  determining which algorithms will be used for the XAI system. Various
  algorithms, such as DT, neural networks, and support vector machines, can
  be used to create a predictive model. It is important to select an algorithm
  best suited to the data and can provide an accurate and reliable prediction
  of customer preferences.
- **Explainability techniques:** Once the algorithm has been selected, the next
  step is to apply explainability techniques. Explainability techniques make the
  algorithm's predictions more transparent, allowing for a better understanding of the customer's behavior. These techniques can involve visualizations
  of the predictions, providing descriptions of the predictions, or providing a
  detailed explanation of the underlying logic behind the predictions.
- **Customer feedback:** Finally, customer feedback is an important part of the
  XAI system. This feedback can be used to assess the accuracy and reliability of the predictions and identify areas for improvement. Additionally, customer feedback can be used to refine the explainability techniques, such as
  providing more detailed explanations or adding additional visualizations, to
  make the predictions more understandable and transparent.

3.6   UTILIZING XAI TO IMPROVE CUSTOMER EXPERIENCES

Once the working model is in place, the next step is to use XAI to improve customer experiences in e-commerce. XAI can make e-commerce more personalized,
accurate, and efficient. Here are some examples of how XAI can be used to improve
customer experiences in e-commerce:

- Recommending products based on customer profiles and past purchase behavior
- Automatically detecting anomalous customer behavior and alerting cus-
  tomer service
- Automating customer segmentation and personalization
- Automating customer service tasks such as order processing and customer
  service inquiries
- Automatically identifying customer problems and offering solutions
- Automatically detecting fraudulent transactions
- Automatically detecting and responding to customer sentiment
- Automating customer feedback analysis and product optimization

3.7 TRADITIONAL AI TRANSITION TO EXPLAINABLE AI (XAI) TO IMPROVE CUSTOMER EXPERIENCES IN E-COMMERCE

This section will discuss the transition from traditional AI to XAI. Traditional AI is largely based on black box algorithms that are difficult to interpret and understand; the output is often unpredictable and can lead to errors or misclassifications [37]. To increase the trustworthiness of AI systems, XAI has been developed to provide a more transparent and explainable approach to AI. XAI seeks to make AI systems more interpretable by providing explanations for the decisions they make. This can be done by using interpretable models, such as DT, which can be used to visualize the decision-making process. It also involves using techniques such as feature importance, which can be used to identify the most influential factors in the AI system's decision [38]. XAI also seeks to explain why certain decisions were made, such as by providing a breakdown of the weights assigned to the different features of the data. This can help increase transparency and trust in the AI system, as users can understand the decisions and reasoning behind them.

Figure 3.3 compares AI-powered demographics and XAI for enhancing customer experiences. AI-powered demographics are a type of AI that uses customer data to create customer profiles and segment them into meaningful groups. This allows businesses to focus their marketing efforts on the right target audiences and create more tailored customer experiences. XAI, on the other hand, provides a more transparent and interpretable method for businesses to make decisions and understand the underlying logic behind AI decisions. XAI provides a more holistic view of customer needs, allowing businesses to understand customer behaviors better and build better customer relationships. AI-powered demographics and XAI can enhance customer experiences, but XAI provides a more comprehensive view of customer data and can create more personalized experiences. Overall, XAI seeks to make AI systems more

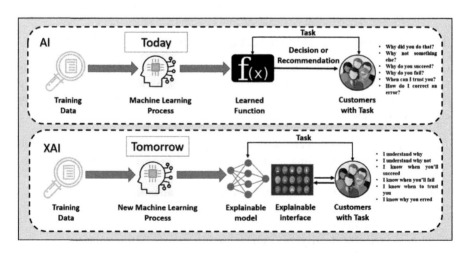

FIGURE 3.3 Comparing AI-powered demographics and XAI for enhancing customer experiences.

TABLE 3.3

Comparison of Traditional AI and Explainable AI

Traditional AI	Explainable AI (XAI)
• It uses algorithms that are not transparent or understandable to humans	• It uses algorithms that allow humans to understand and explain the decision-making process of the AI system
• Makes decisions on its own, without human input	• It empowers humans to make decisions by understanding the AI system's rationale and logic
• The decisions made by the AI system are opaque and non-transparent	• The decisions made by the AI system are transparent and explainable
• Data-driven decisions are based on large amounts of data	• Decisions are based on the AI system's understanding of the data and its ability to explain the rationale behind its decision
• Difficult to debug and troubleshoot errors	• Easier to debug and troubleshoot errors

interpretable and transparent by explaining the decisions made. In this way, users can better understand how the AI system operates and increase trust in it.

Table 3.3 compares traditional AI to XAI. It outlines the differences between the two, such as the ability to understand and explain the decision-making process of XAI, the transparency and explainability of the decisions made by XAI, and the difficulty in debugging and troubleshooting errors.

3.8   WORKING MODEL OF XAI FOR E-COMMERCE

In this section, the XAI model used in the e-commerce industry combines several AI technologies, such as ML, NLP, and DL. According to [39], the authors developed a smart framework for executing real-world applications in the cloud environment. By combining IoT and cloud technologies [40, 41], e-commerce models can be characterized in a more sophisticated way. Therefore, these technologies help to improve customer experiences by providing personalized services, product recommendations, and customer support. According to Figure 3.4, the working model of XAI for e-commerce is discussed step-by-step.

- **Data collection:** The first step in the working model of XAI for E-commerce is data collection. This involves gathering the necessary data from various sources, such as customer reviews, product descriptions, ratings, and other relevant sources. The data should be collected in a structured format for better analysis.
- **Data-preprocessing:** After collecting the data, it needs to be preprocessed to remove any irrelevant information, normalize the data, and make it ready for use. This step also involves cleaning the data, removing any incorrect or missing values, and formatting the data for use in ML models.

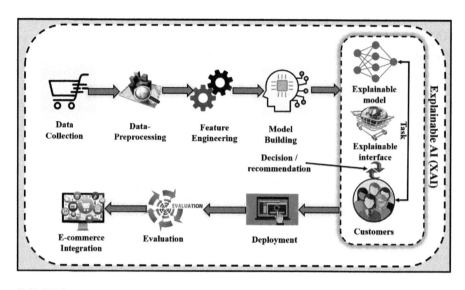

FIGURE 3.4 Working model of XAI for e-commerce application.

- **Feature engineering:** This step involves creating new features from the data that can be used for predictive modeling. This includes extracting features from the text data and transforming the data into a format that the ML models can use.
- **Model building:** After the features have been created, the next step is to build the model. This involves selecting a suitable algorithm, training the model on the data, and testing the model to assess its accuracy.
- **Explainable AI:** This step involves using XAI techniques to explain the model's decisions. This includes using techniques, such as feature importance, DT, and rule-based explanations to explain the model's decisions. In XAI, a Model of Explainability, an Interface of Explainability, and Customers are all involved, which are described as follows:
  - **Explainable model:** As part of the XAI process, this step involves creating an explainable model that can be used to explain the model's decisions to customers. This could include using techniques such as NLP to generate explanations that customers can understand.
  - **Explainable interface:** This involves developing an interface allowing customers to interact with the explainable model. In addition, the model can be explained through visualizations, or questions and answers can be provided in an interactive mode.
  - **Customers:** As part of this process, customers will be engaged with the XAI system. Customers can receive information about the model's decisions and feedback regarding its performance from this department.
- **Deployment:** After the XAI system has been tested and evaluated, it needs to be deployed in an e-commerce environment. This involves setting up the system, configuring the necessary settings, and ensuring that the system is secure and reliable.

- **Evaluation:** This step involves evaluating the performance of the XAI system on e-commerce data. This could include using metrics, such as accuracy, precision, recall, and F-measure to assess the system's performance.
- **E-commerce integration:** The final step in the working model of XAI for e-commerce is integrating the system with existing e-commerce platforms. This could include integrating the system with platforms like Amazon, eBay, or Shopify. This would enable customers to use the XAI system to make better online shopping decisions.

3.9   BENEFITS OF XAI FOR CUSTOMERS AND E-COMMERCE BUSINESSES

XAI has the potential to improve the customer experience in e-commerce by providing customers with more transparency and control over their interactions with e-commerce platforms. XAI-based explanations can help customers better understand product recommendations and make more informed decisions. Additionally, XAI-based explanations can help to build trust and loyalty between customers and e-commerce businesses. XAI can also be used to optimize e-commerce business operations, such as personalizing product recommendations and pricing. The following benefits can be achieved by using XAI to improve customer experience in e-commerce:

- **Improved decision-making:** XAI enables customers to make better decisions by providing personalized and contextualized recommendations. This helps customers make informed decisions faster and easier. For businesses, this means improved customer engagement, loyalty, and reduced churn.
- **Increased conversions:** XAI algorithms can help generate more conversions by providing customers with personalized recommendations and content. This helps businesses increase their revenue and gain a competitive advantage.
- **Improved customer experience:** XAI algorithms can help personalize the customer experience by providing them with tailored content and recommendations. This helps businesses create a better customer experience that increases satisfaction and loyalty.
- **Better targeting:** XAI algorithms can help businesses better target their customers by providing them with more relevant content and recommendations. This helps businesses improve their marketing efforts and increase their reach.
- **Improved engagement:** XAI algorithms can help businesses engage customers more effectively by providing personalized content and recommendations. This helps businesses improve customer engagement and loyalty.
- **Optimized operations:** XAI algorithms can help businesses optimize their operations by providing them with personalized product recommendations and pricing. This helps businesses reduce costs and improve efficiency.

3.10   CHALLENGES TO SUCCESSFULLY ADOPTING XAI

Despite XAI's potential benefits, several challenges must be addressed before XAI can be successfully adopted in e-commerce. Firstly, ML models must be made more transparent and explainable. Secondly, trust-building measures must be implemented to ensure that customers understand and trust the explanations provided by XAI-based systems. Finally, XAI-based systems must be able to provide accurate and up-to-date explanations of the decision-making process. The following challenges must also be addressed to utilize XAI in e-commerce effectively:

- **Data availability:** XAI requires large amounts of data to be effective, and it cannot be easy to obtain sufficient data to train algorithms. This can be especially problematic in cases where data is confidential or proprietary or if the data is not standardized across different sources. Companies need to invest in data collection, aggregation, and validation processes to ensure that the data is available for XAI.
- **Explainability:** XAI must be able to explain why it makes certain decisions, which can be a challenge since the algorithms are often complex and difficult to understand. Companies must find ways to make their XAI algorithms as transparent and interpretable as possible.
- **Algorithm bias:** Algorithms can sometimes be biased due to the data they are trained on, leading to inaccurate or unfair decisions. Companies must be aware of this and ensure their algorithms are trained in unbiased data sets.
- **Security and privacy:** With XAI, companies must ensure that customer data is secure and private and that the algorithms are not used for malicious purposes.
- **Cost:** XAI can be expensive to implement, and companies will need to consider the cost of training the algorithms and maintaining the system.
- **Regulatory compliance:** Companies must ensure that their XAI-based systems comply with applicable laws and regulations related to privacy and data security. They must also be aware of any changes in regulations that may impact on their systems.

3.11   POTENTIAL SOLUTIONS TO OVERCOME CHALLENGES

This section will discuss potential solutions to e-commerce businesses' challenges when implementing XAI. XAI has been gaining considerable traction in recent years due to its ability to provide users with clear and understandable explanations for the decisions made by AI systems. To unlock the full potential of XAI and benefit e-commerce businesses, it is important to consider solutions to the most common challenges associated with its implementation. These solutions can range from incorporating user feedback into the decision-making process to improving the system's transparency to developing a better understanding of how XAI works. By addressing these challenges, e-commerce businesses can improve customer experiences and increase trust in their AI systems. The following strategies can be used to overcome the challenges of XAI in e-commerce:

- **Adaptive personalization:** Adaptive personalization is a powerful tool that can be used to improve customer experiences in e-commerce. Through AI-driven algorithms and ML, adaptive personalization can track user behavior and provide tailored content, product recommendations, and other features that meet a customer's needs.
- **Automated customer service:** Automated customer service can reduce the burden on customer service representatives by automating basic customer interactions. Using AI-powered chatbots and voice assistants, e-commerce businesses can quickly provide customers with the information they need without waiting for a human representative.
- **Machine learning-powered fraud detection:** ML can be used to detect fraud in e-commerce. By analyzing customer behavior and data, ML algorithms can identify patterns that may indicate fraudulent activity. This can help e-commerce businesses reduce the risk of fraudulent transactions and protect their customers.
- **Explainable AI:** XAI is an emerging technology that can improve customer experiences in e-commerce. XAI can provide customers with an explanation of why a certain product was recommended or why a certain decision was made. This can help customers understand why they see certain content and make better decisions.
- **Augmented reality:** Augmented reality (AR) can provide customers with a more immersive shopping experience. Customers can visualize products in their own space using AR-powered features, try on clothes virtually, and compare products side-by-side. This can help customers make better informed decisions and reduce the risk of buyer's remorse.
- **Leveraging chatbots:** Chatbots can improve customer experiences in e-commerce by providing automated customer service and support. Chatbots can answer frequently asked questions, provide product recommendations, and proactively help. This can help to reduce wait times and improve customer satisfaction.

3.12   DISCUSSION

XAI is an emerging technology that has the potential to revolutionize customer experiences in e-commerce. By providing more insight into the workings of AI systems, XAI can help e-commerce companies better understand their customers and tailor their services accordingly. XAI can also enable more accurate predictions of customer behavior, allowing e-commerce companies to anticipate customer needs and create experiences tailored to their individual preferences. XAI can improve customer service by providing customers with more detailed explanations of why a decision was made. For example, an AI system used to recommend products to customers could use XAI to explain why a particular product was chosen. This gives customers more insight into the system and can help them better understand its workings.

XAI can also improve product recommendations by allowing e-commerce companies to understand customer preferences better. With XAI, companies can understand why a customer has made a particular purchase decision and use this to make more accurate predictions about future purchases. This helps companies create better product recommendations and provides customers with more personalized experiences. Finally, XAI can also be used to improve the security of e-commerce systems. By providing detailed explanations of why certain decisions were made, XAI can help detect potentially malicious activity and help companies identify the source of any security breaches. Overall, XAI has the potential to improve customer experiences in e-commerce significantly. By providing more insight into the workings of AI systems, XAI can help e-commerce companies better understand their customers and tailor their services accordingly. Additionally, XAI can be used to improve product recommendations, provide more detailed explanations of decisions, and improve the security of e-commerce systems. As such, XAI is an invaluable tool for improving customer experiences in e-commerce.

3.13 CONCLUSION AND FUTURE DIRECTIONS

XAI has the potential to revolutionize customer experiences in e-commerce by enabling personalized, targeted, and transparent experiences. XAI can enable e-commerce retailers to give customers a better understanding of the decisions being made, allowing them to make more informed purchases. Additionally, XAI can enable personalized experiences by providing customers with more tailored recommendations, creating a more engaging and engaging customer experience. Although XAI has great potential to improve customer experiences in e-commerce, many challenges still exist. These include improving the accuracy and speed of XAI models and their ability to explain complex decisions. Additionally, further research into methods of leveraging XAI to create more personalized experiences is needed. With continued research and development, XAI has the potential to unlock the potential of e-commerce and create a more positive customer experience.

REFERENCES

1. Lukyanenko, R., Maass, W., & Storey, V. C. (2022). Trust in artificial intelligence: From a foundational trust framework to emerging research opportunities. Electronic Markets, 32(4), 1993–2020.
2. Arya, V., Bellamy, R. K., Chen, P. Y., Dhurandhar, A., Hind, M., Hoffman, S. C., ... & Zhang, Y. (2019). One explanation does not fit all: A toolkit and taxonomy of AI explainability techniques. arXiv preprint arXiv:1909.03012.
3. Castillo, M. J., & Taherdoost, H. (2023). The impact of AI technologies on e-business. Encyclopedia, 3(1), 107–121.
4. Hagras, H. (2018). Toward human-understandable, explainable AI. Computer, 51(9), 28–36.
5. Wang, D., Yang, Q., Abdul, A., & Lim, B. Y. (2019, May). Designing Theory-Driven User-Centric Explainable AI. In: Proceedings of the 2019 CHI Conference on Human Factors in Computing Systems (pp. 1–15).
6. Bartle, A. S., Jiang, Z., Jiang, R., & Bouridane, A., & Almaadeed, S. A critical appraisal on deep neural networks: Bridge the gap from deep learning to neuroscience via XAI.
7. Lamy, J. B., Sekar, B., Guezennec, G., Bouaud, J., & Séroussi, B. (2019). Explainable artificial intelligence for breast cancer: A visual case-based reasoning approach. Artificial Intelligence in Medicine, 94, 42–53.

8. Liao, M., & Sundar, S. S. (2022). When e-commerce personalization systems show and tell: Investigating the relative persuasive appeal of content-based versus collaborative filtering. Journal of Advertising, 51(2), 256–267.

9. Gerlach, J., Hoppe, P., Jagels, S., Licker, L., & Breitner, M. H. (2022). Decision support for efficient XAI services – A morphological analysis, business model archetypes, and a decision tree. Electronic Markets, 32(4), 2139–2158.

10. Chaudhary, K., & Alam, M. (2022). Big Data Analytics: Applications in Business and Marketing. Boca Raton, FL: Auerbach Publications.

11. Chaudhary, K., & Alam, M. (Eds.). (2022). Big Data Analytics: Digital Marketing and Decision-Making. Boca Raton, FL: CRC Press.

12. Naiseh, M., Al-Thani, D., Jiang, N., & Ali, R. (2023). How the different explanation classes impact trust calibration: The case of clinical decision support systems. International Journal of Human-Computer Studies, 169, 102941.

13. Chaudhary, K., Alam, M., Al-Rakhami, M. S., & Gumaei, A. (2021). Machine learning-based mathematical modelling for prediction of social media consumer behavior using big data analytics. Journal of Big Data, 8(1), 1–20.

14. Malhotra, S., Chaudhary, K., & Alam, M. (2022). Modeling the use of voice based assistant devices (VBADs): A machine learning base an exploratory study using cluster analysis and correspondence analysis. International Journal of Information Management Data Insights, 2(1), 100069.

15. Ansari, M., & Alam, M. (2023). An intelligent IoT-cloud-based air pollution forecasting model using univariate time-series analysis. Arabian Journal for Science and Engineering, 1–28.

16. Ansari, M., & Alam, M. (2022). IoT-Cloud Enabled Statistical Analysis and Visualization of Air Pollution Data in India. In: Proceedings of Data Analytics and Management: ICDAM 2021, Volume 2 (pp. 125–139). Singapore: Springer Singapore.

17. Ali, S. A., Ansari, M., & Alam, M. (2020). Resource management techniques for cloud-based IoT environment. Internet of Things (IoT) Concepts and Applications, 63–87.

18. Atakishiyev, S., Salameh, M., Yao, H., & Goebel, R. (2021). Explainable artificial intelligence for autonomous driving: A comprehensive overview and field guide for future research directions. arXiv preprint arXiv:2112.11561.

19. Blazek, P. J., & Lin, M. M. (2021). Explainable neural networks that simulate reasoning. Nature Computational Science, 1(9), 607–618.

20. Ciravegna, G., Barbiero, P., Giannini, F., Gori, M., Lió, P., Maggini, M., & Melacci, S. (2023). Logic explained networks. Artificial Intelligence, 314, 103822.

21. Shi, S., Xie, Y., Wang, Z., Ding, B., Li, Y., & Zhang, M. (2022, April). Explainable Neural Rule Learning. In: Proceedings of the ACM Web Conference 2022 (pp. 3031–3041).

22. Ali, A., Aliyuda, K., Elmitwally, N., & Bello, A. M. (2022). Towards more accurate and explainable supervised learning-based prediction of deliverability for underground natural gas storage. Applied Energy, 327, 120098.

23. Morichetta, A., Casas, P., & Mellia, M. (2019, December). EXPLAIN-IT: Towards Explainable AI for Unsupervised Network Traffic Analysis. In: Proceedings of the 3rd ACM CoNEXT Workshop on Big DAta, Machine Learning and Artificial Intelligence for Data Communication Networks (pp. 22–28).

24. Vilone, G., & Longo, L. (2020). Explainable artificial intelligence: A systematic review. arXiv preprint arXiv:2006.00093.

25. Khrais, L. T. (2020). Role of artificial intelligence in shaping consumer demand in e-commerce. Future Internet, 12(12), 226.

26. Pallathadka, H., Ramirez-Asis, E. H., Loli-Poma, T. P., Kaliyaperumal, K., Ventayen, R. J. M., & Naved, M. (2021). Applications of artificial intelligence in business management, e-commerce and finance. Materials Today: Proceedings.

27. Rifat, M. R. I., Amin, M. N., Munna, M. H., & Al Imran, A. (2022, September). An End-to-end Machine Learning System for Mitigating Checkout Abandonment in E-Commerce. In: 2022 17th Conference on Computer Science and Intelligence Systems (FedCSIS) (pp. 129–132). IEEE.

28. Yılmaz Benk, G., Badur, B., & Mardikyan, S. (2022). A new 360° framework to predict customer lifetime value for multi-category e-commerce companies using a multi-output deep neural network and explainable artificial intelligence. Information, 13(8), 373.

29. Matuszelański, K., & Kopczewska, K. (2022). Customer churn in retail e-commerce business: Spatial and machine learning approach. Journal of Theoretical and Applied Electronic Commerce Research, 17(1), 165–198.

30. Ekhart, N. (2022). Taking down malicious webshops: Designing explainable AI against growing e-commerce fraud.

31. Ravi, M., Negi, A., & Chitnis, S. (2022, April). A Comparative Review of Expert Systems, Recommender Systems, and Explainable AI. In: 2022 IEEE 7th International conference for Convergence in Technology (I2CT) (pp. 1–8). IEEE.

32. Qian, K., Danilevsky, M., Katsis, Y., Kawas, B., Oduor, E., Popa, L., & Li, Y. (2021, April). XNLP: A Living Survey for XAI Research in Natural Language Processing. In: 26th International Conference on Intelligent User Interfaces-Companion (pp. 78–80).

33. Emmert-Streib, F., Yli-Harja, O., & Dehmer, M. (2020). Explainable artificial intelligence and machine learning: A reality rooted perspective. Wiley Interdisciplinary Reviews: Data Mining and Knowledge Discovery, 10(6), e1368.

34. Hasan, N., Chaudhary, K., & Alam, M. (2021). Unsupervised machine learning framework for early machine failure detection in an industry. Journal of Discrete Mathematical Sciences and Cryptography, 24(5), 1497–1508.

35. Kenny, E. M., & Keane, M. T. (2021). Explaining deep learning using examples: Optimal feature weighting methods for twin systems using post-hoc, explanation-by-example in XAI. Knowledge-Based Systems, 233, 107530.

36. Wäldchen, S., Pokutta, S., & Huber, F. (2022, June). Training Characteristic Functions with Reinforcement Learning: Xai-Methods Play Connect Four. In: International Conference on Machine Learning (pp. 22457–22474). PMLR.

37. Adadi, A., & Berrada, M. (2018). Peeking inside the black-box: A survey on explainable artificial intelligence (XAI). IEEE Access, 6, 52138–52160.

38. Arrieta, A. B., Díaz-Rodríguez, N., Del Ser, J., Bennetot, A., Tabik, S., Barbado, A., … Herrera, F. (2020). Explainable artificial intelligence (XAI): Concepts, taxonomies, opportunities and challenges toward responsible AI. Information Fusion, 58, 82–115.

39. Ansari, M., & Alam, M. (2023). IoT-Cloud-Enabled Smart Framework for Real-World Applications. In: Intelligent Systems and Applications: Select Proceedings of ICISA 2022 (pp. 87–105). Singapore: Springer Nature Singapore.

40. Ansari, M., Ali, S. A., & Alam, M. (2022). Internet of things (IoT) fusion with cloud computing: Current research and future direction.

41. Parween, S., & Hussain, S. Z. (2022). A comparative analysis of CoAP based congestion control in IoT. In: 2021 4th International Conference on Recent Trends in Computer Science and Technology (ICRTCST) (pp. 321–324). IEEE.

4 Business Intelligence

Kingsley T. Igulu[1], Friday E. Onuodu[2],
Richa Chaudhary[3], and Palimote Justice[4]
[1]Department of Computer Science, Kenule Beeson
Saro-Wiwa Polytechnic, Bori, Rivers State, Nigeria
[2]Department of Computer Science, University
of Port Harcourt, Port Harcourt, Nigeria
[3]School of Computer Science, UPES University,
Dehradun, India
[4]Department of Computer Science, Kenule Beeson
Saro-Wiwa Polytechnic, Bori, Rivers State, Nigeria

4.1 INTRODUCTION

Every day, enormous new volumes of data are being collected. They frequently become incredibly difficult to maintain and process, particularly in light of the enormous volume of data that is flowing from social media platforms and the internet. These data are presented in a different format and follow a distinct organizational scheme. These data originate from a wide variety of sources as well. To handle, preserve, and manage these data to monetize them, several kinds of tools and software are being developed by enterprises.

Business intelligence (BI) is a term that encompasses a wide range of methods, structures, systems, tools, applications, and technologies that take raw data and transform it into actionable insight for strategic, tactical, and operational decision-making. The term "BI tools" refers to all of these techniques, architectures, workflows, programs, and technologies. These approaches, architectures, processes, applications, and technologies are in charge of gathering and processing raw data into information that is pertinent and valuable to drive corporate performance according to Evelson and Nicolson (2008). The BI process often includes a wide range of auxiliary procedures or duties, covering data sourcing and collection, data cleansing, data storage, data analysis, data display and communication, and data delivery. For instance, the BI procedure can involve the following: data cleansing (Zheng et al., 2014). Data presentation involves the display and provision of findings of a query or analysis given in a human-comprehensible formats (e.g. charts, tables, and diagrams), which aid in the making of decisions at both the low-level and the high-level. The presentation of data will frequently make use of interactive searches and data explorations to provide users with assistance in obtaining information that is pertinent to their needs. BI systems include a variety of data visualization and interaction forms and approaches inside the technical stack, such as digital dashboards, reports (both static and interactive reports), and advanced analytical and visual tools. These can be accessed through the reports (Chiang, 2011).

DOI: 10.1201/9781032614083-4

As a catch-all phrase, "business intelligence" can be used to many different types of data-analysis software. Some examples of these uses are online analytical processing (OLAP), real-time BI, enterprise reporting, mobile BI, operational BI, open source BI, cloud and software as a service BI, location intelligence, and collaborative BI. Software for data visualization is also part of BI tools, and it can be used to make charts and other infographics. Additionally, BI technology includes tools for the construction of BI dashboards and performance scorecards, which display data visualizations of business key performance indicators (KPIs) in a manner that is easy to understand.

Statistical analysis, data mining, predictive analytics, text mining, and big data analytics are all examples of advanced analytics techniques that could be incorporated into a BI program. The data scientists, predictive modelers, statisticians, and other professional analytics specialists who work on and manage advanced analytics projects often work in siloed groups.

There has been a demand for showing massive volumes of data in a format that is not just straightforward to acquire but also straightforward to comprehend. Data are created by organizations daily. Following that, there has been a substantial increase in the amount of information that can be retrieved via the web. For customers to traditionally visualize, analyze, and make use of such huge amounts of data presents a daunting challenge (Zheng, 2017). The capacity to visualize data is a skill that is essential for conducting scientific research. These days, computers can process enormous amounts of data. Data visualization refers to the process of designing, developing, and putting into action the creation of graphical representations of data that are generated by a computer. It does an effective job of representing data that comes from a variety of sources. The visualization of analytics for decision makers is facilitated because of this, and it also makes it simpler for decision makers to analyze the data. Children benefit from this because it enables them to recognize patterns, comprehend information, and formulate views (Zheng, 2017).

4.2   BUSINESS INTELLIGENCE: HISTORY AND DEFINITIONS

4.2.1   What Is Business Intelligence (BI)?

Howard Dresner is credited as being the first modern author to use the term "business intelligence" in its current form. Although the phrase "business intelligence" has been in use for a number of decades, this particular usage dates back to 1988. According to Dresner, the BI could be defined as "concepts and ways to enhance business decision making through the application of fact-based support systems."

When it comes to making strategic, tactical, and operational insights and decisions, BI is defined by Forrester as "a collection of techniques, processes, systems, and technologies that transform raw data into meaningful and valuable information." As of the date of publishing, this definition is complete and correct.

Other definitions include:

- *"A variety of software applications used to analyze an organization's raw data by CIO.com"*

- *"A broad category of computer software solutions that enables a company or organization to gain insight into its critical operations through reporting applications and analysis tools by Information Builder".*
- *"Technologies, applications and practices for the collection, integration, analysis, and presentation of business information by OLAP.com"*
- *"The use of computing technologies for the identification, discovery and analysis of business data – like sales revenue, products, costs and incomes by Technopedia."*

The BI software is the primary topic of discussion in many of these definitions. BI encompasses more than only the use of computing tools, even though the term is typically linked to businesses in the software industry. In addition, the primary aim of BI is left out of many standard definitions of the term "business intelligence." The following definitions were taken from Better Buys (2015) and will be used throughout this work:

Business Intelligence helps derive meaningful insights from raw data. It's an umbrella term that includes the software, infrastructure, policies, and procedures that can lead to smarter, data-driven decision making. And

(Evelson and Nicolson, 2008):

Business Intelligence (BI) is a collection of methods, architectures, processes, applications, and technologies that gather(collect) and transform raw data into meaningful and useful information used to enable more effective strategic, tactical, and operational insights and decision-making to drive business performance.

Business intelligence platforms are those that, according to the technical definition provided by Gartner, "allow organizations to build BI applications by providing capabilities in three categories: analysis, such as online analytical processing (OLAP); information delivery, such as reports and dashboards; and platform integration, such as BI metadata management and a development environment."

In their most basic form, BI systems aid decision makers by providing them with information that can be acted upon, which is then given at the appropriate time, in the right location, and in the right form. This project's goal is to simplify management responsibilities by improving both the timeliness and the quality of the information that is fed into the decision-making process. On occasion, the term "business intelligence" will refer to the process of making decisions online, which is also sometimes referred to as "instant response." The majority of the time, this phrase is referring to reducing the amount of time that has passed in order to increase the likelihood that the intelligence will still be useful to the person making the decision when it is finally time to make the choice. The implementation of strategies derived from BI is commonly acknowledged to be a preventative strategy.

BI is a technology-driven process that analyzes data and provides users with insights to help them make better business decisions. The term "business intelligence" (BI) refers to a broad category of technologies, programs, and approaches that facilitate the gathering of information from various internal and external systems, the cleaning and organizing of that information in preparation for analysis, the formulation and execution of queries against that information, and the generation of various types of outputs (such as reports, dashboards, and data visualizations) to make the findings of that analysis accessible to end users and operational staff. These procedures are routinely performed as part of the data collection process.

Because BI data may incorporate both historical and real-time information from source systems, it can be used to assist both strategic and tactical decision-making processes. Data analysts and other members of the information technology (IT) sector were the earliest adopters of BI software. These experts would investigate issues and compile reports detailing the outcomes of queries for corporate clients. Nonetheless, BI software is increasingly being used by executives, economists, analysts, and employees on their own. The emergence of DIY tools for business analytics and information discovery is a contributing factor.

In its study on the evaluation of BI for the year 2022, Gartner (2022) evaluates that there are 12 functional capabilities that are required for BI platforms. The requirements are discussed as follows:

1. **Security:** Features that provide managing users, monitoring platform access, authenticating users, and authenticating the platform itself.
2. **Governance** (formerly called "manageability"): Capabilities for managing the generation and exchange of information, as well as measuring usage, from the prototype stage all the way through production.
3. **Cloud-enabled analytics:** The capacity to create, install, and maintain analytic applications and analytics in the cloud, while making use of data stored both in the cloud and on-premises and facilitating cooperation between various different cloud implementations.
4. **Data source connectivity:** Features that facilitate interaction between users to a variety of on-premises and cloud-based storage systems, as well as import data from those locations, are referred to as connectivity capabilities.
5. **Data preparation:** The capacity to develop analytical models, as well as support for user-driven data aggregation, drag-and-drop, and the mixing of data from many sources, are all features that are included in this capability (such as user-defined measures, groups, sets, and hierarchies).
6. **Catalog:** The capacity to display content in a way that makes it simple to locate and take in. The catalog allows users to search for items and provides them with recommendations.
7. **Automated insights:** This is one of the most essential features of augmented analytics, and it refers to the capacity to use machine learning (ML) methods in order in order to instantly offer users helpful information (by prioritizing a dataset's properties, for instance).
8. **Data visualization:** The ability to study data by changing images of charts, including support for highly dynamic dashboards. Other than the more commonplace pie, bar, and line charts, this includes more specialized visualizations like heat maps, tree maps, geography maps, scatter plots, and

many more. This does not contain, for instance, pie charts, bar charts, or line graphs.

9. **Natural language query:** Then, users can ask for specific information by typing a query into a box or talking into a microphone.
10. **Data storytelling:** The capacity to produce data stories in the style of news articles, including headlines, narrative prose, data visualizations, and audiovisual content in response to ongoing monitoring of discoveries.
11. **Natural language generation:** Data-driven insight generation is the process of creating such descriptions automatically. An analytics report's narrative will change in real time as the user explores the data, elaborating on new findings and clarifying the value of visualizations like charts and dashboards.
12. **Reporting:** This functionality enables the generation of reports that are pixel-perfect, parameterized, and paginated, as well as those that can be scheduled and broadcast to a large user population.

4.2.2   BI History and Progression

The phrase "business intelligence" was first used by Richard Millar Devens in his book "Cyclopedia of Commercial and Business Anecdotes" published in 1865. To our knowledge, this is the first time this term has been used. Devens came up with the term to characterize the success of a banker known as Sir Henry Furnese over his rivals by anticipating market shifts and acting on new information before they did. He maintained an impeccable and comprehensive stream of commercial intelligence on the entire Dutch territory, as well as Flanders, France, and Germany. He was able to improve his earnings by being the first to learn of the several conflicts that had been waged. He also benefited from the collapse of Namur, which he learned about in advance, increasing his earnings. See (Devens, 1865, p. 210) for citation. BI still relies heavily on the original capacity to gather data and act suitably in response to it. The answer is yes; Furnese was exceptional in this regard.

Modern BI is widely regarded to have originated with the development of decision support systems (DSS) in the 1960s and its subsequent refinement through the mid-1980s. DSS evolved from computer-aided models first designed to streamline the planning and decision-making processes. Since the 1980s, when DSS were first introduced, other technologies, including executive information systems (EIS), data warehouses (DWs), OLAP, and BI, have taken center stage.

BI has evolved similarly to other IT technologies and concepts. The development of BI is depicted in Figure 4.1 from Better Buys (2015):

BI is able to generate actionable data since it accepts inputs from multiple sources. Data from organized and unstructured sources may be among the several potential inputs to a BI system. Structured category includes OLAP, DW, EIS, data mining, DSS, enterprise resource planning (ERP), and databases. Unstructured sources include, but are not limited to, business processes, conversations and posts (Twitter, Instagram, and Facebook—social media), graphics, photos, videos, text, web pages, and news articles, among others.

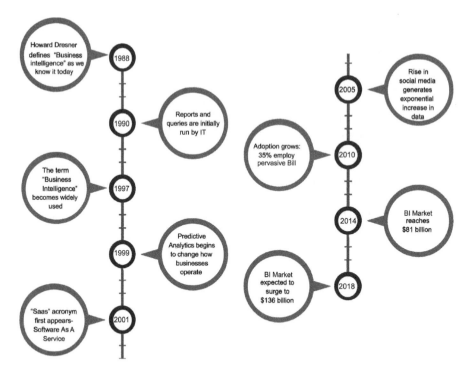

FIGURE 4.1   Progression of BI (Better Buys, 2015).

4.3   COMPONENTS OF BI

Proactive BI necessitates the following elements, as outlined by Langseth and Vivatrat (2003):

- data mining.
- geographic information systems.
- real-time data warehousing.
- automatic identification of anomalies and exceptions.
- data visualization.
- a smooth workflow that follows through on everything.
- proactive alerting combined with automatic determination of the recipient.
- automated learning and enhancing of performance.

This article (Better Buys, 2015) provides a concise summary of these aspects, which are as follows:

4.3.1   SOURCE DATA

The foundation of BI is the collection and analysis of relevant data. As was just mentioned, companies today have access to data on a scale that has never been seen before. This may largely be attributed to transactional systems, which include customer relationship management systems, ERP systems, inventory database systems, human resources and payroll system systems, and a great deal of other system types. A significant portion of the data that is utilized by BI comes from outside sources. In today's world, it is common practice to gather remarks made by individuals in which a corporation is mentioned by using social media as a source for the collection of these statements. Other sources can vary widely depending on the issues that the company is attempting to answer, but some examples include government reports, data from meteorological stations, and news stories from the relevant industry.

4.3.2 ETL (EXTRACT, TRANSFORM, AND LOAD)

Even while we have access to the data, this does not mean that it is currently in a state where it can be utilized for intelligence purposes. When it comes to the process of data preparation before analysis, BI focuses a substantial amount of stress on the programs and methods that are applied. It is extremely unlikely that the data generated by a number of different applications will all be in the same format. In addition, it is not always simple to compare the data provided by one application with the data produced by another application. This is because the data may be formatted differently. In addition, businesses that rely on BI to make significant decisions have the additional responsibility of ensuring that the data they utilize is accurate before moving forward with those decisions.

The processes of data extraction, transformation, and loading are collectively known as "Extract, Transform, and Load" (abbreviated as "ETL") in the industry. The data, after being collected from a variety of different sources, both internal and external, are then given a uniform format before being placed in a DW. This procedure, in most instances, additionally involves completing data integrity tests in order to guarantee that the information being utilized is correct and consistent.

4.3.3 DATA WAREHOUSE

Data from all of an organization's internal applications and systems, as well as data from other sources, may be stored and analyzed in a single location formally known as DW. The ETL operation is finished once the data are imported into the warehouse where they are stored. This is due to the fact that the information included inside its separate sources is of little value when used for intelligence purposes. There are two key factors contributing to this result. The majority of the time, these sources consist of apps that were developed for transaction processing rather than for analysis. In this particular circumstance, the process of analyzing data would take up an excessive amount of time and impede the performance of essential company tasks. The second goal of BI is to acquire a more in-depth understanding of the company. In order to acquire a complete picture of everything that is going on within the business, the data coming from all of these different systems need to be merged together.

4.3.4 Online Analytical Processing (OLAP)

Data warehousing and ETL methodology provide the back end of a BI system, whereas OLAP. An OLAP system facilitates the grouping, summing, and ordering of data according to a wide variety of criteria. This feature allows users to retrieve the specific information they need and run the appropriate comparisons to find the solutions to their problems.

4.3.5 Visualizations

As was said before, one of the primary objectives of BI is to streamline and improve the availability of data for business users who do not possess technical expertise. It is typically essential to convert the data into formats other than numerical lists and spreadsheets in order for it to be accurately digested. Other formats include: displaying data with the assistance of visualization tools, such as charts, graphs, and other formats, help to make the information easier to comprehend. Conventional presentation formats include things like scorecards, bar graphs, and pie charts, among other things. On the other hand, more advanced methods of data visualization can give content that is interactive and dynamic. This particular method of displaying data can also select the most useful form of representation and tailor the display to the requirements of each individual user.

4.3.6 Dashboards

The dashboard serves as the primary graphical user interface (GUI) for a wide array of business information systems of varying types. The most pertinent information and data visualizations are shown to the user in a format that is tailored according to the function that the user performs on the system. This information and these visualizations are displayed on the user's dashboard. The dashboard is an interface that is simple to operate and gives users access to a fundamental way for organizing data in a single spot. Additionally, it provides the user with the capability to drill down for additional information on particular subjects.

It is sufficient to mention that most of the BI systems rely on AI techniques (including neural networks, data mining, fuzzy logic, and general ML) to provide users with highly accurate data that can be put into practice.

4.4 USES OF BI

Decisions, both strategic and operational, can benefit from the use of BI. According to the results of a survey conducted by Gartner (Willen, 2002), the following is the order of importance for the strategic usage of BI:

1. Methods for monitoring and improving business performance
2. Customer relationship optimization, activity tracking, and conventional decision-making
3. Independent BI software packages tailored to a given set of tasks or methods.
4. Management BI reporting

BI transforms raw data into actionable information that can then be analyzed by humans to produce knowledge. BI is responsible for the following activities, among others:

- Developing projections for the future by drawing on past and current performance, as well as historical data, and making educated guesses about where the future will head.
- Analyses of "what if" scenarios that take into account the potential consequences of changes.
- Access to the data on an as-needed basis in order to provide answers to inquiries that are not routinely asked.
- Perspective on strategy.

4.5 TYPE OF DATA: STRUCTURED, SEMI-STRUCTURED AND UNSTRUCTURED DATA

Both structured and semi-structured data are used by analysts in BI (Rudin, 2003; Moss, 2003). Semi-structured data refer to any data that does not neatly fit into either relational or flat files. The phrase "structured data" refers to the data that does fit neatly into these file types. Instead of the more prevalent term "unstructured," the phrase "semi-structured" is used to acknowledge that the vast majority of data possesses some level of organization. Formally, we recognize any data that is not structured as semi-structured rather than unstructured in order to allow data that have the appearance of being structured but are not genuinely structured. This is done to accommodate data that are seemingly structured but are not truly structured. E-mail, for instance, is broken up into individual messages, and these individual messages are then compiled into folders. To be fair, the word "semi-structured data" can refer to a few different things depending on the setting in which it is used. Data that cannot be organized into rows and columns are said to be "unstructured" when discussing relational databases. These data have to be saved as a BLOB, which stands for binary big object. BLOBs are catch-all data types that are included in the majority of DBMS programs. The use of classification and taxonomy is necessary when working with unstructured data (Blumberg and Atre, 2003a) [citation needed].

Sixty percent of all CTOs and CIOs agreed that semi-structured data are crucial for improving operational efficiency and creating new business opportunities (Blumberg and Atre, 2003b).

We have between 50,000 and 100,000 conversations with our customers daily, and I don't know what was discussed. I can see only the end point – for example, they changed their calling plan. I'm blind to the content of the conversations.

It is difficult to search through semi-structured data using the tools that are currently available for conventional databases (Blumberg and Atre, 2003c). However, both the analysis and the decision-making processes require the use of a wide variety of semi-structured data (Negash, 2004). The following types of information can be considered semi-structured: marketing materials, business processes, graphics, memos, movies, user group files, image files, letters, news items, phone conversations, presentations, white papers, word processing text reports, research, e-mails, web pages, spreadsheet files, video files, and chats. This list is not exhaustive.

The Gartner Group predicts that between 30 and 40 percent of the time spent by white-collar workers in 2003 was spent on handling semi-structured data, which is an increase from the 20 percent spent in 1997 (Blumberg and Atre, 2003b). For instance, Merrill Lynch believes that over 85 percent of all firm information is stored as semi-structured data (Blumberg and Atre, 2003b). In addition, spreadsheets, which are not part of structured database systems, are commonly used to house about 15 percent of the structured data (Blumberg and Atre, 2003b).

Structured data from databases are the primary focus of DWs, ERP systems, CRM systems, and databases; nevertheless, the vast amounts of semi-structured data that exist within organizations are largely overlooked. Blumberg and Atre (2003b) argue that despite vendors' best attempts to develop ever-more-complex document management software, the handling of semi-structured data remains one of the most critical unsolved problems in the IT industry.

4.6 DATA VISUALIZATION

People are able to "see" data more clearly as a result of technological advancements in data visualization, which translate vast quantities of quantitative data into knowledge that can be applied in practical situations. A wide variety of businesses, not just the ones mentioned above, rely extensively on BI tools as a source of decision support (Alazmi, 2012; Baltzan, 2014). Data visualization is used to "make sense of the ever-increasing stream of information with which we are besieged" and "provides a creative antidote to the analytical paralysis that can arise from the strain of processing such a massive volume of data" (Baltzan, 2014). Heat maps are a type of data visualization that uses color to represent numeric data in a matrix ((Wilkinson and Friendly, 2009; Iliinsky and Steele, 2011; Rodeh et al., 2013; Nandeshwar, 2013). Data visualization in the form of colors makes it much easier for analysts to spot trends in the numbers (Nandeshwar, 2013). The use of color in heat maps allows for regions that have seen large shifts, values that are outside of their typical range, or other elements that are of importance to be brought to the attention of the viewer (Wilkinson and Friendly, 2009; Iliinsky and Steele, 2011). Displaying datasets in a visual format, testing hypotheses, and drawing attention to trends that could otherwise be concealed inside datasets are all made easier with the assistance of heat maps and other methods of data visualization (Alazmi, 2012).

Your data could be visually represented as a narrative using data visualization. Interacting with customers in order to better understand patterns, trends, and insights by putting data into a visual context is the process that we call data visualization.

4.6.1 CATEGORIZING BUSINESS DATA VISUALIZATION FORMS

Dashboards, reports, and other analytical tools are the typical formats used to show the BI results. The majority of dashboards' decisions are based on the visualization of data. The data in reports are typically presented in greater depth, and the format of the report is normally non-interactive and static. The readability of modern reports is significantly improved by the numerous aspects of visualization (diagrams, charts, and embedded visuals) and interaction that are included in these reports. Additionally moving toward a more visual orientation are analytical tools.

Reporting and analysis carried out with BI usually makes use of a wide variety of technologies and kinds of visualization. Embedded visuals, block visuals, and standalone visuals are the three primary types of visual forms that can be broken down further into subcategories dependent on how visualizations are presented on screen. Table 2 provides a summary of the characteristics along with some examples of each one (Zheng, 2017).

4.6.1.1   Embedded Visuals

The term "embedded visuals" refers to any visual effects that are included in another method of presentation. They are never delivered as stand-alone presentations; rather, they are constantly layered on top of several other kinds of presentation. Conditional formatting and inline micro charts are the two basic kinds of embedded visuals that can be used (or Sparkline).

When referring to the direct style or formatting of content, such as numbers, text, and other elements, the term "conditional formatting" refers to the use of visual factors like color and size. Text, numbers, shapes, and other elements are all examples of this type of data (Bertin, 2010). Due to the fact that conditional formatting does not substantially modify the style or flow of the content, it has less of an impact on readability than other types of formatting. Instead, it adds a decorative touch that highlights certain information or language to either provide more context or emphasize its significance.

A Sparkline is a simplified chart that may be embedded into the context of tables, text, photos, or any other form of data.

> *[A Sparkline is a concise and compact chart that can be used in this context]. It does it in a straightforward and compact fashion, exposing the essential data pattern (variation, trends, differentiations, etc.) (Tufte, 2006). The chart lacks any sort of title, label, data point, or legend to provide context or explanation. Their name, "sparkline," comes from the fact that these charts are often shown in the form of a small line chart. However, they can also be presented in the form of alternative charts, such as bar charts, bullet graphs, and so on.*

4.6.1.2   The Use of Graphs and Diagrams

Even though it takes up more room, a block graphic is still considered to be a component of a dashboard or report and appears alongside other content. This visual unit is more autonomous and self-sufficient than the others. In some cases, it is possible for it to function as an independent visual if there are sufficient amounts of complexity of data or visuals and interactions. Block graphics come in a variety of formats, the two most prevalent of which are charts and diagrams.

Symbols (such as points, lines, and areas) and visual factors (such as color, shape, and size) are combined visually to form charts, which represent data. All of these icons and numbers add up to a picture of the information. These symbols and variables combine to provide a visual representation of the data. Sometimes, the phrases "chart" and "diagram" might be used synonymously because there are no discernible differences between the two. When the word "diagram" is used, charts are typically included. To better depict structures, relationships, and sequences, a diagram can also visualize qualitative information alongside quantitative data. To contrast, a chart is more abstract in that it emphasizes displaying numerical quantities (such as business performance measures and indicators). Most BI users are likely to be familiar with the use of charts and diagrams when it comes to visualizing corporate data. In a great number of reports and presentations, they serve as the primary component of the data display.

Fundamental chart styles include, but are not limited to, line charts, bar charts, pie charts, and other types that are comparable. Organizational structure diagrams, tree diagrams, network diagrams, process diagrams, and other similar sorts of diagrams are all examples of diagrams. Abela (2008) presents a fundamental categorization of charts according to their roles; the visual guide has been applied extensively for directing selections of charts. In order to provide a more comprehensive comparison, we have also included the objective of profiling in the table. Comparison of several data points can be thought of as an umbrella concept that includes profiling.

Other business contexts make use of other, more specific types of charts to accomplish various, specialized aims. These charts are extensions of more fundamental sorts of charts, such as bar charts and line graphs. These charts go beyond the capabilities of the aforementioned fundamental chart kinds by including supplementary visual features or by rearranging the elements in a novel method to express supplementary, domain-specific meaning. For instance, in project management, Gantt charts, which are derived from data tables and bar charts, are employed; in sales, funnel charts; in stock technical analysis, candlestick charts; and in performance measurement, bullet charts, which are derived from bar charts.

4.6.1.3 Location-Based Visuals

The concept of location as a dimension plays a crucial role in a variety of the many factors that are included in the data analysis and decision-making processes of corporations. There is a significant link between the locations of a business and the various business processes that it conducts. It has been getting a lot of attention recently, particularly because location sensors that collect location data have become so widely deployed (such as GPS and other location capture technologies). Consumers are provided with a background or context that is similar to one that they are already familiar with by using location-based images, which are often based on a map. The user will have an easier time understanding and perceiving the data that is related to the location as a result of this. A study that is done annually and was done in 2015 (Dresner, 2015) discovered that more than 95 percent of respondents view it as being at least somewhat important. This study found that map-based display of information was ranked as the top priority, and it also found that this was found to be the case. More than 60 percent of those who participated in the survey stated that the skills for layered visualizations were either "very significant" or "critical" to the organization they worked for.

The location-based visuals are made up of three primary components: the type of location data, the visual shapes, and the depiction of the data points on the map. These elements work together to create the final product.

4.6.1.4   Dashboards

Independent visualizations are more comparable to applications than they are to visualizations. They take up an even greater size, sometimes even filling the screen entirely. In addition, they provide a variety of content kinds as well as tools for interacting with that content. A digital dashboard is defined by Wikipedia as "a visual presentation of the most critical information required to achieve one or more objectives; condensed and presented on a single screen so the information can be monitored at a glance" (Few, 2004). The term "dashboard" was first used to refer to a visual display for the purpose of providing operational status monitoring on equipment. This allowed for more efficient reading. Its application has been broadened to include the visualization on screens of digital data related to the performance of businesses. To put it simply, a dashboard is a front-end application that integrates data (content), visual views, and user interface and interaction.

Metrics, KPIs, and textual information are all kinds of data that can be presented on dashboards. Metrics are quantitative measurements of facets of an organization's operations. They are also known as measurements or indicators. A KPI is a metric that may be compared both to the target (also known as the objective) and to other relevant benchmarks (such as time periods, historical averages, or other KPIs) (Barr, 2009). Performance-oriented dashboards make considerable use of KPIs. Statistics that show patterns, distributions, breakdowns, predictions, or any other kind of comparisons or linkages are also commonplace on dashboards. Textual information is not normally provided on most dashboards; however, this component can be added if it is relevant to the dashboard's primary function.

4.6.2   Data Visualization Tools

There are two distinct audiences that can benefit from data visualization: those who are not developers and those who are. The first seven tools that are discussed below are geared toward users who are not developers, while the remaining ones are geared toward developers.

4.6.2.1   Tableau (http://www.tableau.com/)

Tableau is a business tool for the visualization of large amounts of data (Figure 4.2). You may make charts, graphs, maps, and a wide variety of other visualizations with Tableau. Visual analytics can be performed using a desktop application. You don't want to install software on your desktop, or you can't for some reason? Using a server-side solution, you can see reports graphically on the web as well as on mobile devices. Cloud-hosted services offer an alternative for those who need a server solution but don't want to deal with the setup themselves.

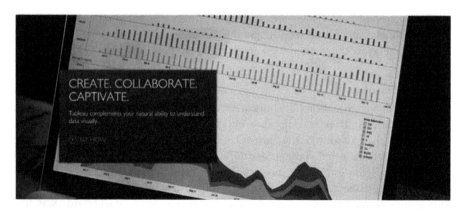

FIGURE 4.2   Tableau interface.

4.6.2.2   Infogram (https://infogr.am/)

Infogram's visualizations and infographics can be connected to streaming big data utilizing the system (Figure 4.3). Indeed, that's one of its strongest selling points. By following a straightforward three-step approach, you may select from a wide variety of pre-made templates, modify them with extra visualizations like charts, maps, photos, and videos, and then easily share the results with others. Infogram allows for the creation of team accounts for news organizations and journalists, branded designs for businesses, and classroom accounts for schools working on a wide range of projects.

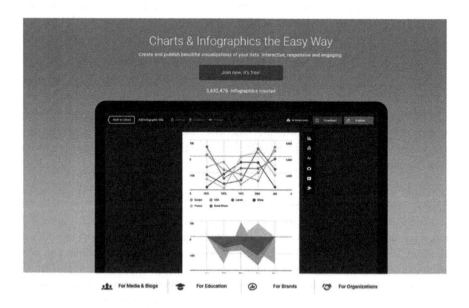

FIGURE 4.3   Infogram interface (https://infogr.am/).

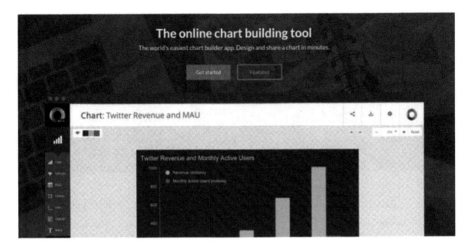

FIGURE 4.4 Interface of ChartBlocks.

4.6.2.3 ChartBlocks (http://www.chartblocks.com/en/)

ChartBlocks is a web program that makes it easy to build visualizations from scratch with data from spreadsheets, databases, and even real-time feeds, without the need for any coding (Figure 4.4). All the hard work disappears when you employ a chart-making wizard. A powerful JavaScript framework called D3.js will be used in the background to create your chart in HTML5; for a review of D3.js published by our developers, continue reading. Your visualizations will also adapt to any screen size and run smoothly on any device. You can also embed your charts into other websites or share them on social media like Facebook or Twitter.

4.6.2.4 Datawrapper

The Datawrapper library has been adopted by a wide variety of media outlets and social media platforms, including Twitter, The Guardian, The Washington Post, BuzzFeed, Vox, and The Wall Street Journal (Figure 4.5). This is because Datawrapper is firmly focused at publishers and journalists. Datawrapper is simple to use and calls for no coding at all. Simply upload your data, and you can quickly construct a chart or even a map and share it. In addition to providing access to local area maps, we also provide individualized layouts that flawlessly include your visualizations into your website.

4.6.2.5 Plotly (https://plot.ly/)

Starting with a basic spreadsheet, Plotly will walk you through the process of developing a sleek and professional-looking chart in just a few minutes. The folks over at Google, in addition to the United States Air Force, Goji, and New York University, are some of the organizations that make use of Plotly. Plotly is an online tool that is very simple to use and can get you started in a matter of minutes. If you have a team of developers who are interested in giving it a try, there is an application programming interface (API) accessible for languages such as JavaScript and Python.

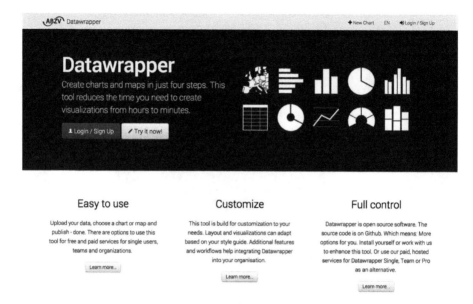

FIGURE 4.5   Interface of Datawrapper.

4.6.2.6   Raw (http://raw.densitydesign.org/)

On its homepage, RAW boasts that it is "the missing connection between spreadsheets and vector drawings," among other things (Figure 4.6). Your Big Data could be created in a variety of formats, including Google Docs, Microsoft Excel, Apple Numbers, or simply a simple list with commas delineating each item. Because RAW is compatible with Sketch, Adobe Illustrator, and Inkscape, a designer may rapidly export your visualization and make it seem finished in one of those tools. Easy to use, with noticeable effects appearing very instantly.

FIGURE 4.6   Raw icon.

FIGURE 4.7   Visual.ly interface.

4.6.2.7   Visual.ly (http://visual.ly/)

Visual.ly is an online platform for sharing visual content. Incorporating them was an easy decision because their portfolio is already fairly robust and they do provide a unique service in the form of big data visualization (Figure 4.7). Their resume boasts illustrious clients, including Twitter, VISA, Nike, Ford, National Geographic, and The Huffington Post. Through a streamlined online approach, you may completely outsource your visualizations to a third party. After explaining your project, you will be connected with a creative team that will stay with you throughout the duration of the project. If you'd like, you can send all of your visualization work to an outside company. We'll let you know through email when you've reached a new milestone and facilitate continuous input to the creative team via Visual.ly. Once your project is complete, you may use Visual.ly's distribution network to show it off.

4.6.2.8   D3.js (http://d3js.org/)

D3.js, the most powerful data visualization library available, is written in JavaScript and makes use of CSS, HTML, and SVG. D3.js is a data-driven transformation tool that applies to webpages and, as you can see from the samples they provide, makes it possible to create stunning visualizations in a very short amount of time (Figure 4.8). Incorporating real-time data-driven interactivity, D3.js is the best option. Warning: because this library is both strong and up-to-date, it does not come with any pre-built charts, and only versions of Internet Explorer 9 and later are supported.

FIGURE 4.8   d3.js interface.

4.6.2.9   Ember Charts (http://emberjs.com/)

Ember Charts makes use of D3.js behind the scenes and is built on top of the Ember.
js framework, as the product's name might imply. It is possible to create time
series, bar, pie, and scatter charts using Ember Charts (Figure 4.9). It is incredibly

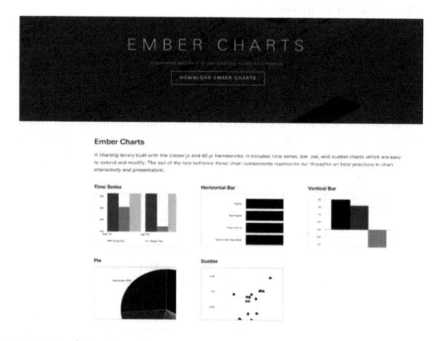

FIGURE 4.9   Ember Charts home.

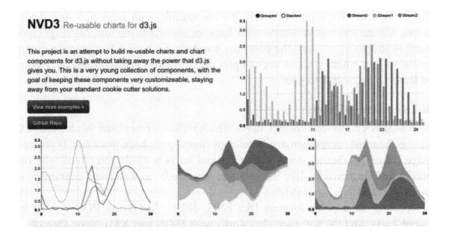

FIGURE 4.10 NVD3 charts.

sophisticated yet simple to extend. Best practices and user interaction were given a great deal of attention by the team that developed Ember Charts, which is the same team that was responsible for developing Ember.js. Your application will not crash even when given incorrect data since it has a graceful error-handling system.

4.6.2.10 NVD3 (http://nvd3.org/)

NVD3 operates on top of D3.js, which should come as no surprise, and seeks to create charts and components that can be reused (Figure 4.10). The project's objective is to facilitate the organization and personalization of all your charts. On top of D3.js, NVD3 provides a more user-friendly interface while concealing all the framework's robust capabilities. The front-end engineers at Novus Partners are responsible for the development of NVD3, which makes use of their expertise in charting technology.

4.6.2.11 Google Charts (https://developers.google.com/chart/)

With its foundation in HTML5 and SVG, Google Charts aims to be entirely cross-browser compatible (Figure 4.11). This includes support for VML-enabled versions

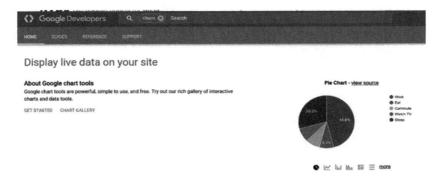

FIGURE 4.11 Google Charts.

of older Internet Explorer browsers. It's compatible with both iOS and Android devices. Create interactive charts with features like zooming and filtering. Google Charts is simple to use, and the company's website features a fantastically comprehensive gallery where you can see samples of the various visualizations and interactive features accessible to you.

4.6.2.12 FusionCharts

The company claims that FusionCharts, which includes more than 90 charts and 900 maps, is the most comprehensive JavaScript charting package available. If you're not a huge fan of JavaScript, don't worry; FusionCharts is easily integrated with other libraries and frameworks, like ReactJS and AngularJS, as well as programming languages like ASP.NET and PHP.

Exporting to popular formats like PNG, JPEG, SVG, and PDF is easy with FusionCharts, and the software also works with JSON and XML data. One of their products, a pre-built dashboard for running a business, is something you should investigate further.

4.6.2.13 Highcharts (https://www.highcharts.com/)

Highcharts is a JavaScript API that is compatible with jQuery and used by 61 of the Fortune 100 (Figure 4.12). The charts are displayed in SVG format, with a VML fallback for support of older browsers. Highstock and highmaps, two specialist chart kinds, are available on top, and many other plugins are included. You can use it without cost for personal projects, or you can get a license to create a business software. You should look into their Highcharts cloud service as well.

FIGURE 4.12 Highcharts home.

FIGURE 4.13 Charts.js.

4.6.2.14 Charts.js

Chart.js should be your first stop when working on a simple chart project. It is open source, very small (it only ships at 11kb), very quick, and very simple to use, and it supports six different chart types: doughnut, pie, polar, line, and bar charts (Figure 4.13). In addition, you can lower your carbon footprint by adding or removing any of these six categories of activities. Chart.js is built on top of HTML5 Canvas and ships with polyfills to support IE6 and IE7. If you've decided that your project may benefit from some straightforward and speedy charts, you should keep a watch on the Chart.js GitHub page, which is experiencing a meteoric rise in popularity.

4.6.2.15 Leaflet

Are you looking for a customized solution for mapping Big Data? You won't need any bar graphs or pie charts, will you? Leaflet uses the data from OpenStreetMap and adds visuals built using HTML5 and CSS3 as well as interactivity on top of it all to guarantee that everything is responsive and ready for mobile use. You are able to incorporate heat maps, masks, and animated markers by making use of their huge plugin repository. Leaflet is available free of charge and weighs in at just 33 kilobytes.

4.6.2.16 Chartist.js

Are you looking for a customized solution for mapping Big Data? You won't need any bar graphs or pie charts, will you? Leaflet uses the data from OpenStreetMap and adds visuals built using HTML5 and CSS3 as well as interactivity on top of it all to guarantee that everything is responsive and ready for mobile use. You are able to incorporate heat maps, masks, and animated markers by making use of their huge plugin repository. Leaflet is available free of charge and weighs in at just 33 kilobytes.

4.6.2.17 n3-charts

This n3-charts project is for all those AngularJS fans out there. It is based on D3.js and gives you dynamic, user-friendly graphs for your data. n3-charts caters to a certain subset of AngularJS developers that are looking for chart visualizations that are simple, easy, and elegant. Keep in mind that if it is a significant undertaking, you are going to want to search in other places. You should use n3-charts if you want to keep things as simple as possible.

4.6.2.18   Sigma JS

To achieve the desired level of interactivity, use Sigma JS. In its default state, WebGL is used for rendering, with HTML5 Canvas as a backup, and it supports mouse and touch input out of the box. Other features include the ability to refresh and resize the image. JSON and GEXF are now the two most popular formats for storing data. Their selection of plugins for interactive features is quite extensive. The rendering engine known as Sigma JS is exceptional in terms of the degree to which it may be customized. Its primary focus is on the representation of graphs and networks on web pages.

4.6.2.19   Polymaps

Polymaps is a visualization tool that, you guessed it, displays maps. Polymaps is a JavaScript package that makes use of SVG to depict geographical data on scales ranging from the level of an entire country to the level of an individual street. In order to style your visualization, you make use of CSS rules, and the data you provide may simply be processed by Polymaps thanks to the GeoJSON standard. If you are interested in making heat maps, this is the most effective tool available to you. Interactivity can be added to any and all of your custom maps. OpenStreetMap, CloudMade, Bing, and a plethora of other map sources can also be visualized.

4.6.2.20   Processing JS

The Processing visual programming language is supported by the Processing.js library, which is written in JavaScript. Processing.js is web-oriented, much like every other JavaScript library, and it gives you the ability to bring the power of Processing to your websites. This is the most insightful and innovative visual interactive library that exists. In order for Processing.js to work its magic, an HTML5-compatible web browser is required. Make sure you have a look at the exhibition page to get a better idea of what this great JavaScript library can do.

4.7   BUSINESS INTELLIGENCE TOOLS AND PLATFORMS

(Haije, 2019) gave a list of top BI tools and are discussed below.

4.7.1   SAP BI

SAP BI has you covered with regards to ML, planning, and predictive analytics (Figure 4.14). Reporting and analysis, data visualization and analytics apps, office connection, and mobile analytics are just some of the many benefits offered by the BI platform. SAP is a reliable piece of software that serves the needs of all roles, from IT to end users to management, and does so by offering a wide range of features in a unified environment.

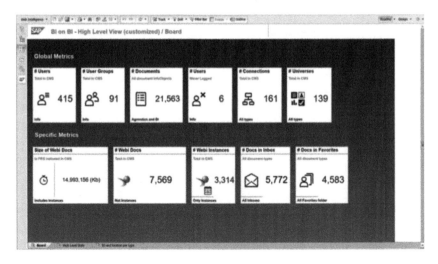

FIGURE 4.14   Interface of SAP BI.

4.7.2   MICROSTRATEGY

You can keep tabs on trends, spot new opportunities, boost productivity, and more with the help of MicroStrategy's powerful (and fast) dashboarding and data analytics. A user can link to a single source or multiple sources, with data flowing in from anywhere, including a local computer, the cloud, or specialized business programs (Figure 4.15). You can use a computer or a mobile device to access it.

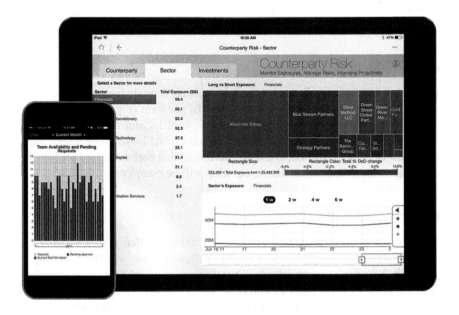

FIGURE 4.15   Interface of MicroStrategy.

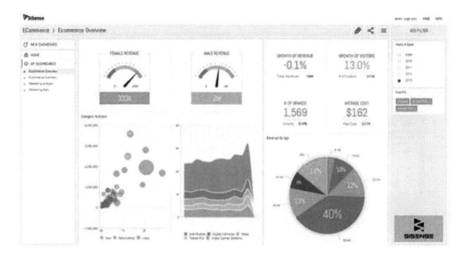

FIGURE 4.16   Interface of Sisense.

4.7.3   SISENSE

This user-friendly program eliminates the need for assistance from the IT department, allowing any employee to easily manage large, complex datasets and do analysis and visualization without assistance (Figure 4.16). It also lets you compile data from a wide variety of sources, like AdWords, Google Analytics, and Salesforce, among many others. Not to add, in comparison to other instruments, the data are processed relatively quickly using the in-chip technology that is utilized by the system.

4.7.4   SAS BI

Although SAS's most well-known product, advanced predictive analytics, is quite popular, the company also offers an excellent BI platform (Figure 4.17). It is a self-service platform that enables users to make informed decisions about their company by leveraging data and metrics. Using their library of APIs, you have a wide variety of options for personalization, and SAS guarantees that both advanced analytics and reporting on top of high-level data integration will be completed.

4.7.5   YELLOWFIN BI

Yellowfin BI is a platform for "end-to-end" analytics that mixes visualization, ML, and collaboration. It is a tool for BI. Yellowfin Labs was the company that created it. You can also effortlessly filter through loads of data using straightforward filters (such as checkboxes and radio buttons), and because to this tool's versatility in accessibility, you can open up dashboards virtually anywhere (mobile, webpage, etc.).

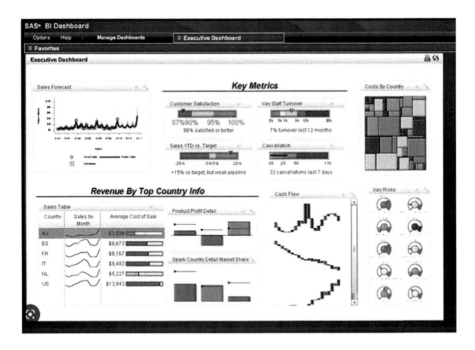

FIGURE 4.17 Interface of SAS BI.

4.7.6 DUNDAS BI

Users are able to connect to a wide variety of data sources in real time using Dundas BI, which is a BI solution that is both adaptable and browser-based (Figure 4.18). It provides excellent data visualizations in the form of charts, tables, and graphs, all of which

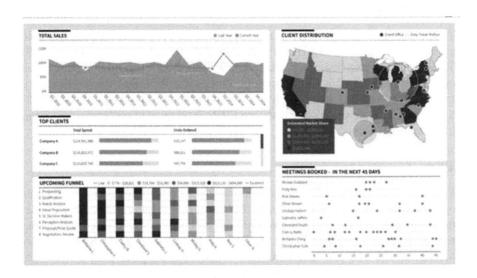

FIGURE 4.18 Interface of Dundas BI.

FIGURE 4.19 Interface of TIBCO Spotfire.

are modifiable and can be accessed and seen from desktop computers as well as mobile devices. Users also have the ability to construct their own reports, complete with drill-down capabilities and specific performance measures for examination. Dundas offers support to businesses of varying sizes and operating in a wide variety of fields.

4.7.7 TIBCO SPOTFIRE

TIBCO Spotfire is a self-service BI tool that delivers executive dashboards, data visualization, and analytics, in addition to pushing KPIs to mobile devices (Figure 4.19). TIBCO Spotfire also pushes KPIs to mobile devices. Because users can specify their own KPIs and alerts can be sent to both iPhones and Androids, this application is fantastic for working together with your digital team. It is possible to link TIBCO Spotfire with a wide variety of CRMs and ERPs, in addition to spreadsheet programs like Excel and Access.

4.7.8 SYSTUM

Systum is a BI platform that assists companies in streamlining and consolidating operations across numerous B2B and B2C channels (Figure 4.20). This enables the companies to increase their levels of both productivity and efficiency. It comes with a variety of capabilities related to sales, such as an integrated CRM, Inventory Management, a B2B site, and more. Additionally, Systum gives users a wide variety of choices for integrating their businesses with third-party platforms, such as Amazon, eBay, and Quickbooks, among others.

FIGURE 4.20 Interface of Systum.

4.7.9 MICROSOFT POWER BI

Data visualization is a particular strength of Microsoft's Power BI suite of web-based business analytics solutions (Figure 4.21). The software was developed by Microsoft. The software was developed by Microsoft. It provides users with the ability to discover patterns in real time and comes equipped with brand new connectors that make

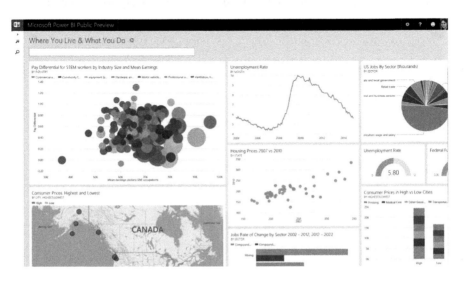

FIGURE 4.21 Interface of MS Power BI.

it possible to step up your game when it comes to marketing. Microsoft Power BI is a web-based service, which means that users may use it from virtually any internet-connected device. Users of this program are also able to integrate their own applications as well as deliver reports and dashboards that display data in real time.

4.7.10 LOOKER

Looker is just one more BI tool that you want to be on the lookout for. Due to the fact that this platform is capable of interacting with any SQL database or warehouse, it is a good option for start-up businesses, businesses operating in the medium range, and corporations functioning at the enterprise level. The ease of use, the helpful visualizations, the robust collaboration options (The information and reports may be transferred via email or USL, and the software can be linked to others.), and the dependability of the support are just some of the benefits that come along with making use of this particular service (tech team).

4.7.11 CLEAR ANALYTICS

Where have all of those people gone that take pleasure in working with Excel? This BI tool is an Excel-based program that is extremely user-friendly and can be handled by staff members that have even the most elementary acquaintance with Excel (Figure 4.22). What you receive is a self-service BI solution that includes a variety of BI capabilities, such as the ability to produce, automate, analyze, and visualize the data of your company. In addition, what you get is what is known as a BI platform.

4.7.12 Tableau

Tableau is a software for BI that enables users to identify hidden patterns in data and visualize that data (Figure 4.23). It is not necessary to include IT in the

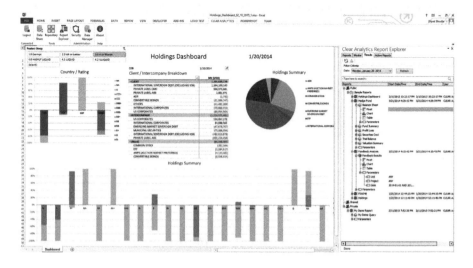

FIGURE 4.22 Interface of clear analytics.

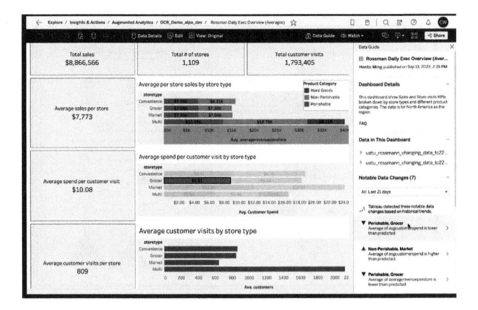

FIGURE 4.23 Interface of Tableau.

process because the software makes it simple to analyze, visualize, and exchange data. Tableau is compatible with a wide variety of data sources, including Oracle, Microsoft Excel, Microsoft SQL Server, Salesforce, and Google Analytics. Tableau is available for free for individual use. However, if you desire more, the price may increase significantly in a short amount of time. But of course, you'll get something in return for doing this, and that something is well-designed dashboards that are very simple to operate. In addition, Tableau provides three standalone solutions, which are as follows: Tableau Desktop, which is available to anybody; Tableau Server, which provides analytics for enterprises; and Tableau Online, which may be operated locally (hosted analytics for organizations).

4.7.13 ORACLE BI

Oracle BI is an enterprise portfolio of BI software and services (Figure 4.24). Users of this technology are provided with virtually all of the BI features, including dashboards, proactive intelligence, alerts, ad hoc, and many more. As Oracle is a very resilient system, it is an excellent choice for businesses that require the analysis of enormous volumes of data (both from Oracle and from sources other than Oracle).

4.7.14 DOMO

Domo is a BI platform that works entirely in the cloud and can connect to a wide variety of external data stores, such as spreadsheets, databases, and social media platforms (Figure 4.25). Domo is used by businesses of various sizes, from sole proprietorships to international conglomerates. The platform provides visibility and

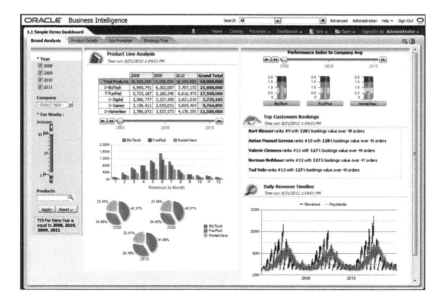

FIGURE 4.24   Oracle BI.

FIGURE 4.25   Interface of Domo.

analytics at both the micro and the macro level. Everything is considered, whether it be the current cash balances, a list of your best selling products broken down by region, or the ROI for each marketing channel. The only thing that can be considered a drawback to using Domo is that it can be challenging to retrieve studies from the cloud for individual usage.

4.7.15   SPLASHBI

SplashBI is a business analytics platform that enables organizations to understand the whole narrative behind their data. It also enables users to make data-driven decisions by giving the essential actionable intelligence. SplashBI empowers enterprises to understand their data. This BI tool is the answer to all of your data problems, whether you work in sales or marketing, accounting or finance, human resources, or customer support. SplashBI is available in the cloud or on-premise, and it comes with a substantial quantity of content (reports/dashboards) and data models that have been pre-built to assist users in getting started quickly. The Data Connector library offered by SplashBI enables users to simultaneously connect to a wide variety of databases and applications, which in turn enables users to combine, report on, visualize, and analyze data. Google Analytics, SAP, Oracle, Salesforce, Marketo, Hadoop, and Quickbooks are just few of the data connections platforms that are available to customers.

4.8 TRENDS AND PROSPECTS

4.8.1 COMBINING SOFTWARE WITH CONSULTING SERVICES

"Information as a service" and the provision of intelligence to clients is something that vendors are beginning to offer as an alternative to the practice of selling the software and equipment that businesses require in order to acquire intelligence on their own. This is in contrast to the traditional model of selling software.

- Enhancing the Capability of Users to Carry Out Their Own Tasks Software developers are placing a growing emphasis on expanding the range of tasks that may be carried out without the assistance of data scientists or members of the IT staff.

4.8.2 CLOUD-BASED BI

Cloud computing is beginning to gain traction in BI, as it has in other fields. As technology advances, businesses will be able to employ intelligence without devoting internal resources to infrastructure administration and software modifications. This will become possible as a result of the convergence of cloud computing and big data.

4.8.3 MOBILE INTELLIGENCE

The use of mobile technology in many aspects of business operations, including BI, is becoming increasingly common. Mobile tools allow decision makers to access information regardless of where they are, not just at their workstations as was previously the case.

4.8.4 BIG DATA

The availability of data to businesses is higher than it has ever been, and a sizeable amount of it comes from sources that are external to the company in an unstructured format. BI is being rapidly combined with big data analytics so that companies may make decisions based on all of the information that is accessible to them, notwithstanding the format that the information may take.

4.8.5 The BI Market

The total value of the worldwide market for BI in 2023 is estimated to be USD 29.22 billion. Corporations and other sectors are rapidly using cutting-edge automation technology in their sphere. In order for businesses to make intelligent real-time judgments regarding the market, BI systems are utilized to process and examine data via integration apps for the cloud and big data. In the past, BI was utilized for tasks, such as the resolution of queries, the development of reports, and dashboards. The use of cutting-edge technology in BI is increasing the level of competition in the market, and the leaders of the market are using BI software (GlobeNewswire, 2022).

North America held the largest revenue share and was the dominant player in the BI market. This was due to the region's dominance. It is anticipated that rapid technical innovation, as well as the presence of important industry players in the region, such as IBM Corporation, Microsoft Corporation, Tableau Software, and Oracle Corporation, among others, will fuel expansion throughout the region. The expansion of the market for BI in this region is being driven, in part, by measures taken by European governments and the growing research and development infrastructure in Europe. For instance, the European Commission announced an expenditure of €292 million in digital technologies in February of 2022. During the course of the projection period, it is predicted that the market for BI in the Asia-Pacific region would witness profitable expansion. The most significant firms from other regions are putting a lot of focus on growing their operations in this region so that they can take a larger portion of the market there.

4.9   CONCLUSION

The term "business intelligence" refers to much more than the mere display and reporting of data. In addition to that, it consists of tools for analytics, data governance, and other specialized forms of productivity. Any firm has the potential to acquire a competitive advantage and make decisions that are accurate and based on facts if they implement the appropriate BI strategy. The chapter focuses on BI. It begins with defining BI and discussions on various components of BI.

There are several BI technologies available for the capture, integration, cleansing, search, analysis, and dissemination of structured data. However, additional work is required in order to combine these technologies and to offer information that may be acted upon. On the other hand, BI tools for semi-structured data are not yet at their full maturity. On the other hand, a substantial amount of work is being done in industry to deal with data that are semi-structured (MacIntyre, 2004; Kontzer, 2023;).

The trend toward providing end users with improved and more useful methods of data presentation and visualization is a phenomenon that is taking place on a scale that encompasses the entire planet. The process of BI as a whole is becoming increasingly dependent on data visualization, which is why it is quickly becoming an essential component of every BI solution. Users of BI software and those responsible for making decisions might benefit on varying levels and from varying points of view from the utilization of various types of data visualization. BI managers and developers should understand the features, strengths, and weaknesses of their tools, and then use those tools in conjunction with one another to produce a suitable mix that serves a variety of user types whose requirements differ.

This chapter presents a complete analysis of BI, with a particular emphasis on visualization forms and tools; reading it will assist BI managers, decision makers, analysts, and developers in making more informed decisions regarding how to pick and apply these tools. The combination of cloud and mobile capabilities is the current trend in BI.

REFERENCES

Alazmi, A. R. (2012). "Data Mining and Visualization of Large Databases," *International Journal of Computer Science and Security, 6*(5), 295–314.

Baltzan, P. (2014). *Business driven information systems* (4th ed.). New York: McGraw-Hill.

Barr, S. (2009). What Does "KPI" Really Mean? *Dashboard Insight.* Retrieved January 10, 2023.

Better Buys. (2015, December). The Definitive Guide to Business Intelligence. Retrieved from www.betterbuys.com

Blumberg, R., & Atre, S. (2003a). Automatic Classification: Moving to the Mainstream. *DM Review.*

Blumberg, R., & Atre, S. (2003b). The Problem with Unstructured Data. *DM Review.*

Blumberg, R., & Atre, S. (2003c). "More than Search," *DM Review, 13*(3), 42–47.

Devens, R. M. (1865). "Cyclopædia of Commercial and Business Anecdotes," *Appleton and Company,* 210.

GlobeNewswire. (2022, December 6). Business Intelligence Market Size to Worth Around USD 54.9 Bn by 2023. Retrieved from globenewswire.com/en/news-release/2022/12/06/2568432/0/en/Business-Intelligence-Market-Size-to-Worth-Around-USD-54-9-Bn-by-2032.html#:~:text=According%20to%20Precedence%20Research%2C%20the,7.26%25%20from%202023%20to%202032

Haije, E. G. (2019, November 6). Top 15 Business Intelligence Tools. *An Overview.* Retrieved January 2019, from https://mopinion.com/: https://mopinion.com/business-intelligence-bi-tools-overview/

Iliinsky, N., & Steele, J. (2011). *Designing data visualizations.* Sebastopol: O'Reilly Media.

Kontzer, T. (2023). Companies Are Choking on Information Employees Create. And a Spate of Vendor Mergers Has Yet to Deliver Tools to Deal with the Problem. *InformationWeek,* http://www.informationweek.com/story/showArticle.jhtml?articleID=17301874. Current January 19, 2023.

Langseth, J., & Vivatrat, N. (2003). "Why Proactive Business Intelligence Is a Hallmark of the Real-Time Enterprise: Outward Bound," *Intelligent Enterprise, 18*(5), 34–41.

MacIntyre, B. (2004). "Information Technology Challenges Keep Rising," *The Business Journal of Portland,* January 23, 2004. http://portland.bizjournals.com/portland/stories/2004/02/23/focus8.html

Moss, L. (2003). "Nontechnical Infrastructure of BI Applications," *DM Review, 13*(1), 42–45.

Nandeshwar, A. (2013). *Tableau data visualization cookbook.* Birmingham: Packt Publishing.

Negash, S. (2004). "Business Intelligence," *Communications of the Association for Information Systems, 13*(2), 177–195.

Rodeh, O., Helman, H., & Chambliss, D. (2013). *IBM Research Report: Visualizing Block IO Workloads.* Retrieved from http://domino.watson.ibm.com/library/cyberdig.nsf/papers/9E29FDDED06E5DE785257C1 D005E7E9E/$File/rj10514.pdf

Rudin, K. A. (2003). "Will the Real Analytic Application Please Stand Up," *DM Review*, *13*(3), 30–34.

Wilkinson, L., & Friendly, M. (2009). "The History of the Cluster Heat Map," *The American Statistician*, *63*(2), 179–184.

Willen, C. (2002, January 14). "Airborne Opportunities," *Intelligent Enterprise*, *5*(2), 11–12.

Zheng, J. G. (2017, December). *Data Visualization for Business Intelligence.* doi:10.4324/9781315471136-6

5 Sentiment Analysis of Social Media

Bibliometric Analysis

Meera Mehta and Shivani Arora
Shaheed Bhagat Singh College, Delhi University,
Delhi, India

5.1 INTRODUCTION

The world is being driven by data today. The data in terms of views, posts, and subscriptions is of immense importance to the academic and business worlds. The various techniques used to analyse this new currency (data) are expanding.

Social media is where conversations are happening at lightning speed, and what is discussed there, matters. Whether these discussions are political, moral, and religious or to boycott a movie, or criticise a song – each string of conversation has tremendous results. Social listening is what the academics and companies need to consider to stay abreast of the trends and changes in their respective field.

Over the years, social media has been studied extensively, and the researchers have focussed on sentiment analysis of social media (Mohammad, Garcia, Jou, Schuller, Chang and Pantic, 2017). The broad aspects have been covered by various experts in the field of sentiment analysis of social media, including toxic culture towards feminist movements (Suarez Estrada, Juarez and Piña-García, 2022), customer reviews of Tripadvisor and other travel websites (Paolanti et al., 2021; Abeysinghe and Bandara, 2022, Dangi, Bhagat and Dixit, 2022; Habek, Toçoğlu and Onan, 2022), on COVID-19 vaccination (Amoudi and Shearah, 2022; Aygun, Kaya and Kaya, 2022; Arora and Piplani, 2022; Irfan, 2022; Diviya, 2022), and cryptocurrency (Habek, Toçoğlu and Onan, 2022). These are just a few of the papers and only miniscule areas of research. The rest of the chapter details the areas, trends, research papers, collaborations of research, etc. This chapter aims to highlight the work done on sentiment analysis of social media with the following objectives:

The research aims to address the following aspects of sentiment analysis of social media:

1. What are the current trends in the research of sentiment analysis of social media?
2. Who are the impactful and influential contributors to the field, and which sources take the lead?
3. Which are the most cited research papers in social media sentiment analysis?

DOI: 10.1201/9781032614083-5

4. Which countries lead in the research on this domain?
5. Which are the leading publishing sources and affiliations of social media sentiment analysis?

To arrive at meaningful and factual inferences related to the above mentioned queries, Bibliometric analysis was done.

5.2 RESEARCH METHODS AND STUDY DESIGN

The research aims to analyse the research undertaken in the sentiment analysis of social media. The research progress made in the field so far would help researchers in the field decide on the future course of their research. Bibliometric analysis techniques were applied on the data collected from the Scopus database. Scopus is one of the richest databases and covers most research in any field. This study has used Scopus as its base for answering the research questions.

Bibliometric Analysis has gained popularity in recent years. The purpose is to give a crisp analysis of the areas of any particular research being undertaken and all aspects related to it. The interest in the technique has been pushed due to the user-friendliness of the software supporting it, viz., Biblioshiny and VOSviewer, and digital databases like Scopus, Web of Science. Bibliometric Analysis can help in general understanding of the work being done in any field, but that is just the tip of the iceberg. The various layers can help unearth the structure of a problem being discussed and allow academia and the industry to use it to solve practical problems.

5.2.1 SEARCH STRATEGY

The search criteria, keywords, inclusion criteria, exclusion criteria, and extraction process are discussed in detail in this section. The keywords used for searching were *"Sentiment Analysis"* AND *"Social Media"* and limited to the access of available articles from the Computer science field, published between 2002 and 2022 and indexed in the Scopus database. The retrieval of meta-data is explained in Table 5.1. The raw data extraction leads to the extraction of 7141 documents on the topic.

TABLE 5.1
Bibliographic Data Retrieval Process

Stage	Filtering Data	Eliminated	Accepted
1.	First Extraction (on 27 December 2022)		7141
2.	Publication Year (Exclude 2023)	58	7083
3.	Type of Work (include only Published)	1562	5521
4.	Subject Area (Computer Science)	948	4573
5.	Document Type (only Articles) and Final Publication stage and Source (Journals)	3430	1143
6.	Language (English)	20	1123
7.	TOTAL ACCEPTED PAPERS		1123

On applying the filtration on the subject, document type, type of publication and excluding the year 2023, the result was 1123 papers.

5.2.2 BIBLIOMETRIC ANALYSIS

The current study gives a bibliometric overview of the sentiment analysis of social media research that is now dominating the computer sciences section of the journals in the Scopus database. The total number of publications and citations is part of our descriptive analysis (Tsay, 2009), and keyword analysis is utilised to find new ideas and trends in the proposed study (Hu et al., 2018). Bibliographic couplings (BCs), co-occurrences and co-authorship, co-words, citation, and co-citation analyses are a few examples of science mapping analyses. For the primary analysis, we employed Excel, VOSviewer, and Scopus analysis. Science mapping and bibliometric analyses are displayed using VOSviewer, BIblioshiny, and data files are extracted using CSV excel.

5.3 RESULTS AND FINDINGS

5.3.1 CURRENT RESEARCH TRENDS

Figure 5.1 presents the research trends of publication of the Scopus database on sentiment analysis of social media in the last 12 years; the research trends show increasing growth in the publication work in this field. Except for 2017, when the research

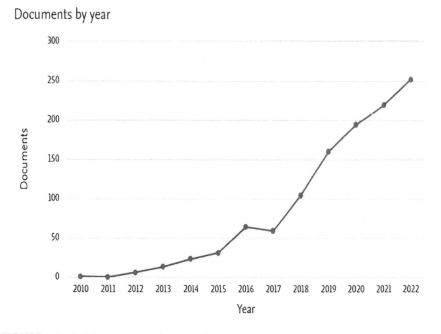

FIGURE 5.1 Publication trends between 2010 and 2022.

Documents by subject area

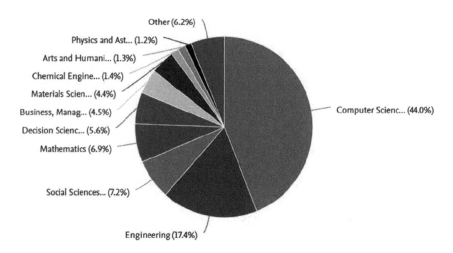

FIGURE 5.2 Distribution of documents by subject area.

in this field slowed down for a year, it continued to grow to the extent that in 2022, the publications reached 250 documents indicating that academicians are working on sentiment analysis of social media.

To identify the subject areas of research, 1123 documents were extracted from the Scopus dataset, wherein computer science dominated 44.0% of the total area, followed by engineering with a share of 17.4%. Social Sciences, Mathematics, and Decision Sciences accounted for 7.2%, 6.9%, and 5.6%, respectively (Figure 5.2). According to this analysis, the progress in the subject area of computer science is prominent, and hence, researchers are expected to pursue these streams to study sentiment analysis of social media.

5.3.2 LEADING, INFLUENTIAL, AND IMPACTFUL SOURCES

Table 5.2 lists the top ten leading journals on the basis of the number of documents published and their citations in the sentiment analysis of the Social Media domain.

Although IEEE Access has the maximum number (74) of documents published in this area; documents published in the journal Knowledge-Based System have the highest citations of 1619. The above ten sources have been the most impactful influence on researchers. Artificial Intelligence Review with only six documents published has a citation score of 379. The citations support the impact of the journals on the research on sentiment analysis of social media.

TABLE 5.2
The Top Ten Leading Journals

Source	Documents	Citations
Knowledge-Based System	21	1619
IEEE Access	74	1126
Information Processing and Management	20	1033
Decision Support Systems	9	258
Expert Systems with Application	20	790
International Journal of Information Management	12	628
Neurocomputing	10	556
Information Sciences	9	506
Multimedia tools and Applications	26	463
Artificial Intelligence Review	6	379

5.3.3 Most Prolific Authors on Sentiment Analysis of Social Media

Figure 5.3 has incorporated the data of the top authors of sentiment analysis of social media depicting the number of research papers published. The top authors with more than three papers have been considered in the field. He, W is the most prolific author in our database, with 11 papers to his credit. Akula, Asgar, and Tian are the next in line with all of them having published six papers each.

5.3.4 Co-Authorship Analysis

Co-authorship analysis (Table 5.3) studies the collaboration among academicians on the specific research area. F.H. Khan, U. Qamar and S. Bhasir have the highest

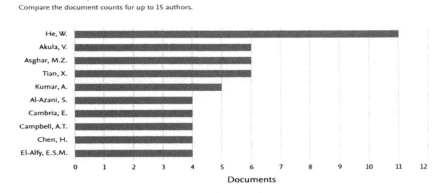

FIGURE 5.3 Top ten leading authors on sentiment analysis of social media.

TABLE 5.3

Co-Authorship of Top Nine Authors in the Research Area

Author	Documents	Citations
Khan F.H.; Qamar U.; Bashir S.	3	179
Ceron A.; Curini L.; Lacus S.M.	2	151
Vashishtha S.; Susan S.	2	102
Nemes L.; Kiss A.	2	92
Deng S.; Sinha A.P.; Zhao H.	2	91
Kumar A.; Garg G.	2	75
Xu J.; Huang F.; Zhang X.; Wang S.; Li C.; Li Z.; He Y.	2	58
Aloufi S.; Saddik A.E.	2	37
Liu S.; Lee I.	2	26
Martí Bigorra A.; Isaksson O.; Karlberg M.	2	21

collaboration of three documents and their research work has received the maximum citations (Khan, Qamar and Bashir, 2016) A. Ceron.; L. Curini; S.M. Lacus have collaborated on two papers that have been cited 151 times. The above analysis indicates that although researchers have collaborated on a few documents (maximum three) their work has been acknowledged (in terms of citations) well.

5.3.5 MOST INFLUENTIAL ARTICLES

Table 5.4 shows the research papers with the maximum citations in the field. The research paper of 2015, "A survey on opinion mining and sentiment analysis: Tasks, approaches and applications", has the maximum number of citations, 829. The distant second is the 2016 paper, "Fusing audio, visual and textual clues for sentiment analysis from multimodal content", with 321 citations, followed by others (Pandey, Rajpoot and Saraswat, 2017; Poria, Cambria, Howard, Huang and Hussain, 2016; Thien Hai, Shirai and Velcin, 2015; Yu, Duan and Cao, 2013) The last in the list of ten most cited papers is "Sentiment analysis using deep learning architectures: a review" from 2020, with 202 citations (Yadav and Vishwakarma, 2020). This chapter from 2020 is relatively new and will increase in citations in due course. The number of citations adds credibility to the chapter's quality and relevance.

These top-cited papers discuss the pervasiveness of social media and how sentiment analysis or opinion mining is required to be undertaken. The papers elaborate on required and prevalent tasks, various approaches, and the applications of sentiment analysis (Ravi and Ravi, 2015). The paper by Portia (2016) elaborates on how audio and video content on social media require analysis and the methodology to do it. Facebook, YouTube, WhatsApp, and Instagram are the most used social media apps in 2022, worldwide (https://www.wordstream.com/blog/ws/2022/01/11/most-popular-social-media-platforms). Videos on YouTube and Instagram have pushed

TABLE 5.4

Top Ten Leading Articles Based on Citations with Author Name and Year of Publication

S. No.	Name of the Paper	Authors	Year of Publication	Citations
1	A survey on opinion mining and sentiment analysis: Tasks, approaches and applications	Ravi K.; Ravi V.	2015	829
2	Fusing audio, visual and textual clues for sentiment analysis from multimodal content	Poria S.; Cambria E; Howard N.; Huang G.-B.; Hussain A.	2016	321
3	A review of natural language processing techniques for opinion mining systems	Sun S.; Luo C.; Chen J.	2017	315
4	The impact of social and conventional media on firm equity value: A sentiment analysis approach	Yu y.; Duan w.; Cao q.	2013	314
5	Sentiment analysis on social media for stock movement prediction	Nguyen t.h.; shirai k.; velcin j	2015	294
6	Sentic patterns: Dependency-based rules for concept-level sentiment analysis	Poria S.; Cambria e.; Winterstein G.; Huang G.-B.	2014	255
7	A survey of multimodal sentiment analysis	Soleymani M.; Garcia d.; Jou B.; Schuller B.; Chang S.F.; Pantic M.	2017	231
8	Using hashtags to capture fine emotion categories from tweets	Mohammad S.M.; Kiritchenko S.	2015	229
9	Twitter sentiment analysis using hybrid cuckoo search method	Chandra Pandey A.; Singh Rajpoot D.; Saraswat M.	2017	210
10	Sentiment analysis using deep learning architectures: a review	Yadav A.; Vishwakarma D.K.	2020	202

their popularity, and conversations are happening there. Portia et al. have used both features – and decision-level fusion methods to extract the information from the various modalities.

Natural language processing (NLP) has been discussed in detail by Sun, Luo and Chen (2017). The authors looked into several degrees and scenarios for opinion mining methodologies and then explored deep learning and comparative opinion mining as methods for mining opinions. The paper covers sophisticated themes and opinion summaries and discusses the unsolved and complicated aspects of sentiment analysis.

5.3.6 Co-Occurrence Author Keywords (Co-Words) with Ten Most Frequent Author Keywords

The occurrences of the author's keywords as shown in Figure 5.4 validate the research for this chapter. Sentiment analysis (n = 755), opinion mining (n = 114), and text mining (n = 84) support the extractions of the research papers is covering the topic with its synonyms since opinion mining, sentiment analysis, and text mining are sometimes used interchangeably. Social media (n = 268) and Twitter (n = 163) imply that Twitter is the most commonly studied social media for sentiment analysis. COVID-19 is a keyword coming up 46 times since the number of publications in 2020–2022 is the highest, and every research around this time did revolve around the pandemic. Machine learning (n = 151), NLP (n = 107), and deep learning (n = 105) are the underlying techniques helping in opinion mining.

Figure 5.5 shows a visual overlay of 50 most frequently used (trending keywords) author keywords in the form of a Tree Map. As expected, "sentiment analysis" is

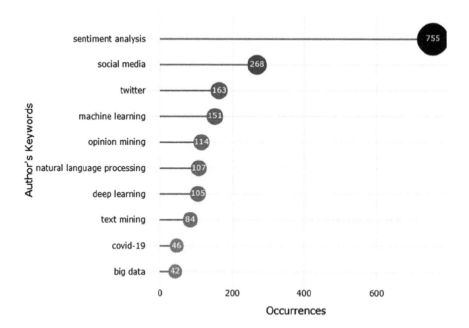

FIGURE 5.4 Top ten authors' keywords in sentiment analysis of social media.

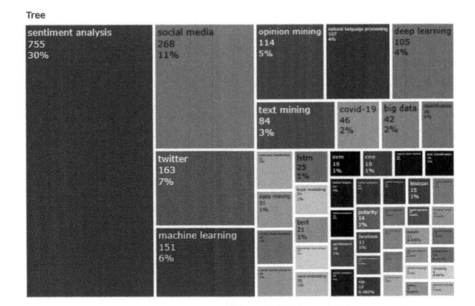

FIGURE 5.5   Tree-map of trending keywords (authors).

the most trending keyword. However, newer terms like "Social Media Analytics", "Social Media Data", "Sentiment Classification" are also visible.

5.3.7   BIBLIOGRAPHIC COUPLING OF COUNTRIES

A scientific mapping technique called BC makes the assumption that two papers with equivalent references would have similar content (Kessler, 1963). Figure 5.6 shows the top 30 countries' BC networks. On the network, two clusters can be seen; each cluster contains 15 items. USA, India, and China are the nations with the highest citations. These countries appear in the IST cluster. Australia, France, Greece, and Germany constitute the second cluster with lesser work in this research area. The bibliographic analysis identifies the empirical components common in sentiment analysis and social media research in general on a large scale.

5.3.8   HIGHEST PUBLICATION SOURCES

Table 5.5 lists the top nine most preferred journals with more than 200 articles, with their CiteScore, SNIP, and SJR. These nine journals account for 19.15% of total publications, indicating that almost 20% of the total papers were published in these nine journals. Authors prefer IEEE Access, International Journal of Advanced Computer Science and Applications, Multimedia Tools and Application, Applied Sciences, and Knowledge-Based System are the most preferred journals for publication. Table 5.5 also showcases the CiteScore, SNIP, and SJR values

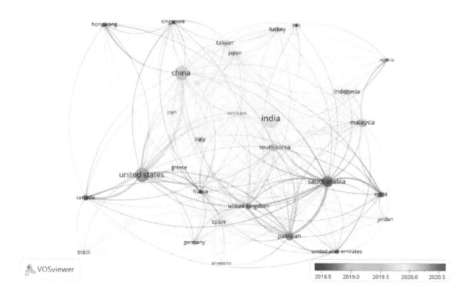

FIGURE 5.6   Bibliographic coupling of countries.

TABLE 5.5

Top Nine Journals That Have the Highest SNIP, SJR, and CiteScore

S. No.	Journal	Countries	No. of Papers	SNIP (2021)	SJR (2021)	CiteScore
1	IEEE Access	USA	74	1.326	0.927	6.7
2	International Journal of Advanced Computer Science and Applications	UK	50	0.528	0.284	1.8
3	Multimedia Tools and Application	Netherlands	26	1.055	0.716	5.3
4	Applied Sciences	Switzerland	22	1.026	0.507	3.7
5	Knowledge-Based System	Netherlands	21	2.611	2.192	12.0
6	Iranian Journal of Information Processing and Management	Iran	20	0.138	0.131	0.3
7	Expert Systems with Applications	UK	20	2.985	2.07	12.2
8	Social Network Analysis and Mining	Austria	20	1.248	0.682	4.8
9	Journal of Theoretical and Applied Information Technology	Pakistan	20	0.394	0.195	1.3
	TOTAL PAPERS IN TOP NINE JOURNALS		**215**			
	TOTAL EXTRACTED PAPERS		**1123**			
	SHARE OF TOP NINE JOURNALS IN TOTAL EXTRACTED PAPERS		**19.15%**			

for the top nine in 2021. To calculate the CiteScore SJR and SNIP values for the top nine journals. The CiteScore is determined by dividing the total number of citations a journal obtained from works published in the preceding three years by the total number of publications indexed in Scopus during the same period. It requires an organised, objective technique of ranking the most esteemed journals in the world to provide quantitative, statistical statistics based on citation data. SJR – SCImago Journal Ranking is the average weighted citations per year split by articles in a journal during the past three years. It is founded on the idea that not every citation should be evaluated equally. Higher the SJR more prestigious is the journal based on the SJR IEEE Access, Knowledge-Based System and Expert Systems with Applications are the top three journals with SJR 0.927, 2.192, 2.07, respectively. SNIP analyses citations based on the overall number of citations in a topic field to calculate the contextual citation efficacy of a source. It enables you to perform direct source comparisons on a variety of subjects. The top three journals by SNIP values are Knowledge-Based System (2.611), Expert System with Applications (2.985), and IEEE Access (1.326). Thus, based on the above analysis from among the top nine journals, SNIP, SJR, and CiteScore for IEEE Access are the highest.

5.3.9 LEADING INSTITUTES

Figure 5.7 shows the top ten institutional affiliations in Sentiment Analysis and Social Media in the Scopus Dataset. King Abdul Aziz University of Saudi Arabia, K.L. Deemed to be University, India, and King Saud University of Saudi Arabia are the top three institutions with highest contribution in this research area.

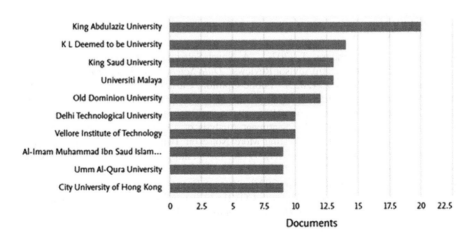

FIGURE 5.7   Top ten leading affiliations of sentiment analysis and social media.

5.4 CONCLUSION

The surge of publications in 2022 implies the growing interest in the research on sentiment analysis of social media. Social media is changing the way people live their lives, where fear of missing out has been driving the growth of it exponentially. The offline conversations are becoming a rarity, and the conversations on social media mean more to people, businesses, and academia. The pandemic pushed the conversations further and sentiment analysis took a significant position in the research community. Any aspect of life or business should be continued to be analysed to yield meaningful inferences.

Social Sciences contribution to the field is approximately 7%, the researchers in the Social Sciences should also focus more on analysing the sentiments of social media trends on various aspects that affect the society. It is highly recommended since the fibre of the society is changing and social listening is what gives a clear perspective on the issue or the trend.

A list of top ten institutions with maximum publications can help researchers in the field look for collaborations, research funding, or inviting experts in the field. The top authors contributing to the field are a ready reckoner for the research collaborations and learning from their experience. The collaborations bring fresh perspectives and since social media is expanding and taking over the lives of people, the sentiment analysis of the social media is going to be an inexhaustible field of research in the future.

The journals IEEE Access and Knowledge-Based System are more receptive to the discussing Sentiment analysis of social media and hence need to be explored and also considered highly while submitting the papers in this field.

The top ten cited research papers provide an enriching outlook to the understudied area, where the techniques to analyse the video, audio, and text have been explored. NLP has also been discussed in detail, with its challenges and future prospects. The reviews of the customers regarding various aspects have been studied in the papers and analysed in detail (He, 2017).

BIBLIOGRAPHY

Abeysinghe, P., & Bandara, T. (2022). "A Novel Self-Learning Approach to Overcome Incompatibility on TripAdvisor Reviews," *Data Science and Management, 5*(1).

Amoudi, G., & Shearah, Z. (2022). "Public Opinion, Clusters, and Statistics of COVID-19 Vaccination: A Twitter Analysis," *Journal of Theoretical and Applied Information Technology, 100*(20), 6036–6048.

Arora, S., & Piplani, K. (2022). "Sentiment Analysis of Tweets on Vaccination Vaxxers or Anti-Vaxxers – Who Is Creating More Noise on Twitter?" *International Journal of Research in Business Studies, 7*(1), 79–90. 79–90. http://www.ijrbs.com/pdf/IJRBS2022.pdf#page=79

Aygun, I., Kaya, B., & Kaya, M. (2022). "Aspect Based Twitter Sentiment Analysis on Vaccination and Vaccine Types in COVID-19 Pandemic with Deep Learning," *IEEE Journal of Biomedical and Health Informatics, 26*(5).

Dangi, D., Bhagat, A., & Dixit, D. K. (2022). "Sentiment Analysis of Social Media Data Based on Chaotic Coyote Optimization Algorithm Based Time Weight-AdaBoost Support Vector Machine Approach," *Concurrency and Computation: Practice and Experience 34*(3), 1–17. https://doi.org/10.1002/cpe.6581

Habek, G. C., Toçoğlu, M. A., & Onan, A. (2022). "Bi-Directional CNN-RNN Architecture with Group-Wise Enhancement and Attention Mechanisms for Cryptocurrency Sentiment Analysis," *Applied Artificial Intelligence, 36*(1).

Kessler, M. M. (1963). "Bibliographic Coupling between Scientific Papers," *American Documentation, 14*(1), 10–25. https://doi.org/10.1002/asi.5090140103

Khan, F. H., Qamar, U., & Bashir, S. (2016). "eSAP: A Decision Support Framework for Enhanced Sentiment Analysis and Polarity Classification," *Information Sciences, 367–368*, 862–873. ISSN 0020-0255. https://doi.org/10.1016/j.ins.2016.07.028. (https://www.sciencedirect.com/science/article/pii/S0020025516305096.)

Mohammad, S., Garcia, D., Jou, B., Schuller, B., Chang, S.-F., & Pantic, M. (2017). "A Survey of Multimodal Sentiment Analysis," *Image and Vision Computing, 65*, 3–14. ISSN 0262-8856. https://doi.org/10.1016/j.imavis.2017.08.003. https://www.sciencedirect.com/science/article/pii/S0262885617301191

Mohammad, Saif M., and Kiritchenko, Svetlana. 2015. "Using Hashtags to Capture Fine Emotion Categories from Tweets – Mohammad - 2014 - Computational Intelligence - Wiley Online Library." *Computational Intelligence* 31(2).

Pandey, A. C., Rajpoot, D. S., & Saraswat, M. (2017). "Twitter Sentiment Analysis Using Hybrid Cuckoo Search Method," *Information Processing & Management, 53*(4), 764–779. ISSN 0306-4573. https://doi.org/10.1016/j.ipm.2017.02.004. https://www.sciencedirect.com/science/article/pii/S0306457316302205

Paolanti, M., Mancini, A., Frontoni, E., Felicetti, A., Marinelli, L., Marcheggiani, E., & Pierdicca, R. (2021). "Tourism Destination Management Using Sentiment Analysis and Geo-Location Information: A Deep Learning Approach," *Information Technology and Tourism, 23*(2), 2.

Poria, S., Cambria, E., Howard, N., Huang, G.-B., & Hussain, A. (2016). "Fusing Audio, Visual and Textual Clues for Sentiment Analysis from Multimodal Content," *Neurocomputing, 174*(Part A), 50–59. ISSN 0925-2312. https://doi.org/10.1016/j.neucom.2015.01.095. (https://www.sciencedirect.com/science/article/pii/S0925231215011297)

Ravi, K., & Ravi, V. (2015). "A Survey on Opinion Mining and Sentiment Analysis: Tasks, Approaches and Applications," *Knowledge-Based Systems, 89*, 14–46. ISSN 0950-7051. https://doi.org/10.1016/j.knosys.2015.06.015. (https://www.sciencedirect.com/science/article/pii/S0950705115002336.)

Suarez Estrada, M., Juarez, Y., & Piña-García, C. A. (2022). "Toxic Social Media: Affective Polarization After Feminist Protests," *Social Media and Society, 8*(2).

Sun, S., Luo, C., & Chen, J. (2017). "A Review of Natural Language Processing Techniques for Opinion Mining Systems," *Information Fusion, 36*, 10–25. ISSN 1566-2535. https://doi.org/10.1016/j.inffus.2016.10.004. (https://www.sciencedirect.com/science/article/pii/S15662 53516301117.)

Thien Hai, N., Shirai, K., & Velcin, J. (2015). "Sentiment Analysis on Social media for Stock Movement Prediction," *Expert Systems with Applications, 42*(24), 9603–9611. ISSN 0957-4174. https://doi.org/10.1016/j.eswa.2015.07.052.

Yadav, A., & Vishwakarma, D. K. (2020). "Sentiment Analysis Using Deep Learning Architectures: a Review," *Artificial Intelligence Review*, *53*, 4335–4385. https://doi.org/10.1007/s10462-019-09794-5.https://doi.org/10.1007/s10462-019-09794-5

Yu, Y., Duan, W., & Cao, Q. (2013). "The Impact of Social and Conventional media on Firm Equity Value: A Sentiment Analysis Approach," *Decision Support Systems*, *55*(4), 919–926. https://doi.org/10.1016/j.dss.2012.12.028.

6 Exploring Hugging Face Transformer Library Impact on Sentiment Analysis
A Case Study

Aashita Chhabra[1], Kiran Chaudhary[2], and Mansaf Alam[1]
[1]Department of Computer Science, Jamia Millia Islamia, New Delhi, India
[2]Department of Commerce, Shivaji College, University of Delhi, Delhi, India

6.1 INTRODUCTION

The world is glowing based on artificial intelligence, especially when discussing E-commerce Industry. Any E-commerce industry takes the favor from a social media platform to work for their marketing team. With the help of a technical team having expertise in machine learning (ML), generate optimum results. Social Media is one of the prominent tools for marketing strategies as it contains content in the form of images, reviews, ratings, and hit ratio of the consumers, which leads to more profitable sales and product management. Various Social media platforms are "LinkedIn," "Facebook," "Instagram," "Twitter," "Pinterest," and "YouTube"; much data can be accessed through these sites. As billions and millions of customers visit popular social media platforms regularly, it should be handled with care and admiration to bring fruitful results. It shapes your brand and brings growth and density to the firm. Millions of customers visit e-commerce websites to buy and explore new products and services and gain information about new technologies. Now every vendor who sits and observes the to and fro of the product daily knows the customer's requirements. One has to shake hands with artificial intelligence to acquire more prominent and accurate results. Usually, a customer shows interest only after seeing the reviews of other buyers' opinions. ML plays a significant role in attracting online customers, increasing the hit ratio of the website, and receiving textual reviews. The technology named sentiment analysis (SA) joins in with different functionalities to gather the genuine opinion of the visitor. This helps to lead any company or firm to analyze customer choice. The accuracy of emotional verdicts can be improvised only by recognizing the relationship between product features provided by online customers [1]. The author explains the process for using SA in some steps. It starts with gathering the reviews, identifying sentiments, classification, and feature selection. Finally, the sentiments are

DOI: 10.1201/9781032614083-6

polarized in three forms (Positive, Negative, and Neutral) to get the acquired result and predict the further ability of the products [2]. To uplift your sales, it becomes mandatory to know the customer's opinion on social media, whether positive or negative [3]. When a seller works on accessing market intelligence, it holds the idea of SA to gain the customer interpretation of the product through reviews and ratings. It helps reach customer satisfaction, forecast new prices of products, strategize market campaigning, and develop new products [4]. The challenge with some current SA approaches is that it won't be able to analyze informal, sarcasm-based sentences and abrupt information [5]. Online reviews are not only an asset for the distributor of the product but also for the consumers. It becomes the real gold for every organization to attract more users for beneficiaries [6]. Many classification techniques are applied for sentimental mining, which goes through various processes to extract the premium data [7]. One of the techniques, Cluster computing, has been explained by an author that helps in customers' decision-making by making a cluster of online reviews [8]. Working with ML-Social Media Marketing with the combination of WEKA tool outperforms other data mining tools for data analysis and business process in terms of reporting capability. This work can be extended to other business domains like the healthcare industry, education, and many more [9]. Semantic analysis with LSTM (long short-term memory) has been shown where the analysis of emojis takes place [10]. Next, one does the aspect-based SA (ABSA) to predict the business failure and survival of the industry. It has numerous types of ABSA for restaurant survival behavior, which help identify the required features to be considered for the analysis, for example, taste, price, location, service, and atmosphere. The condition-based forest model was compared with ABSA by employing ML, finding that the former is less efficient [11]. Another ABSA has been integrated with the external knowledge implemented using a graph convolution neural network. A statistical study of all the sentiments or parts of speech has been constructed in a matrix form to visualize the impact of degree words, denying words, and other parameters. A word–sentence interaction network (WSIN) is created to gather the current word with the contextual meaning of that word to filter out the useful information [12]. Another application is Tripadvisor application where travel advisor wants to predict the number of revisits to a destination, checking the online forums of their customers help in gaining insight by using factor-augmented autoregressive and bridge model [13]. The author uses two kinds of model tree kernel and feature-based model to identify the polarity of the sentiments in two categories positive or negative and third one is neutral. It's been demonstrated that both the models outperform unigram baseline [14]. SA helps to predict the election result on the basis of likes of tweets and performed a tremendous work to accomplish it [15]. A comparative study is shown between two models named KNN(K- nearest neighbor) and support vector machine (SVM) to check the opinion polarity of views over social media websites, where SVM performs better than KNN in the same case [16].

6.2   ISSUES ADDRESSED BY EXPERTS

SA means touching the real emotions or attitude though textual information, images, score rating and many more. Purchase behavior is analyzed through SA that indirectly motivates any business process to accommodate the demand of the customers. Experts have taken this issue very seriously in regard to business intelligence and have gathered much perspective to work upon. They have access to reviews of both their own product and the advancement of competitors [17]. This helps them to maintain their competitive advantage, which is again a beneficiary for them. It deals with much functionality to work upon and till now, a much number of authors have worked on different criteria to meet the challenges of recent times. SAs are done to evaluate the micro post of the intended reviews, but some matters are culturally varied, which is the main challenge depicted [18]. Some of the issues are addressed in the diagram given in Figure 6.1.

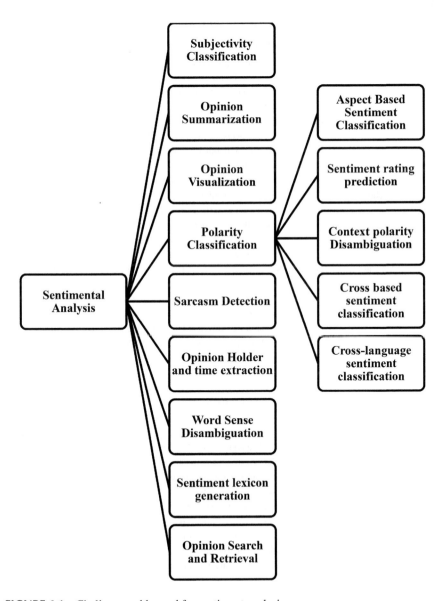

FIGURE 6.1   Challenges addressed for sentiment analysis.

6.3 RELATED WORK

One of the prominent tasks of natural language processing is SA, an analytical technique that uses statistics and ML to determine the real context of the product. Some of its related work performed with different proposed methodologies has been shown in Table 6.1.

TABLE 6.1
Key Features Provided by Experts on Semantic Analysis

S. No	Reference	Key Features
1	Revathy et al. [19]	The author approaches the technique of a double-feed neural network. It optimizes the classified information but is compared with neuro-fuzzy algorithms. DFFNN outperforms a double-feed neural network.
2	Rahman and Islam [20]	Public opinion is considered the most critical and valuable input for any decision-maker to combat coronavirus. Hence, sentiment analysis of public opinion mining is performed using various algorithms like stacking classifier (SC), voting classifier (VC), and bagging classifier (BC).
3	Machova et al. [21]	To detect the troll comments, lexicon-based sentiment analysis has been used with the comparative study of the detective model and found that the support vector machine performed the best among all. However, the detection model is more successful in terms of F1 accuracy.
4	Albadani et al. [22]	Sentiment detectors like TSDs are efficient in finding the opinion from tweets, but the gap area is the time constraint that compels the demander to enforce automated workflow. Here deep learning strategies come into the picture, which offers the architecture by combining "universal language model fine-tuning" (ULMFiT) with a support vector machine (SVM) to perceive more accurate and refined results in no time.
5	Rodrigues et al. [23]	Many fake accounts on popular websites are malicious and generated by different chatbots. These can be detected in real-time using machine learning models and creating a model for some specific tweets using association for sentiment analysis.
6	Basiri et al. [24]	Twitter product reviews for sentiment analysis are performed using the Bidirectional CNN-RNN model. The efficiency is recognizing the polarity of sentiments, which is the major task of SA. With the enhancement of the process with time, it does not provide a negative product review for business management utilities.
7	Huang et al. [25]	An ensemble learning approach has been provided by participating in speech for Chinese products. First, some fixed pattern has been taken with higher frequency inputted to the random subspace algorithm. The base classifiers are centered on product attribute to associate contextual meaning for sentiment analysis.

(Continued)

TABLE 6.1 (Continued)
Key Features Provided by Experts on Semantic Analysis

S. No	Reference	Key Features
8	Yang et al. [26]	Formulation of a model named SLCABG works upon sentiment lexicon. Here, gated unit network and CNN is implemented, which takes out the sentiment features and use this mechanism to weigh. It recognizes the polarity of positive and negative, but it requires more refined sentiment features; hence, the work can be enhanced.
9	Denecke and Deng [27]	The utility of sentiment analysisis very less in medical domain but the most appropriate usage can be found by studying the clinical document and maintaining the new lexion database for medical words and accessing the impact of patients' history in positive or negative term
10	Kiran Chaudhary et al. [28]	Authors have predicted the consumer behavior of social media platforms using mathematical modeling with pre-processed data. Sentiments taken from different platforms are tested and trained to get the beneficial data.
11	S Malhotra et al. [29]	As AI has evolved rapidly with many new features to acquire data in form of voice. It is taken from Voice-Based Assistant Devices (VBADs) which not only ease the lifestyle but gives a relieve from boredom
12	N Hasan et al. [30]	Another perspective is to check the early failure detection in an industry. A comparative study is performed using various algorithms and performance is analyzed.
13	Kiran Chaudhary et al. [31]	Some more applications have been discussed for Big Data Analytics. Author gives the broader idea of Big data utilities in which they mentioned about the dynamic data which is tremendously increasing with growing social media
14	Kiran Chaudhary et al. [32]	Sentiment analysis can only be performed with Digital marketing. It gathers the requirements in a different form and analyze it to make better decision making for any kind of organizations

6.4 METHODOLOGY

SA using ML is observed to be implemented in different fields. Everyone has another motivation to proceed, but one thing common among all is that datasets are trained as per the requirement. Now, another utility has come up: Hugging Face, a natural language processing startup that works in a transformer library of Python. Many APIs expose transformer architecture, such as BERT, GPT-2, DistilBERT, and XML. The criterion it follows is that it uses a pre-trained model, and test cases can be directly applied to predict the result. The library downloads a pre-trained model for NLP. The tasks that are performed by it are text classification, text summarization, masking, opinion mining, feature extraction, etc. In recent times, AutoNLP has come up to train and deploy the model. Now pipeline is used to call a pre-trained model, as shown in Figure 6.2.

```
from transformers import pipeline
classifier = pipeline("Sentiment Analysis", model = model, tokenizer = tokenizer)
```

FIGURE 6.2 To import pipeline for implementing the pre-trained model.

```
from transformers import pipeline
from transformers import AutoTokenizer, AutoModelForSequenceClassification
import torch
import torch.nn.functional as F

model_name = "distilbert-base-uncased-finetuned-sst-2-english"
model = AutoModelForSequenceClassification.from_pretrained(model_name)
tokenizer = AutoTokenizer.from_pretrained(model_name)

from transformers import pipeline
classifier = pipeline("sentiment-analysis", model = model, tokenizer = tokenizer)
results = classifier(["We are happy to show you the transformer library.","we hope you don't hate it"])

for result in results:
    print(result)

tokens = tokenizer.tokenize("We are very happy to show you transformer")
token_ids = tokenizer.convert_tokens_to_ids(tokens)
input_ids = tokenizer()
```

FIGURE 6.3 A function that converts token to ids is used for fast accessibility.

Case Study: Now, we will use a concrete model and a concrete tokenizer. We will specify the model name, a DistilBERT model, and a smaller but faster version of BERT. It is also pre-trained and finely tuned. Here, a dataset is taken from Stanford sentiment tree bank version 2. We will use a different tokenizer approach and import two different classes, AutoTokenizer and AutoModelForSequenceClassification, as shown in Figure 6.3. Now, after importing, we can create two instances for the same. The results are the same for both tokenizers as they are by default. Now, the function converts the token to ids, which prints the token ids and input ids. Tokenizer will provide us with the string of characters and behave as a separate token with unique token ids within the list. Here, we have shown two sentences for showing the results with their highest probability. Now the predictions are saved in save directory using a torch given in Figure 6.4. Now many other models are available for hugging faces in a transformer library, which makes it accessible and enables reliable binary semantic analysis for various types of text. Output is shown in Figure 6.5.

6.5 DISCUSSION WITH RESULTS

In Table 6.2, some of the random instances have been taken to depict the result after using the DistilBERT transformer library. Hugging Face has provided the opportunity to access the maximum lexion without even training. It has built a strong lexion structure that has got numerous amount of databases with all types of synonyms to generate the accurate result. The hugging face will serve different services of natural language processing with complicated models having big infrastructure to access the better and timely quality.

```
print(f'Tokens:{tokens}')
print(f'Token IDs:{token_ids}')
print(f'Input IDs:{input_ids}')

x_train = ["We are happy to show you the transformer library","we hope you dont hate it"]
batch = tokenizer(x_train, padding = True, truncation = True, max_length =512, return_tensors = "pt")
print(batch)


with torch.no_grad():
    outputs = model(**batch, labels = torch.tensor([1,0]))
    print(outputs)
    predictions = F.softmax(outputs.logits, dim =1)
    print(predictions)
    label = torch.argmax(predictions, dim=1)
    labels = [model.config.id2label[label_id] for label_id in labels.tolist()]
    print(labels)

    save_directory ="saved"
    tokenizer.save_pretrained(save_directory)
    model = AutoModelForSequenceClassification.from_pretrained(save_directory)
```

FIGURE 6.4   Predictions are saved in a save directory using a torch.no_grad.

```
['POSITIVE', 'NEGATIVE']
{'input_ids': tensor([[    3,  1433,   976, 26897,   120, 26951,   312, 26773,  6187,    19,
          4273, 23158,  2088,     2,  5415, 22445, 26902, 17491,  6572,  2328,
         26914,     4],
        [    3,  1433,  1438,  3500, 23158, 13463, 26898, 26979,   209,   193,
         26897, 23568, 26914,     4,     0,     0,     0,     0,     0,     0,
             0,     0]]), 'token_type_ids': tensor([[0, 0, 0, 0, 0, 0, 0, 0, 0, 0, 0, 0, 0, 0, 0, 0, 0, 0, 0, 0, 0, 0],
        [0, 0, 0, 0, 0, 0, 0, 0, 0, 0, 0, 0, 0, 0, 0, 0, 0, 0, 0, 0, 0, 0]]), 'attention_mask': tensor([[1, 1, 1, 1, 1,
         1, 1, 1, 1, 1, 1, 1, 1, 1, 1, 1, 0, 0, 0, 0, 0, 0]])}
tensor([0, 1])
['positive', 'negative']

Process finished with exit code 0
```

FIGURE 6.5   Polarity is shown after using a pre-trained model.

TABLE 6.2

Outcomes for Random Instances Using DistilBERT Library

S. No	Different Instances	Outcome
1	We are happy to show you the transformer library	Positive
2	We hope you don't hate it	Negative
3	I think weather is going to be worse than before	Negative
4	Bert library has got better APIs than others	Positive

6.6 CONCLUSION

The crux of the chapter concludes with the latest utility of an API of Python library, i.e., Transformer, which brings many pre-trained and finely tuned models to access SA of text classification, text summarization, masking, opinion mining, feature extraction, etc. Different models have been applied in many papers with the dataset training before utilizing it for extracting polarity. However, the challenge here is to work without training the data. Hugging Face brings the utility that works with the tested data to be performed rather than training the data, which is also time-consuming. Moreover, it has many security features to ensure that code and data remain secure. For future scope, one can adopt other models of Transformer other than BERT, which have more scalable features and reduce cost and time.

REFERENCES

1. Du, Y., & Yang, L. (2019). A sentiment measurement model for online reviews of complex products. In *Proceeding of IEEE International Conference on Communications, Information System and Computer Engineering (CISCE)* (pp. 199–202), 10.1109/CISCE.2019.00053
2. Chakraborty, K., Bhattacharyya, S., Bag, R., & Hassanien, A. A. (2018). "Sentiment Analysis on a Set of Movie Reviews Using Deep Learning Techniques", *Social Network Analytics: Computational Research Methods and Techniques*, 127. https://doi.org/10.1016/B978-0-12-815458-8.00007-4
3. Bavakhani, M., Yari, A., & Sharifi, A. (2019). A deep learning approach for extracting polarity from customers' reviews. In *Proceeding of IEEE 5th International Conference on Web Research (ICWR)* (pp. 276–280).
4. Tubishat, M., Idris, N., & Abushariah, M. A. M. (2018). "Implicit Aspect Extraction in Sentiment Analysis: Review, Taxonomy, Oppportunities, and Open Challenges," *Information Processing & Management*, 54(4), 545–563.
5. Dashtipour, K., Gogate, M., Li, J., Jiang, F., Kong, B., & Hussain, A. (2020) "A Hybrid Persian Sentiment Analysis Framework: Integrating Dependency Grammar Based Rules and Deep Neural Networks", *Neurocomputing*, 380, 1–10. 10.1016/j.neucom.2019.10.009
6. Qiu, J., Liu, C., Li, Y., & Lin, Z. (2018). "Leveraging Sentiment Analysis at the Aspects Level to Predict Ratings of Reviews", *Information Sciences*, 451, 295–309. https://doi.org/10.1016/j.ins.2018.04.009
7. Raj, V. (2019). Sentiment analysis on product reviews. In *2019 International Conference on Computing, Communication, and Intelligent Systems (ICCCIS)* (pp. 5–9).
8. Zhang, W., Kong, S.-x, & Zhu, Y.-c (2019). "Sentiment Classification and Computing for Online Reviews by a Hybrid SVM and LSA Based Approach," *Cluster Computing*, 22(5), 12619–12632.
9. Arasu, B. S., Seelan, B. J. B., & Thamaraiselvan, N. (2020). "A Machine Learning-Based Approach to Enhancing Social Media Marketing," *Computers & Electrical Engineering*, 86, 106723.
10. Ghica, D. R., & Alyahya, K. (2019). "Latent Semantic Analysis of Game Models Using LSTM," *Journal of Logical and Algebraic Methods in Programming*, 106, 39–54.
11. Li, H., Bruce, X. B., Li, G., & Gao, H. (2023). "Restaurant Survival Prediction Using Customer-Generated Content: An Aspect-Based Sentiment Analysis of Online Reviews," *Tourism Management*, 96, 104707.

12. Gu, T., Zhao, H., He, Z., Li, M., & Ying, D. (2023). "Integrating External Knowledge into Aspect-Based Sentiment Analysis Using Graph Neural Network," *Knowledge-Based Systems*, *259*, 110025.
13. Colladon, A. F., Guardabascio, B., & Innarella, R. (2019). "Using Social Network and Semantic Analysis to Analyze Online Travel Forums and Forecast Tourism Demand," *Decision Support Systems*, *123*, 113075.
14. Agarwal, A., Xie, B., Vovsha, I., Rambow, O., & Passonneau, R. J. (2011, June). Sentiment analysis of twitter data. In *Proceedings of the Workshop on Language in Social Media (LSM 2011)* (pp. 30–38).
15. Sharma, A., & Ghose, U. (2020). "Sentimental Analysis of Twitter Data with Respect to General Elections in India," *Procedia Computer Science*, *173*, 325–334.
16. Singh, N. K., Tomar, D. S., & Sangaiah, A. K. (2020). "Sentiment Analysis: A Review and Comparative Analysis Over Social media," *Journal of Ambient Intelligence and Humanized Computing*, *11*, 97–117.
17. Serrano-Guerrero, J., Olivas, J. A., Romero, F. P., & Herrera-Viedma, E. (2015). "Sentiment Analysis: A Review and Comparative Analysis of Web Services," *Information Sciences*, *311*, 18–38.
18. Wankhade, M., Rao, A. C. S., & Kulkarni, C. (2022). "A Survey on Sentiment Analysis Methods, Applications, and Challenges," *Artificial Intelligence Review*, *55*(7), 5731–5780.
19. Revathy, G., Alghamdi, S. A., Alahmari, S. M., Yonbawi, S. R., Kumar, A., & Haq, M. A. (2022). "Sentiment Analysis Using Machine Learning: Progress in the Machine Intelligence for Data Science," *Sustainable Energy Technologies and Assessments*, *53*, 102557.
20. Rahman, M., & Islam, M. N. (2022). "Exploring the performance of ensemble machine learning classifiers for sentiment analysis of covid-19 tweets. In *Sentimental Analysis and Deep Learning* (pp. 383–396). Springer.
21. Machova, K., Mach, M., & Vasilko, M. (2022). "Comparison of Machine Learning and Sentiment Analysis in Detection of Suspicious Online Reviewers on Different Type of Data," *Sensors*, *22*(1), 155.
22. AlBadani, B., Shi, R., & Dong, J. (2022). "A Novel Machine Learning Approach for Sentiment Analysis on Twitter Incorporating the Universal Language Model Fine-Tuning and SVM," *Applied System Innovation*, *5*(1), 13.
23. Rodrigues, A. P., Fernandes, R., Shetty, A., Lakshmanna, K., & Shafi, R. M. (2022). Real-Time Twitter Spam Detection and Sentiment Analysis Using Machine Learning and Deep Learning Techniques. *Computational Intelligence and Neuroscience*, *2022*, 1–14.
24. Basiri, M. E., Nemati, S., Abdar, M., Cambria, E., & RajendraAcharya, U. (2021). ABCDM: An Attention-Based Bidirectional CNN-RNN Deep Model for Sentiment Analysis. *Future Generation Computer Systems*, 115, 279–294. 10.1016/j.future.2020.08.005
25. Huang, J., Xue, Y., Hu, X., Jin, H., Lu, X., & Liu, Z. (2019). "Sentiment Analysis of Chinese Online Reviews Using Ensemble Learning Framework," *Cluster Computing*, *22*(2), 3043–3058.
26. Yang, L., Li, Y., Wang, J., & Sherratt, R. S. (2020). "Sentiment Analysis for E-Commerce Product Reviews in Chinese Based on Sentiment Lexicon and Deep Learning," *IEEE Access*, *8*, 23522–23530.
27. Denecke, K., & Deng, Y. (2015). "Sentiment Analysis in Medical Settings: New Opportunities and Challenges," *Artificial Intelligence in Medicine*, *64*(1), 17–27.
28. Chaudhary, K., Alam, M., Al-Rakhami, M. S., & Gumaei, A. (2021). "Machine Learning-Based Mathematical Modelling for Prediction of Social Media Consumer Behavior Using Big Data Analytics," *Journal of Big Data*, *8*(1), 1–20.

29. Malhotra, S., Chaudhary, K., & Alam, M. (2022). "Modeling the Use of Voice Based Assistant Devices (VBADs): A Machine Learning Base an Exploratory Study Using Cluster Analysis and Correspondence Analysis," *International Journal of Information Management Data Insights*, 2(1), 100069.
30. Hasan, N., Chaudhary, K., & Alam, M. (2021). "Unsupervised Machine Learning Framework for Early Machine Failure Detection in an Industry," *Journal of Discrete Mathematical Sciences and Cryptography*, 24(5), 1497–1508.
31. Chaudhary, K., & Alam, M. (2022). *Big Data Analytics: Applications in Business and Marketing*. Auerbach Publications.
32. Chaudhary, K., & Alam, M. (Eds.). (2022). *Big Data Analytics: Digital Marketing and Decision-Making*. CRC Press.

7 Data Analytics in Business Intelligence

Kingsley T. Igulu[1], Ebenezer Osuigbo[1], and Thipendra P. Singh[2]
[1]Department of Computer Science, Kenule Beeson Saro-Wiwa Polytechnic, Bori, Rivers State, Nigeria
[2]School of Computer Science Engineering and Technology, Bennett University, Greater Noida, India

7.1 INTRODUCTION

Discovering, interpreting, and communicating the significance of important patterns in data is what analytics is all about. Quantifying performance with analytics is possible through the concurrent use of three disciplines: statistics, computer programming, and operations research. This method is especially useful in fields that have a large amount of recorded information. When it comes to communicating insights, analytics frequently favors data visualization.

The relevance of data analytics is only going to continue to rise in the current world. In order to find patterns and trends, it requires the collection and examination of enormous amounts of data. The enhancement of marketing efforts, the development of new products and services, and the optimization of company operations are all examples of the many uses that can be found for data analytics. By adopting data analytics, businesses have the potential to enhance their operations, significantly boost their efficiency, and make more informed decisions.

Data analytics is a vast discipline that encompasses a variety of methodologies and technologies. Predictive analytics, data mining, machine learning (ML), and natural language processing are included. Data mining involves the extraction of patterns from massive databases, whereas ML employs algorithms to learn from data and create predictions. Natural language processing employs algorithms to analyze and comprehend human language, whereas predictive analytics uses data to make predictions about the future (el Morr & Ali-Hassan, 2019).

In the commercial sector, data analytics are becoming increasingly vital. Utilizing data analytics, businesses are gaining customer insights, enhancing operations, and developing new products and services. Additionally, data analytics is utilized to enhance marketing efforts, detect fraud, and enhance customer service (Fan et al., 2015).

In addition to healthcare, finance, and education, data analytics is employed in a variety of other industries. By utilizing data analytics, healthcare companies may spot trends in patient health, while financial institutions are developing new goods and services. Data analytics is used in education to monitor student performance and enhance teaching methods (Duan & da Xu, 2021).

DOI: 10.1201/9781032614083-7

Data analytics is gaining importance in modern society. Utilizing data analytics, businesses are gaining customer insights, enhancing operations, and developing new products and services. With the emergence of new technologies, the importance of data analytics is growing (Alsunaidi et al., 2021).

In today's ever-evolving and competitive business climate, it has become increasingly vital for firms to stay ahead of the curve by using the power of data analytics. With the proper data, organizations can develop a deeper understanding of their consumers, optimize their operations, and make more informed decisions. This comprehensive tutorial will provide a complete understanding of the importance of harnessing the potential of data analytics in business intelligence (BI). It will provide a comprehensive overview of the fundamental concepts, fundamental principles, and best practices for exploiting data to obtain a competitive advantage. Finally, it shall discuss the most popular tools and technologies available to help companies make the most out of their data. By the end of this chapter, you will have a solid understanding of the application of analytics in BI efficiently.

7.2   KEY PRINCIPLES OF DATA ANALYTICS

Data can be a powerful resource for any organization. The challenge, though, is choosing the right data to create insights from, using that data to create value, and then communicating those insights to your stakeholders. This chapter will provide an overview of the key principles of data analytics.

7.3   TYPES OF ANALYTICS

Data analytics can be broken down into four categories: descriptive analytics, diagnostic analytics, predictive analytics, and prescriptive analytics (Lim et al., 2013; Richards, 2016).

7.3.1   DESCRIPTIVE ANALYTICS

Descriptive analytics is a type of data analysis that involves summarizing data to draw conclusions about the data. It is typically the first step in data analysis, as it provides the most detailed view of the data available. Descriptive analytics is often used to understand the characteristics of the data, such as the average, median, and range of the data. It can also be used to identify patterns or relationships in the data that can be used to make better decisions (Richards, 2016).

The main purpose of descriptive analytics is to give a more detailed view of the data. It helps to summarize the data and identify any trends or patterns that can be used to improve decision-making processes. Descriptive analytics can be used to provide insights into customer behavior, marketing campaigns, or product performance. It allows businesses to better understand their customers and their needs, enabling them to make more informed decisions and improve the efficiency of their operations.

Descriptive analytics can be used in many different areas, including marketing, finance, and operations. In marketing, descriptive analytics can be used to identify which products are most popular, as well as which customers are most likely to purchase a particular product. In finance, descriptive analytics can be used to identify patterns in financial data, such as spending patterns or trends in stock prices. In operations, descriptive analytics can be used to identify which processes are most efficient, as well as which processes need to be improved.

In addition to providing detailed insights into data, descriptive analytics can also be used to identify potential risks and opportunities. For example, descriptive analytics can be used to identify areas where a company may be vulnerable to fraud or other risks. It can also be used to identify areas where a business can capitalize on new opportunities or increase its efficiency. By using descriptive analytics, businesses can make more informed decisions and get better insights from their data.

7.3.2 DIAGNOSTIC ANALYTICS

Diagnostic analytics is a form of data analytics that focuses on understanding the past history of a business to identify the underlying cause of a problem. It is the process of analyzing large volumes of data to identify patterns, trends, and correlations. This type of analytics is used to gain insight into the current state of a business and to uncover the root cause of any problem (Wu & Härdle, 2020).

Diagnostic analytics can be used to identify potential business risks, opportunities for improvement, and areas for further investigation. It allows businesses to improve their existing strategies, processes, and systems. It enables them to develop strategies for better decision-making and to identify areas where further research is needed. By using diagnostic analytics, businesses can identify problems and opportunities in a timely manner. This type of analytics helps businesses to understand trends and patterns in their data, including customer behavior and financial performance. It can also be used to identify the underlying cause of a problem, such as a decrease in customer satisfaction or a drop in sales.

Diagnostic analytics can be used to develop strategies to improve business performance. It can help businesses to identify new opportunities, enhance existing processes, and improve decision-making. It is an effective way to gain insight into a business's current state and identify areas for improvement. Diagnostic analytics is an important part of data analytics and BI. It is used to analyze large volumes of data to identify patterns, trends, and correlations. This type of analytics helps businesses to understand the underlying causes of a problem and develop strategies for improvement. By using diagnostic analytics, businesses can make informed decisions and improve their performance.

7.3.3 PREDICTIVE ANALYTICS

Predictive analytics is a data analytics process that uses sophisticated algorithms and advanced data science techniques to analyze data and make predictions about future events. It is a powerful tool for businesses to gain actionable insights into their operations. Predictive analytics can be used in a variety of ways, from forecasting sales and predicting customer behavior to identifying trends and risks in the market. Predictive analytics uses data from a variety of sources, including customer interactions, sales data, financial data, and market research. This data is then analyzed using advanced algorithms that identify patterns and trends in the data. By doing so, predictive analytics can provide businesses with valuable insights into how their operations are likely to develop in the future.

Businesses can use predictive analytics to make decisions about their operations, such as when to launch a new product or which markets to enter. It can also be used to predict customer behavior and identify trends in the market. Predictive analytics can also be used to identify risks and opportunities, allowing businesses to make informed decisions and stay ahead of the competition.

Predictive analytics is becoming increasingly important in the business world. As businesses become more data-driven, predictive analytics is becoming an essential tool for businesses to gain actionable insights into their operations. By utilizing predictive analytics, businesses can use data to make better decisions, identify trends, and stay ahead of the competition. Data analytics and BI are becoming increasingly intertwined, as predictive analytics helps businesses gain a better understanding of their data.

7.3.4 PRESCRIPTIVE ANALYTICS

Prescriptive analytics is an advanced form of data analytics and BI that uses data-driven insights and predictive analytics to recommend specific actions that organizations can take to optimize their operations and achieve their desired outcomes. It goes beyond descriptive and predictive analytics by providing actionable solutions that help organizations improve their performance (Ram Mohan Rao et al., 2018).

Prescriptive analytics uses mathematical algorithms, ML, and artificial intelligence (AI) to analyze data and find solutions to complex problems. It helps organizations identify opportunities and make decisions that will maximize their results. For example, prescriptive analytics can be used to identify the best way to allocate resources, optimize supply chains, and anticipate customer demand. It can also be used to identify potential risks, identify areas for improvement, and evaluate the effectiveness of strategies. Prescriptive analytics can provide valuable insights that can help organizations make more informed decisions. It can be used to identify the best strategies for achieving goals, such as increasing sales or reducing costs. By analyzing data from multiple sources and predicting future outcomes, prescriptive analytics can provide valuable insights that can help organizations achieve their desired results.

Prescriptive analytics can also help organizations identify potential risks and anticipate customer demand. It can be used to evaluate the effectiveness of strategies, identify areas for improvement, and optimize their operations. By analyzing data from multiple sources and predicting future outcomes, prescriptive analytics can help organizations make better decisions and optimize their performance. Prescriptive analytics is an invaluable tool for organizations looking to optimize their operations and maximize their results. By analyzing data and predicting future outcomes, prescriptive analytics can provide valuable insights that can help organizations identify opportunities, make informed decisions, and achieve their desired outcomes. With the help of prescriptive analytics, organizations can make better decisions and maximize their performance.

7.4 BENEFITS OF DATA ANALYTICS

The applications for data analytics are quite varied and extensive. The examination of significant amounts of data has the potential to raise levels of productivity across a wide range of different types of commercial enterprises. Businesses have a better chance of succeeding in today's highly competitive market if they improve their performance. The banking industry was one of the first to utilize the technology. Data analytics plays a significant part in the banking and finance industries, where it is utilized to forecast market trends and evaluate risk. One example of the application of data analytics that everyone deals with is credit ratings. When calculating lending risk, these scores consider a variety of data points. Data analytics is also used to detect and prevent fraudulent activity, which helps financial organizations improve their efficiency and lower their risk.

However, the application of data analytics is not limited to increasing revenues and return on investment (ROI). The analysis of data can yield vital knowledge that can be used in areas, such as healthcare (health informatics), the fight against crime, and the preservation of the environment. These applications of data analytics put these methodologies to work to make the world a better place. Even while statistics and data analysis have always been utilized in scientific study, the application of modern analytical tools and big data has made it possible to get numerous new insights. In complicated systems, these methods can identify patterns and trends. Researchers are currently utilizing ML in their efforts to safeguard endangered species.

The application of data analytics in the medical industry is already very common. Data analytics is having a significant impact on the healthcare industry in a variety of ways, including the ability to predict the outcomes of individual patients more accurately, more effectively allocate resources, and enhance diagnostic procedures. Learning machines are also having an impact on other industries, such as the pharmaceutical sector. The process of finding new drugs is a difficult one that involves a lot of different factors. The discovery of new drugs can be significantly aided by ML. Data analytics are also used by the pharmaceutical industry to better understand the market for medications and to forecast their sales.

The Internet of Things, sometimes known as IoT, is a field that frequently works in conjunction with ML. The analysis of the data produced by these devices presents a significant potential. IoT devices typically have many sensors that are responsible for the collection of useful data points. To control the level of heating and cooling in a home, technological devices such as the Nest thermostat monitor motion and temperature. Intelligent devices such as this one can analyze the data they collect to analyze and predict your behavior. This will deliver advanced home automation that is flexible enough to adjust to how you live (Akhter & Sofi, 2022).

There is no end to the number of uses for data analytics. Every day, more and more data is generated, and this opens the door to new possibilities for applying data analytics to more facets of business, science, and everyday life.

Analytics initiatives can yield several benefits for companies in the areas of increased competitive advantage, increased revenue, increased customer retention and satisfaction, greater employee productivity, increased efficiency, and cost savings. With these benefits in mind, it's clear that businesses are increasingly turning to the power of data analytics (Bentley, 2017).

7.5   DATA ANALYTICS PROCESS

Data analytics is a useful tool for BI that assists firms in making decisions based on accurate information. It is the process of collecting data from numerous sources, such as customer databases, social media platforms, and other sources and then organizing, and analyzing that data. It enables businesses to better understand the requirements and preferences of their customers, recognize emerging trends, and make more informed decisions. The analysis of data requires a few different steps. The gathering of data is the initial stage. This requires collecting data from a wide variety of sources, including customer databases, online analytics, and social media platforms. To ensure that the analysis is accurate, it is essential to make use of data sources that can be relied upon and that provide accurate information (Kumar et al., 2022).

The cleansing of the data is the second phase. This requires correcting any flaws and inconsistencies that have been found in the data. The data are improved in terms of their accuracy and reliability once they have been cleaned. In addition, data transformation is a part of data cleansing. Data transformation entails changing the format of the data so that it can be processed more efficiently.

The analysis of the data is the third step. In order to accomplish this, a number of statistical tools and methods must be utilized to examine the data. This includes the use of predictive analytics, which assists in the identification of trends within the data. This makes it easier to arrive at conclusions that are founded on facts rather than speculations.

BI is the fourth step in the process. Utilizing the information to guide decision-making and proceed with action is the procedure referred to here. This involves utilizing the data to make decisions regarding marketing strategies, providing service to customers, and developing new products.

Data analytics is a significant instrument that assists businesses in improving their performance as well as their ability to make sound judgments. It entails a number of processes, beginning with the collecting of data and ending with BI. It is possible for businesses to improve their relationships with their clientele as well as the choices they make if they have a solid understanding of the data analytics process.

7.6   COMMON DATA ANALYTICS TECHNIQUES

Analytics can be used to gain a better understanding of customers, uncover insights on product usage, and optimize operations. With the right data and tools, companies can gain a better understanding of their customers to gain a competitive advantage, uncover insights on product usage to optimize product designs, and optimize operations to prevent bottlenecks and optimize resource allocation. With the right data and tools, companies can use insights gained from their data to create new products, services, and business processes that can potentially turn their company into a leader in its industry (Sun et al., 2017; Wu & Härdle, 2020).

7.7 POPULAR DATA ANALYTICS PLATFORMS AND VENDORS

There is a large variety of data analytics platforms, each of which can be purchased from a different provider. Based on the most recent data available, this chapter will go over some of the most popular solutions (Kronz et al., 2022). In a recent research that was made available on the company's website, Gartner categorized the many different data analytics platforms using its renowned "Magic Quadrants" as seen in Figure 7.1.

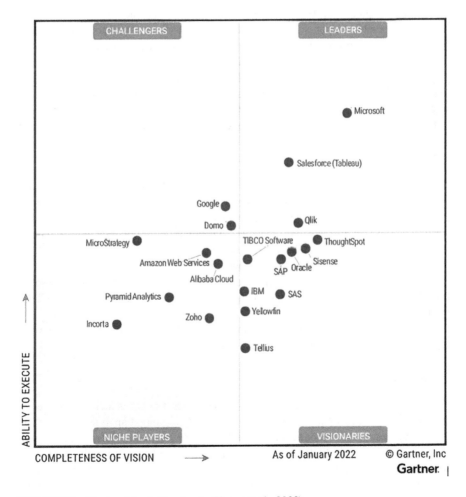

FIGURE 7.1 Gartner Magic Quadrants (Kronz et al., 2022).

A brief description of popular data analytics platforms and vendors are discussed in the following sections according to Kronz et al. (2022).

7.7.1 ALIBABA CLOUD

Alibaba Cloud occupies a unique position in this Magic Quadrant. It mostly competes in the Asia-Pacific region but has worldwide potential. Asia/largest Pacific's public cloud platform is Alibaba Cloud. Quick BI offers data cleansing, visualization, interactive dashboards, and enhanced analytics. This platform offers choices for SaaS, on-premises, and embedded analytics. Quick BI 4.1 offers faster data source access and additional integration options with China's main digital workplace applications, DingTalk, WeChat/WeCom, and Lark.

7.7.2 AMAZON WEB HOSTING

In this Magic Quadrant, Amazon Web Services (AWS) occupies a Niche Player position. Amazon QuickSight is sold mostly to AWS customers. Customers mention integration with the Amazon data stack, scalability, performance, and a price plan that is competitive as the primary reasons for adoption.

Amazon QuickSight took a significant stride toward the area of augmented analytics in 2021 by introducing the Q natural language query (NLQ) capabilities. It has also incorporated essential DATA ANALYTICS features, such as the ability to embed analytic content in other areas and enterprise-level reporting that is scheduled in advance.

7.7.3 DOMO

Domo is a Challenger within the scope of this Magic Quadrant. It has robust functioning and momentum in comparison to its much more established rivals. Domo's cloud-based data analytics platform provides more than 1000 data connectors, data visualizations that are easy to utilize, and a data analytics application development in a low-code/no-code setting. Because of the platform's usability and quick setup time, Domo often sells directly to business lines.

While multicloud, Domo is gaining appeal with enterprises that have selected a non-Microsoft cloud ecosystem and desire a robust native cloud DATA ANALYTICS platform.

Domo's Sandbox was introduced in 2021, enabling clients to use a DevOps approach to the generation and promotion of analytics content.

7.7.4 GOOGLE

Within this Magic Quadrant, Google is a Challenger. Looker is a cloud-architected DATA ANALYTICS platform that provides highly regulated analytics, self-service visualizations, and dashboards based on the LookML semantic layer. Since Google purchased Looker in 2020, the company has continued to offer multicloud situations from the perspective of deployment as well as database connection, and it has continued to strengthen integrations with other products that are part of the Google Cloud stack.

Looker acquired Google Data Studio and its product team in 2021, with the intention of integrating the user experience (UX) across both products. The new extension framework from Looker is a completely hosted development interface that enables developers to create data-driven applications.

7.7.5 IBM

IBM is a Visionary within the scope of this Magic Quadrant. The essential features of IBM Cognos Analytics with Watson are constant across hybrid, multicloud, private, public, and on-premises installations. Cloud Pak for Data works with AWS, Azure, GCP, and IBM Cloud, and it may be used with IBM's containerized stack of D&A services, which includes storage, data refinement, data virtualization, data catalog, and DSML services.

IBM upgraded its user interface and became a Watson-powered BI solution in 2021, incorporating automated insights via "Watson Moments" and NLP, NLG for data storytelling, and NLQ "Assistant" more effectively. It is also investing in the integration of planning and analytics.

7.7.6 INCORTA

Incorta is a Niche Player within the scope of this Magic Quadrant. Incorta's primary value proposition is to minimize users' time to insight by providing an end-to-end D&A platform, including data collection, data administration, and data visualization, with no IT participation.

Incorta introduced Incorta Cloud SaaS and role-specific content for first-time users in 2021 in order to expedite time to insight. The new Data Wizard functionality facilitates self-service content production by guiding users through the process of establishing data pipelines. Additionally, Incorta has expanded its visualization capabilities by enabling end users to develop new visualizations using its Component SDK.

7.7.7 MICROSOFT

Within this Magic Quadrant, Microsoft is placed as a Leader. It has huge market presence and momentum due to Office 365 and a comprehensive, cutting-edge product strategy. Microsoft Power BI includes features, including better analytics, dashboard interactivity, and data visualization, for user convenience.

Key business metrics may now be tracked in a collaborative, data-driven manner, occasioned by the new "goals" function. In most cases, Power BI is deployed as a SaaS service hosted by Microsoft Azure; however, Power BI Report Server offers a less-capable on-premises alternative. Microsoft is constantly adding Power BI features to Office 365, Microsoft Teams, Excel, and SharePoint. By 2022, Microsoft hopes to have established Power BI as the central repository for all business information.

7.7.8 MICROSTRATEGY

In the Magic Quadrant, MicroStrategy is a Niche Player. MicroStrategy excels at IT-desired scalability, manageability, and security. HyperIntelligence is a part of this; it uses a semantic graph to dynamically unearth previously determined insights within running applications. Although the capabilities are substantial, they are no longer as distinctive in a sector that is continually evolving.

MicroStrategy introduced a new containerized and microservices-driven platform architecture in 2021 that is capable of working in a multitenant SaaS setting. It also continued to make substantial Bitcoin investments. Diversifying from its typical DATA ANALYTICS emphasis, it has committed $3.75 billion to acquire 124,391 Bitcoins as of 30 December 2021.

7.7.9 ORACLE

Oracle resides in the Visionary quadrant. Oracle Analytics Cloud (OAC) is a platform that was designed from the ground up to operate in the cloud and provides better analytical capabilities throughout the whole data and analytics workflow. Oracle offers on-premises deployments of its Oracle Analytics Server (OAS) and sells prebuilt data and analytics solutions for an increasing number of Oracle applications via its Fusion Analytics Warehouse (FAW).

Customers were assisted in optimizing the performance of their Oracle environment and collaborating on innovations with other customers through the addition of customer initiatives in 2021. These customer initiatives included Cloud Coach and Code Innovate. In an effort to raise consumers' familiarity with the Oracle brand, the company expanded its sports sponsorships to include high-profile leagues and teams this year, such as the Premier League, Golden State Warriors of the NBA, and Red Bull Racing of Formula 1. OAC is a cloud-first platform that offers enhanced analytics capabilities for the entire data and analytics workflow. Oracle provides OAS for on-premises deployments and delivers prebuilt data and analytics solutions for an expanding number of Oracle applications via FAW.

In 2021, customer initiatives such as Cloud Coach and Code Innovate were added to assist customers in optimizing the performance of their Oracle environment and co-innovating with other customers. Oracle added high-profile sports partnerships this year, including the Premier League, Red Bull Racing in Formula 1, and the Golden State Warriors in the NBA, in an effort to increase brand awareness.

7.7.10 PYRAMIDAL STATISTICS

In the Magic Quadrant, Pyramid Analytics is a Niche Player.

Pyramid delivers an out-of-the-box complete suite for modern DATA ANALYTICS across the data life cycle. This consists of ML-based data preparation, the manipulation of data, the discovery and sharing of data, the creation of dashboards and the production of reports, automated insights, and AutoML model construction with security and governance. Pyramid has a major concentration in the financial services, insurance, retail, and industrial industries, but in 2021, it expanded its customer reach.

Pyramid also increased the speed of its direct query engine, augmented analytics, marketplace of DSML algorithms, and modeling Python and R scripts in 2021.

7.7.11 Qlik

In the Magic Quadrant, Qlik is a Leader. It offers a powerful product concept that is based on augmented analytics and closed-loop decision-making, and it features. Qlik's flagship product, Qlik Sense, leverages its Cognitive and Associative Engines to provide analysts and consumers with self-service analytics and context-aware insights and recommendations.

In 2021, Qlik purchased NodeGraph and Big Squid, expanding its portfolio of acquisitions with more capabilities.

This year, Qlik made the announcement of Qlik Forts, which makes it possible for customers to push down Qlik Sense SaaS capabilities regardless of where their data is stored. In addition to this, it launched Qlik Application Automation, a solution that does not require users to write code and that makes it possible for users to automate data pipelines and actions. Qlik made the decision to announce its plan to go public in January 2022.

7.7.12 Salesforce (Tableau)

In this particular Magic Quadrant, Tableau by Salesforce is positioned as a Leader. It offers business customers a graphical user interface that makes it possible for them to access, prepare, analyze, and display the results of data analysis. Advanced analytics capabilities are available to analysts and citizen data scientists with Tableau CRM, which was formerly known as Einstein Analytics.

Tableau added additional Slack integrations in 2021 and improved its NLQ experience, Ask Data. Ask Data is now a standard feature across all licensing tiers, alongside Explain Data. Ask Data may be added to a dashboard as an integrated feature, and new Lenses make it possible for analysts to curate already existing data sets. Tableau's enterprise capabilities have been improved with the introduction of centralized row-level security as well as virtual data connections, which make it possible for users to extract and manage data tables.

7.7.13 SAP

In the Magic Quadrant, SAP is a Visionary. SAP Analytics Cloud is a multitenant cloud-native platform with extensive data visualization, reporting, and augmented analytics capabilities. It is intimately connected to the enterprise planning capabilities and application ecosystem of SAP.

SAP prioritized usability, performance, and a streamlined UX across SAP Analytics Cloud and Data Warehouse Cloud in 2021.

Its enhanced Story Viewer and Story Designer aid non-technical users in creating, navigating, and interacting with Stories. Analytics Designer, a low-code development environment of SAP Analytics Cloud, employs new SDKs and APIs to enable the construction of analytical applications that leverage all SAP Analytics Cloud features.

7.7.14   SAS

Within the Magic Quadrant, SAS is a Visionary. The SAS Visual Analytics product is a part of the company's end-to-end portfolio, which also includes solutions for visual and augmented data preparation, DSML, AI and data analytics.

In 2021, SAS introduced SAS Viya 4, a cloud-native and containerized platform that was built from the ground up for the cloud. A technological and go-to-market partnership between SAS and Microsoft has been established. As part of this partnership, Microsoft Azure will become a cloud provider for SAS Cloud, and there are plans to integrate SAS with Microsoft's cloud offering in the near future. SAS Visual Analytics added automated explanation and outlier detection, as well as conversational BI and the capacity to create custom chatbots.

7.7.15   SISENSE

Sisense is into the Visionary quadrant. Sisense provides an end-to-end augmented analytics platform that, in addition to easing the construction of analytics apps and simplifying the management of complicated data projects, also enables self-service. More than 50 percent of the clients that use the DATA ANALYTICS platform offered by Sisense make use of the product in OEM form.

Sisense changed the name of their product in 2021 to Sisense Fusion to reflect the fact that the solution focuses on incorporating analytics into corporate operations. The new Sisense Notebooks close the knowledge gap between data specialists and users of visual self-service applications. Users have the option of using one of the prebuilt Infusion Apps or having developers create their own apps or workflows using the Sisense Extend Framework. This allows users to add analytical skills into productivity applications.

7.7.16   TELLIUS

The Visionary in this Magic Quadrant is Tellius. Tellius is an enhanced, specialized analytics and BI platform that provides features for consumers, analysts, and citizen data scientists. It can be installed as a SaaS solution, on-premises, or in the customer's preferred cloud platform.

Tellius provides insights through its "What?", "Why?", and "How?"—style user interface. Using an NLQ search interface, "What?" insights are extracted, and users can construct their own dashboards using typical drag-and-drop techniques. The "Why?" interface reveals automatically hidden significant drivers and trends, together with NLG summaries. The "How?" interface discovers underlying segments and signals that may provide actionable opportunities for decision makers.

7.7.17 THOUGHTSPOT

ThoughtSpot occupies the Visionary position in this Magic Quadrant. It is distinguished by its search-driven UX, its capacity to respond to analytically complicated questions with individualized and pertinent responses, and its scalability.

ThoughtSpot improved its Everywhere embedded analytics in 2021, created a new developer sandbox and additional custom action possibilities, and made available pre-built SpotApps and SpotIQ Monitor for KPIs. Its SpotApp design allows companies to construct analytical applications for vertical and domain use cases. It is investing in a notebook-style SQL workspace, a native voice assistant, and the integration of chatbots with digital office technologies.

7.7.18 TIBCO

In this Magic Quadrant, TIBCO Software is positioned as a Visionary. It has a substantial presence in the health sciences, transport and logistics, high-tech manufacturing, and energy industries, but relative to other vendors, it has less momentum outside of its installed base. With its concept for "hyperconverged analytics," TIBCO Spotfire integrates data science, visual data discovery, and streaming analytics capabilities. It provides extensive analytics dashboard features, interactive visualization, data preparation, and analytic workflows.

In 2021, TIBCO Software will prioritize capabilities that democratize data science features, such as operationalizing characteristics for ML models. It also developed a virtual data catalog that enables users to search and view published data across the enterprise with ease.

7.7.19 YELLOWFIN

Yellowfin resides in the Visionary quadrant. Yellowfin began as a provider of a web-based BI platform for reporting and data visualization. However, the company has since developed to include services for data preparation and augmented analytics, and its pioneering work in the field of data storytelling has gained widespread recognition.

Yellowfin extended its investment in augmented analytics in 2021, including the addition of Guided NLQ for business users to ask questions of data, new Signals for automated business monitoring, and data narrative feeds that directly interact with action-based dashboards. Yellowfin also improved its analytics application creation experience with the Yellowfin JavaScript API and REST API SDKs, which allow citizen developers to select Yellowfin features and assemble them into consumer analytical applications.

7.7.20 ZOHO

In the Magic Quadrant, Zoho is a Niche Player. Zoho Analytics provides data preparation, self-service data visualization, embedded analytics capabilities, and a market for prebuilt analytical applications. Zoho is primarily installed as a pure SaaS solution but may also be deployed through the cloud service provider of the customer's choosing and on-premises.

In addition to the tens of thousands of existing Zoho customers who can already access Zoho Analytics features via their Zoho One suite or CRM Plus, Zoho has a growing base of midmarket and business customers. Zoho Analytics now includes the AI/ML-enabled Zoho DataPrep, and the Ask Zia conversational interface has been improved.

7.8 COMPARISON WITH OTHER CONCEPTS

7.8.1 DATA ANALYTICS AND BUSINESS INTELLIGENCE

Data analytics and BI are two terms that are often used interchangeably, but they are quite different, and each can play a role in decision-making. Data analytics is the process of analyzing raw data and extracting meaningful insights from it. It is used to answer questions, identify patterns, and uncover trends. BI, on the other hand, is the process of collecting, organizing, and analyzing data to inform decisions. It includes data warehousing, data mining, data modeling, and analytics.

When it comes to the comparison between data analytics and BI, the main difference is in the purpose. Data analytics is used to analyze data and understand what it tells us, while BI is used to make decisions. Data analytics is used to uncover patterns and trends, while BI is used to create actionable intelligence. Data analytics is used to identify correlations and causations, while BI is used to identify the best course of action (Tsai et al., 2015; GlobeNewswire, 2022).

Data analytics is focused on the past, while BI is focused on the future. Data analytics examines the data to understand what happened in the past. BI, on the other hand, is used to forecast future trends and make decisions about the future. Data analytics helps us understand the data and uncover insights, while BI helps us make decisions about the future.

7.8.2 DATA ANALYTICS AND MACHINE LEARNING

Data analytics and ML are two distinct technologies, but they often get compared because they are related. Data analytics is the process of collecting, organizing, and analyzing data with the goal of deriving insights and making informed decisions. ML, on the other hand, is a subset of AI that involves teaching computers to learn without being explicitly programmed.

Data analytics and ML have different goals and are used to solve different types of problems. Data analytics is used to identify patterns, relationships, and trends in large data sets. ML is used to automate processes and make predictions based on previously seen data. Data analytics focuses on understanding existing data, while ML focuses on predicting future outcomes.

Data analytics uses descriptive and predictive analytics techniques to analyze data and generate insights. Descriptive analytics techniques are used to summarize data and identify patterns. Predictive analytics techniques are used to make predictions or forecasts based on past data. ML uses algorithms to learn from data and make predictions. It involves training a computer to learn from input data and use that knowledge to make predictions or decisions.

Data analytics and ML are complementary to each other, and both are essential for organizations to make informed decisions. Data analytics provides insights into existing data, which can then be used to make decisions. ML can be used to automate processes and make predictions about future outcomes. Both technologies can be used in combination to make better decisions and improve processes. By combining data analytics and ML, organizations can gain a better understanding of their data and use it to make more informed decisions.

It also suffices to state that most data analytics platforms or tools use ML algorithms to manipulate data.

7.8.3 DATA ANALYTICS AND DATA SCIENCE

Both data analytics and data science are sub-disciplines of computer science that are concerned with the classification, investigation, and interpretation of data sets. There are key distinctions that exist between the fields of data science and data analytics, despite the fact that both fields share many commonalities.

The practice of gathering and analyzing sets of data in order to identify patterns and trends is referred to as data analytics. The primary goals of data analytics are the compilation and examination of previously gathered information, which is subsequently put to use in the formation of well-informed judgments. On the other hand, the primary focus of data scientists is on the development of models and algorithms for the purpose of addressing novel challenges. In order to derive insightful information from the data and create accurate predictive models, they make use of a vast array of different technologies and methods.

Data analytics is primarily concerned with the utilization of previously collected information and various methods in order to obtain new insights and improve decision-making. Data scientists are primarily concerned with the production of new methods, algorithms, and prediction models. Additionally, their focus is on the development of new methodologies. The use of descriptive statistics is a common component of data analytics, whereas the application of predictive analytics is a key component of data science.

The purpose of data analytics is to better understand the link between various variables by locating patterns and trends in already-existing data sets and to identify those data sets. On the other hand, the primary focus of data science is the creation of novel algorithms and models with the purpose of forecasting future occurrences or behaviors. The use of data analytics to guide decisions is common; however, the use of data science to make predictions and develop new insights is more uncommon.

7.8.4 DATA ANALYTICS AND BIG DATA ANALYTICS

Data analytics and big data analytics are two terms that are often used interchangeably, but there are differences between them. To understand the comparison between the two, it is important to understand the meaning of each term. The process of analyzing sets of data in order to develop useful conclusions is referred to as "data analytics." It is used to identify patterns and trends in data and to help companies make better decisions. Big data analytics, on the other hand, is the process of analyzing large amounts of data that cannot be processed using traditional data analytics techniques. It uses advanced analytical techniques, such as ML, AI, and predictive analytics, to identify patterns and trends in large data sets (Chen et al., 2012; Fan et al., 2015; Alsunaidi et al., 2021; Li et al., 2021).

The scale of the data sets that can be processed by data analytics and big data analytics is the primary distinction between the two types of analytics. Data analytics can be used to analyze small-to-medium data sets, while big data analytics can analyze large data sets. Another difference is the depth of analysis that can be performed. Data analytics uses basic methods such as descriptive data analysis, while big data analytics uses advanced methods such as predictive analytics and ML.

In terms of cost, data analytics is usually cheaper to implement than big data analytics. Data analytics typically requires less hardware and software than big data analytics, which means that it is more cost-effective for businesses. Furthermore, data analytics is often used to analyze structured data, while big data analytics is used to analyze unstructured data. Structured data is more organized and easier to analyze than unstructured data.

Big data analytics may be more efficient than traditional data analytics in terms of speed. Big data analytics makes use of sophisticated methods to process massive amounts of data in a short amount of time. These strategies are frequently more effective than more conventional approaches, which ultimately leads to quicker outcomes.

7.9   BEST PRACTICES FOR DATA ANALYTICS

It's important to remember that data analytics relies on acquiring, managing, and utilizing data effectively. With this in mind, it's important to keep in mind the following best practices for data analytics.

i. Make use of data governance best practices. Ensure that all data is collected, managed, and analyzed in accordance with regulations and company policies.

ii. Partner with data scientists to manage the data lifecycle. By partnering with data scientists, companies can manage the entire data lifecycle, including the acquisition, storage, and management of data.

iii. Build data-centric solutions. By building solutions that are rooted in data, businesses can improve customer engagement, increase revenue, and increase efficiency.

iv. Build a data-driven culture. By building a culture that places a high value on data, businesses can utilize data analytics more effectively.

v. Invest in data infrastructure. By investing in data infrastructure, companies can ensure that their data is managed effectively.

vi. Implement monitoring and control solutions. By implementing solutions for monitoring and control, companies can ensure compliance with regulations and policies (Ristevski & Chen, 2018; Sun & Huo, 2021).

7.10   CHALLENGES OF DATA ANALYTICS

There are a number of challenges that businesses should be mindful of when it comes to data analytics. These include the challenge of managing data, the challenge of building scalable solutions, and the challenge of building a culture that values data analytics.

    i. Managing data—The problem with data is that it's extremely valuable. It's important that businesses carefully manage their data. Otherwise, they risk losing value through inaccurate readings and missed insights.
    ii. Scaling solutions—Even the strongest data analytics solutions can be rendered useless if they have an insufficient amount of data.
    iii. Building a culture that values data—Even though data analytics is a powerful tool, it's important to remember that data is still just data. With this in mind, it's important for businesses to cultivate a culture that values all data sources equally.

7.11   EXAMPLES OF SUCCESSFUL DATA ANALYTICS INITIATIVES

There are several successful data analytics initiatives that businesses can take advantage of. Some of the most popular examples include using data to improve product designs, using data to predict customer churn, using data to predict sales trends, using data to forecast costs, using data to predict customer behavior, using data to forecast revenue, using data to plan for future revenue, and using data to manage the data lifecycle.

7.12   DATA ANALYTICS IN THE FUTURE

As data becomes more and more prevalent, analytics will become even more important in business. This is especially true in the area of data science. In the future, IT will play a much larger role in data analytics initiatives, which will require a much deeper understanding of data management, scalability, and programming. Data storage capacity will also become a key challenge, and it will become increasingly important to make use of virtualization and cloud technologies to overcome this challenge. There are many possibilities for data analytics in the future, including using data to build autonomous systems that can make decisions on their own. There are also many possibilities in the areas of using big data and using natural language processing to analyze text. Finally, there are many possibilities in the area of using sensors to collect data and using deep learning to analyze that data.

REFERENCES

Akhter, R., & Sofi, S. A. (2022). Precision agriculture using IoT data analytics and machine learning, *Journal of King Saud University – Computer and Information Sciences*, *34*(8). https://doi.org/10.1016/j.jksuci.2021.05.013

Alsunaidi, S. J., Almuhaideb, A. M., Ibrahim, N. M., Shaikh, F. S., Alqudaihi, K. S., Alhaidari, F. A., Khan, I. U., Aslam, N., & Alshahrani, M. S. (2021). Applications of big data analytics to control covid-19 pandemic, *Sensors*, *21*(7). https://doi.org/10.3390/s21072282

Bentley, D. (2017). Business Intelligence and Analytics. New York, USA: Library Press.

Chen, H., Chiang, R. H. L., & Storey, V. C. (2012). Business intelligence and analytics: From big data to big impact, *MIS Quarterly: Management Information Systems, 36*(4). https://doi.org/10.2307/41703503

Duan, L., & da Xu, L. (2021). Data analytics in industry 4.0: A survey, *Information Systems Frontiers*. https://doi.org/10.1007/s10796-021-10190-0

el Morr, C., & Ali-Hassan, H. (2019). *Healthcare, Data Analytics, and Business Intelligence.* https://doi.org/10.1007/978-3-030-04506-7_1

Fan, S., Lau, R. Y. K., & Zhao, J. L. (2015). Demystifying big data analytics for business intelligence through the lens of marketing mix, *Big Data Research, 2*(1). https://doi.org/10.1016/j.bdr.2015.02.006

GlobeNewswire. (2022, December 6). *Business Intelligence Market Size to Worth Around USD 54.9 Bn by 2032.*

Kronz, A., Schlegel, K., Sun, J., Pidsley, D., & Ganeshan, A. (2022). *Gartner Magic Quadrant for Analytics and Business Intelligence Platforms.* Gatner. Retrieved February 10, 2023, from https://www.gartner.com/doc/reprints?id=1-292LEME3&ct=220209&st=sb

Kumar, S., Sharma, D., Rao, S., Lim, W. M., & Mangla, S. K. (2022). Past, present, and future of sustainable finance: Insights from big data analytics through machine learning of scholarly research, *Annals of Operations Research*. https://doi.org/10.1007/s10479-021-04410-8

Li, W., Chai, Y., Khan, F., Jan, S. R. U., Verma, S., Menon, V. G., Kavita, & Li, X. (2021). A comprehensive survey on machine learning-based big data analytics for IoT-enabled smart healthcare system, *Mobile Networks and Applications, 26*(1). https://doi.org/10.1007/s11036-020-01700-6

Lim, E. P., Chen, H., & Chen, G. (2013). Business intelligence and analytics: Research directions, *ACM Transactions on Management Information Systems, 3*(4). https://doi.org/10.1145/2407740.2407741

Ram Mohan Rao, P., Murali Krishna, S., & Siva Kumar, A. P. (2018). Privacy preservation techniques in big data analytics: A survey, *Journal of Big Data, 5*(1). https://doi.org/10.1186/s40537-018-0141-8

Richards, G. S. (2016). Business intelligence and analytics research, *International Journal of Business Intelligence Research, 7*(1). https://doi.org/10.4018/ijbir.2016010101

Ristevski, B., & Chen, M. (2018). Big data analytics in medicine and healthcare, *Journal of Integrative Bioinformatics, 15*(3). https://doi.org/10.1515/jib-2017-0030

Sun, Z., & Huo, Y. (2021). The spectrum of big data analytics, *Journal of Computer Information Systems, 61*(2). https://doi.org/10.1080/08874417.2019.1571456

Sun, Z., Strang, K., & Firmin, S. (2017). Business analytics-based enterprise information systems, *Journal of Computer Information Systems, 57*(2). https://doi.org/10.1080/08874417.2016.1183977

Tsai, C. W., Lai, C. F., Chao, H. C., & Vasilakos, A. V. (2015). Big data analytics: A survey, *Journal of Big Data, 2*(1). https://doi.org/10.1186/s40537-015-0030-3

Wu, D. D., & Härdle, W. K. (2020). Service data analytics and business intelligence 2017, *Computational Statistics, 35*(2). https://doi.org/10.1007/s00180-020-00968-2

8 Federated Learning for Business Intelligence

Predictive Maintenance in Industry 4.0

Syed Arshad Ali[1], Manzoor Ansari[2],
Mansaf Alam[2], and Sandip Rakshit[3]
[1]Department of Computer Science & Applications,
 School of Engineering & Technology, Sharda
 University, Greater Noida, India
[2]Department of Computer Science, Jamia
 Millia Islamia, New Delhi, India
[3]The Business School, RMIT University Vietnam,
 Ho Chi Minh City, Vietnam

8.1 INTRODUCTION

Manufacturing and industrial operations have been transformed by the fourth industrial revolution, also known as Industry 4.0. One of the key areas where Industry 4.0 has had a major impact is the field of predictive maintenance. Predictive maintenance is a process in Industry 4.0 where the state of a machine is monitored continuously, and the maintenance of the machine is predicted and scheduled based on the data collected [1]. This method allows for the proactive maintenance of machines which can reduce downtime, increase efficiency, and minimize costs. The practice of predictive maintenance leverages advanced technologies, including machine learning (ML), artificial intelligence (AI), big data analytics, and the Internet of Things (IoT), to examine data obtained from machinery and forecast their maintenance requirements, as well as the type of maintenance required. This allows companies to plan maintenance in advance and ensure that machines are running at peak efficiency [2]. With the increasing use of connected devices and the IoT in Industry 4.0, there is a wealth of data available for predictive maintenance. However, the decentralized nature of industrial operations and the sensitive nature of the data make it difficult to share and analyse the data. Federated learning (FL) offers a solution to this problem by allowing data to be analysed locally while still allowing for the sharing of models and insights [3]. A smart framework was developed by the authors for executing real-world applications in the cloud environment [28]. IoT and cloud technologies can be combined to characterize E-Commerce models in a more sophisticated way [31]. IoT and cloud integration can improve the smart industry processing and give better resource utilization [29, 30]. The aim of this manuscript is to investigate the potential of FL in the context of predictive maintenance within the Industry 4.0 framework. In this study, we will analyse the obstacles that are associated with predictive maintenance, the benefits of using FL, and the potential applications of this technique in predictive maintenance. Finally, we will present a summary of the potential of FL for predictive maintenance within the Industry 4.0 paradigm.

There are several motivations for conducting this research on FL for business intelligence (BI):

- **Data privacy:** One of the main motivations for conducting this research is to ensure data privacy. In traditional ML approaches, data is usually centralized, which can be a problem when dealing with sensitive data and multiple devices. FL allows for the training of a predictive maintenance model while keeping data locally on the device, which improves data privacy.
- **Efficiency and reliability:** Predictive maintenance is a critical task in Industry 4.0 to ensure the smooth running of manufacturing processes and to avoid unplanned downtime. FL allows for the training of a high-quality predictive maintenance model on a large and diverse dataset, which can greatly improve the efficiency and reliability of manufacturing processes.
- **Scalability:** The complexity of Industry 4.0, which encompasses numerous devices and systems, poses a challenge for the development of a predictive maintenance model that can be trained on all available data. However, FL offers a solution to this issue by enabling the training of a model across multiple devices and systems. This approach reduces communication costs and enhances scalability, thereby making it feasible to train models on a larger scale.
- **Robustness:** FL algorithms, such as Federated averaging (FedAvg), are robust to non-IID data distributions, which makes it suitable for the industrial environment, where data is distributed among various devices and systems.
- **Advancement in the field:** FL is a relatively new field of ML and there is a lot of room for research and advancement in this area.
- **Conducting research on FL for BI:** Predictive maintenance in Industry 4.0 can help to further develop and improve this technique, which can have a wide range of applications in various fields.

Overall, the motivations for conducting this research are to improve data privacy, efficiency, reliability, scalability, robustness, and advancement in the field of FL.

8.2 BACKGROUND AND RELATED WORKS

Predictive maintenance is an approach to maintenance that takes a proactive stance by utilizing data and analytics to forecast potential equipment failures and optimize maintenance schedules. It is based on the idea that machines and equipment have a predictable failure rate and that by monitoring the condition of the equipment, it is possible to predict when a failure is likely to occur. This allows for scheduled maintenance to be performed at the optimal time, reducing downtime, and increasing efficiency [4].

As part of the fourth industrial revolution, the IoT, big data, and AI will be integrated into industrial operations. As a result of Industry 4.0, predictive maintenance is one of the key areas where the technology is having a major impact. Due to the growing use of connected devices and the IoT, predictive maintenance is becoming increasingly possible. Data sharing and analysis, however, are difficult due to the decentralized nature of industrial operations and the sensitive nature of the data. In ML, FL allows for decentralized training of models. It allows for data to be analysed locally while still allowing for the sharing of models and insights. In this regard, it makes sense to use this approach for predictive maintenance in Industry 4.0, since it allows data to be analysed locally while allowing for the sharing of models and insights.

8.2.1 Evolution of Federated Learning

FL has evolved significantly since its inception in the early 2010s. Figure 8.1 visually depicts the progression and growth of FL. This article outlines several noteworthy milestones that have emerged throughout the development of FL:

Initial research: The inception of FL can be traced back to the early 2010s when researchers at Google introduced the concept. They proposed a novel approach to train ML models utilizing decentralized data, without the need for the raw data to be shared.

Mobile applications: In 2016, Google published a paper on using FL to improve the keyboard on Android devices. This was the first practical application of FL, and it demonstrated the potential of the approach for mobile applications.

Federated optimization: In 2017, Google researchers proposed a new approach called federated optimization, which improved the stability and performance of FL models.

FL for medical research: In 2018, researchers from Stanford and Google proposed using FL to train models for medical research. This demonstrated the potential of FL for sensitive data and highlighted the importance of data privacy and security.

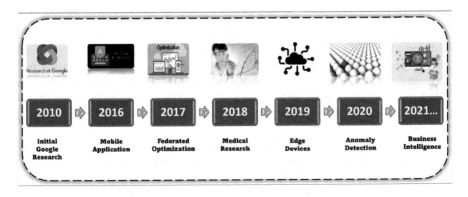

FIGURE 8.1 Evolution of federated learning.

FL for edge devices: In 2019, researchers proposed using FL for edge devices, such as IoT devices. This demonstrated the potential of FL for low-power and low-bandwidth devices.

Anomaly detection: In 2020, a research paper presented an innovative application of FL to detect anomalies in industrial settings, specifically for predictive maintenance in Industry 4.0. This seminal work underscored the immense potential of FL in facilitating industrial-based solutions.

FL for BI: In 2021, Researchers proposed using FL for BI; this highlighted the potential of FL for providing valuable insights and predictions that can be used to optimize the maintenance schedules, reduce downtime, and improve the overall efficiency of the industrial operations.

As the research and development of FL continue to grow, it is expected to see more practical applications and variations of FL in different fields and industries.

8.2.2 RELATED WORKS

In reference to [6], the author conducts an in-depth analysis of the potential of FL to establish a dynamic and open ecosystem for ML within Industry 4.0. The study proposes a multi-level framework that integrates FL, the IoT, and crowdsourcing to generate a robust system of multi-level FL. The framework allows for the creation of intelligent applications, such as predictive maintenance and fault detection in smart manufacturing units. Additionally, the research highlights the various ways in which multi-level FL can contribute to the United Nations Sustainable Goal No. 13, which aims to reduce greenhouse gas emissions.

The paper [7] discusses the application of FL to the prediction of industrial equipment maintenance. Through collaborative efforts, several participants can construct a global predictive model by analysing the technical and contextual characteristics of the intended industrial equipment. The paper proposes an architecture for FL in the context of IoT, considering existing IoT architectures, federated tasks, and computational resources. A cost-efficient method of building the global model is also proposed in the paper using stacking-based aggregation. In contrast to centralized training, the approach reveals its advantages through a real-world use-case scenario.

The study [8] examines how FL can help overcome the obstacles that prevent widespread adoption of ML techniques. This research paper demonstrates the efficacy of FL in conjunction with an Industrial IoT (IIoT) smart manufacturing platform and real-world datasets, employing various ML algorithms to showcase the effectiveness of a decentralized FL-based solution. The findings indicate that FL can achieve comparable performance to that of traditional centralized based learning approaches.

An AI-enhanced architecture for a modular cognitive maintenance system is presented in the paper [9]. By combining structured and unstructured data, the system aims to enhance operational KPIs such as availability and overall equipment effectiveness (OEE). In the context of maintenance, the research question focuses on how to ensure industrial applicability of the system.

In reference to [10], the article outlines the utilization of ML methods to implement predictive maintenance in a toothpaste factory with the objective of augmenting OEE and reducing failure rates. The study compared the performance of two ML algorithms, namely random forest regression and linear regression. The experimental outcomes showed that the random forest regression algorithm achieved an accuracy rate of 88%, while linear regression achieved an accuracy rate of 59%. The results revealed a substantial improvement in OEE by 13.10% and a drastic reduction in unplanned machine failures by 62.38%.

8.3 OVERVIEW OF INDUSTRY 4.0 AND PREDICTIVE MAINTENANCE

In this section, the concept of BI and its importance for organizations, as well as the potential for using FL in this context has been discussed, then the application of BI in the context of Industry 4.0 was discussed, specifically looking at the use of predictive maintenance. BI is a comprehensive process that encompasses the collection, analysis, and transformation of data into actionable insights. It empowers organizations to make informed, data-driven decisions that can significantly enhance performance and provide a competitive edge. BI is instrumental in identifying trends and patterns in data that can be leveraged to make informed decisions that can effectively benefit the organization [11, 25, 26].

The use of FL in BI provides organizations with the ability to securely access and analyse data from multiple sources. FL is a cutting-edge technique that facilitates organizations to train ML models on data that is dispersed across various systems, without compromising the privacy of the data. By using FL, organizations can access and analyse data from multiple sources without needing to share it with one another. This can help organizations to gain insights from data without compromising the privacy of their customers. Predictive maintenance has emerged as an important application of BI in Industry 4.0 [12]. It aims to detect potential failures in machinery or equipment before they occur, thus reducing downtime and improving operational efficiency. By leveraging FL, organizations can create predictive maintenance models that are trained on data from multiple sources, enabling them to detect potential equipment failures proactively and timely.

In conclusion, FL can be used to improve the effectiveness of BI in the context of Industry 4.0, specifically in predictive maintenance. By using FL, organizations can securely access and analyse data from multiple sources without compromising their privacy [27]. This can help organizations to gain insights from data and develop predictive maintenance models that can detect potential failures before they occur, thus improving operational efficiency.

8.4 OVERVIEW OF FEDERATED LEARNING

In this section, we delve into the concept of FL and its application in the realm of BI. We shed light on the advantages of FL as compared to conventional methods of data sharing and storage, while also highlighting the potential challenges that may surface when implementing this approach. Additionally, we analyse the utilization of FL in predictive maintenance scenarios, within the context of Industry 4.0.

8.4.1 DEFINITION OF FEDERATED LEARNING

FL is an advanced distributed ML technique that empowers the collective training of models across several entities, without necessitating the sharing of raw data. Instead of sharing the entire dataset between organizations, FL systems allow each party to train a model on its own data and then share the resulting model parameters with the other parties. By combining individual models, a global model can be created that is more accurate than one created from a single dataset [13].

8.4.2 MATHEMATICAL DEFINITION OF FL

Federated ML (FML) is a distributed ML approach that allows multiple parties to jointly train a model while keeping their data on their own local devices or servers, rather than centralizing the data in a single location. Mathematically, FL can be defined as an optimization problem where the goal is to find the global model parameters, denoted as w*, that minimize the average loss across all parties.

The optimization problem can be defined as follows:

$$w^* = \arg\min(w)(1/n)\sum (i = 1 \text{ to } n)L(w, D(i))$$

where w is the model parameters.

> L (w, D(i)) is the loss function of the model when trained on the local data D(i) of the i-th party.
> n is the number of parties participating in the federation.

In FL, each party holds a local dataset D(i) and computes a local gradient g(i) = ∇L (w, D(i)) using their data. The parties then send their local gradients to a central server, which averages the gradients and updates the global model parameters w. This process is repeated multiple times until the global model parameters converge to the optimal solution w*.

8.4.3 STEPS OF FEDERATED LEARNING APPROACH

This section entails a comprehensive discussion of the fundamental steps of FL, along with a depiction of the operational mechanics of FL in Figure 8.2.

> **Initialize a global model:** To initiate FL, a global model is initialized and communicated to the corresponding participating devices or nodes.
> **Data collection:** Each participating device or node collects data locally and trains the model on its own data.
> **Model updates:** Each device or node updates the global model with its own updates, usually in the form of model weights or gradients.

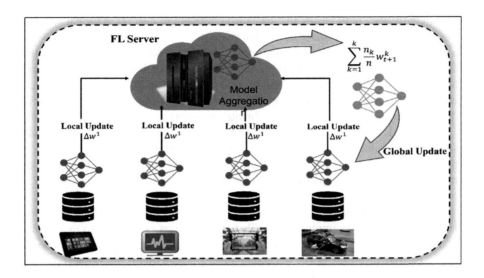

FIGURE 8.2   Steps of federated learning approach.

Averaging: To facilitate the training process in FL, the global model is updated via the averaging of the updates received from all involved devices or nodes.

Repeat: The process is repeated until the model has converged or a stopping criterion is met.

Deployment: The final global model is deployed on the devices or nodes or a central server for the prediction.

8.5   CHALLENGES IN IMPLEMENTING FEDERATED LEARNING FOR PREDICTIVE MAINTENANCE IN BUSINESS INTELLIGENCE

The advent of Industry 4.0, also referred to as the fourth industrial revolution, has triggered a new era of digital transformation, causing a profound impact on the operational dynamics of businesses. In this scenario, BI has emerged as an indispensable tool for enabling informed decision-making. However, the data needed to power BI is often held in different, distributed sources that cannot be easily accessed. This can lead to data silos and privacy issues, preventing companies from obtaining an accurate and holistic view of their operations.

Addressing the challenge of enabling data analysis while maintaining data privacy, FL represents a promising solution, enabling companies to access and combine data from multiple sources without it having to be shared or moved from its original location [5]. This allows for more accurate and up-to-date insights into their operations. However, implementing FL for BI is not without its challenges.

A key challenge in implementing FL is to manage the distributed data sources in a manner that ensures their security and compliance with privacy regulations. This requires companies to have an effective data governance strategy in place that allows them to control who can access and use the data, as well as how it is used.

Additionally, they must ensure that the data is stored in an encrypted format and that it is not shared with any unauthorized parties.

A second challenge is related to the accuracy of the models produced by FL. As the data sources are distributed, it can be difficult to ensure that the models are consistent and accurate across all sources. This can lead to discrepancies in the insights generated, as well as inaccurate predictions. To overcome this, companies must use careful data sampling and model validation techniques to ensure the accuracy of their results.

Finally, FL requires companies to invest in infrastructure, such as hardware and software, to enable the computation of the models. This can be costly, especially if the data sources are spread across multiple locations. To reduce costs, companies may opt to use cloud computing services or specialized hardware to reduce the need for expensive infrastructure investments.

FL has the potential to revolutionize the way businesses access and utilize data. However, successfully implementing FL for BI requires companies to tackle several challenges. These include ensuring data security and privacy, ensuring model accuracy, and investing in the necessary infrastructure. With the right approach, companies can use FL to gain powerful insights into their operations and make more informed business decisions.

8.6 POTENTIAL SOLUTIONS FOR FEDERATED LEARNING FOR PREDICTIVE MAINTENANCE IN BUSINESS INTELLIGENCE

FL is a powerful tool for predictive maintenance in Industry 4.0 because it allows for the training of a high-quality predictive maintenance model while maintaining data privacy and reducing communication costs. Predictive maintenance is a technique that employs ML models and data to anticipate when a machine is likely to fail and schedule maintenance accordingly. This proactive approach to maintenance improves the efficiency and reliability of manufacturing processes, reducing the likelihood of reactive maintenance. However, conventional ML methods for predictive maintenance demand centralized data, which can pose a challenge when handling large amounts of data and numerous devices. FL addresses this issue by enabling several devices or systems to collaboratively train a model while keeping their data locally on the device. Each device or system in a manufacturing facility would have its own data and would use FL to train a predictive maintenance model [23]. By leveraging the advantages of FL, the predictive maintenance model can predict machine failure and schedule maintenance in a proactive manner. With FL, the model is trained collaboratively on a diverse dataset while preserving the privacy of the data and reducing communication overhead. Moreover, FL algorithms, such as FedAvg, can be parallelized and distributed across multiple devices, which accelerates the convergence of the model. This is crucial for predictive maintenance, as frequent updates to the model are necessary to maintain its accuracy [14].

In summary, FL is helpful for predictive maintenance as it allows for the training of a high-quality predictive maintenance model while maintaining data privacy and reducing communication costs. Additionally, FL algorithms can be easily parallelized and distributed across multiple devices, which leads to faster convergence and robustness to non-IID data distributions.

8.6.1   LEVEL OF PRIVACY PROVIDED BY FEDERATED MACHINE LEARNING IN PREDICTIVE MAINTENANCE

Different levels of privacy can be achieved by using different techniques for FML. Some of these techniques include the following:

Secure multi-party computation (SMPC): Secure multi-party computation (SMPC) enables FML in which data is not shared but computations are done on encrypted data [15]. SMPC enables participants to perform computations on their own encrypted data without revealing their data to other participants. In the context of FL, SMPC facilitates collaborative training of a shared model among multiple participants while ensuring that the privacy and security of each participant's data are protected. In addition to distributed training and inference, SMPC allows participants to collaborate on training and running ML models without ever disclosing their identity. By leveraging SMPC, FML can greatly reduce the risk of data breach and improve the security and privacy of data.

Differential privacy: This is a mathematical framework that allows for the sharing of aggregate information about a dataset without revealing any information about individual data points. FML is a powerful tool used to protect data privacy while still allowing data to be used for analysis and learning. Differential privacy is an important technique used in FML to protect data privacy [16]. Differential privacy adds a small amount of noise to the data before it is shared with the server, making it difficult for the server to identify any user's data. This noise blurs the data enough to make it difficult to identify any single user from the dataset. Additionally, differential privacy allows the server to understand the overall trends and patterns in the data, while protecting the individual user's data from being exposed.

Homomorphic encryption: Homomorphic encryption is a cryptographic technique that enables mathematical computations to be performed on encrypted data without requiring it to be decrypted first. This approach allows data to remain secure and private throughout the computation process, as sensitive information is never revealed in plain text form. It is useful in FML, as it allows data to be processed without any of the participating parties having access to the raw data. Homomorphic encryption ensures that data privacy is maintained while allowing the ML model to be trained on encrypted data [17]. It also enables distributed processing, allowing multiple parties to contribute to training the model without any of them having access to the full dataset.

Private Aggregation of Teacher Ensembles with Generative Adversarial Networks (PATE-GANs): A privacy-preserving technique that uses GANs to train models on decentralized data. PATE-GANs ensure that the data remains private by adding noise to the gradients during training. PATE-GANs is a technique used in FML to protect user privacy [24]. With PATE-GANs, a GAN is trained on a dataset of teacher models to create a synthetic dataset.

The GAN is trained to generate synthetic data that is indistinguishable from the original data and can then be used to train a student model [18]. This approach allows the student model to be trained on a large dataset without the need to access individual user data. This helps protect user privacy while still allowing the student model to benefit from the data from all users.

Federated averaging: This is an algorithm used in FML to enable distributed training of a single model across multiple devices. It works by having each device (or "node") calculate its own local model parameters and then share its parameters with the other nodes [19]. The nodes then average their parameters together and update the global model, which can be used to make predictions. FedAvg is an efficient and secure method of training models, as it allows multiple devices to share information without needing to share data.

8.6.2 PROPOSED WORKING MODEL FOR FEDERATED LEARNING– BASED PREDICTIVE MAINTENANCE IN INDUSTRY 4.0

To assess the applicability of FL in the domain of predictive maintenance within Industry 4.0, a case study will be undertaken. The study will entail collecting data from several industrial sites and leveraging FL techniques to develop a predictive maintenance model. The model will be trained on data obtained from diverse industrial sites and evaluated based on its efficacy in predicting equipment failures. The different stages involved in the FML model for predictive maintenance are illustrated in Figure 8.3.

The proposed working model will involve the following phases:

- **Data collection:** Data is collected from multiple industrial sites using IoT devices and sensors. The data includes sensor readings, equipment usage patterns, and maintenance records.

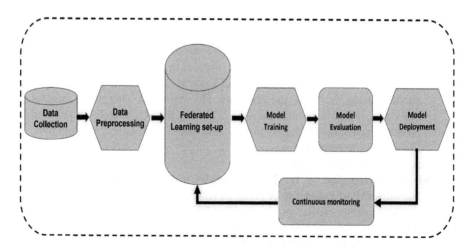

FIGURE 8.3 Phases of working model for federated learning based predicted maintenance.

- **Data pre-processing:** The pre-processing phase of the collected data involves removing any sensitive or irrelevant information, such as personal or identifying data, as well as any data that is not useful for the predictive maintenance model.
- **FL setup:** An FL framework is set up, with one central server and multiple industrial sites as clients. The central server acts as the coordinator, and the clients train their own predictive maintenance models using their local data.
- **Model training:** The predictive maintenance models are trained using FL. The models are trained on the local data of each industrial site, and the models are updated and shared with the central server after each training iteration.
- **Model evaluation:** The predictive maintenance models are evaluated on their ability to predict equipment failures. The evaluation is performed on a separate dataset and is based on metrics, such as accuracy, precision, and recall.
- **Model deployment:** After the models have been trained and evaluated, they are deployed in the industrial sites. The deployed models are used to predict equipment failures and schedule maintenance in real-time.
- **Continuous monitoring:** The deployed models are continuously monitored and updated as new data is collected. This allows the models to adapt and improve over time.
- **BI:** The deployed models provide valuable insights and predictions that can be used to optimize the maintenance schedules, reduce downtime, and improve the overall efficiency of the industrial operations.

8.7 CASE STUDIES AND EXAMPLES OF FEDERATED LEARNING FOR BUSINESS INTELLIGENCE

In this section, we will discuss some case studies and examples of FL for BI.

8.7.1 CASE STUDY 1: AMAZON'S USE OF FEDERATED LEARNING FOR RECOMMENDATION ENGINES

Amazon's success has been partly attributed to its advanced recommendation engine, which is one of the largest online retailers globally. The recommendation engine uses FL to develop personalized recommendations for users based on their past purchases and browsing history. Amazon leverages FL to gather data from various sources, including different mobile devices, and consolidate it in a secure cloud-based environment. Subsequently, this data is used to train an ML model that produces customized product recommendations for each user [20].

The FL process for Amazon's recommendation engine starts with the collection of data from each user's device, which is then transmitted to a secure cloud-based environment. This data is utilized to train an ML model, which is subsequently distributed back to each device. The model is executed on each device, and the outcomes are shared with the cloud. This iterative procedure is repeated multiple times, with the model consistently updated with the newly acquired data, which enhances the accuracy of the recommendations generated.

The result is a highly personalized recommendation engine. Instead of providing generic product recommendations, the model can tailor its recommendations to each user's individual interests and preferences. This allows Amazon to provide a more customized shopping experience for its customers.

8.7.2 Case Study 2: Amazon's Use of Federated Learning for Fraud Detection

Amazon also uses FL to detect fraudulent activity on its platform. As with its recommendation engines, Amazon collects data from multiple sources, such as customers' payment information, and aggregates it in the cloud. This data is then used to train an ML model that can detect fraudulent behaviour [21].

The model is then deployed on each customer's device. Whenever a customer attempts to make a purchase, the model is used to analyse the data and determine whether the purchase is legitimate or not. This allows Amazon to quickly identify and prevent fraudulent transactions from occurring. The use of FL for fraud detection has enabled Amazon to take a proactive approach to keep its customers safe. By detecting fraud before it occurs, Amazon can protect its customers and its own reputation.

8.7.3 Case Study 3: Microsoft's Azure Machine Learning Service

Microsoft's Azure ML service allows customers to use a cloud-based platform to develop and deploy predictive maintenance models. Leveraging Azure ML, customers can create models to predict certain equipment failures, enabling proactive maintenance and reducing costly downtime. Azure ML uses FL as a means of facilitating predictive maintenance, which is a distributed ML approach that enables models to be trained across multiple devices without the need to transfer large datasets across networks [22]. By using FL, customers can securely train models on data that is located on individual devices without having to aggregate the data in a central repository or expose the data to the cloud. This allows customers to protect the privacy of their data while still utilizing the benefits of a cloud-based ML platform. In addition, customers can take advantage of Azure ML's automated model-building features to quickly create models that are tailored to their predictive maintenance needs. These models can then be deployed on the customers' devices, allowing them to monitor and analyse the data in real-time and identify potential maintenance issues before they become costly or cause equipment failure.

Overall, Microsoft's Azure ML service provides customers with an easy and secure way to incorporate predictive maintenance into their BI solutions. By utilizing FL and automated model building, customers can quickly create models that are tailored to their specific needs, enabling them to proactively address potential maintenance issues and reduce costly downtime.

Amazon: Amazon is one of the most advanced companies when it comes to FL for BI. Amazon uses FL to create personalized recommendations for customers based on their past purchases and browsing history. Amazon also uses FL to monitor customer sentiment and provide customer support in real-time.

Google: Google is another company that heavily relies on FL for BI. Google uses FL to develop its search algorithms, which enable it to provide relevant and accurate search results. Google also uses FL to improve its voice recognition software, which allows it to accurately respond to voice commands.

Facebook: Facebook also uses FL for BI. Facebook uses FL to develop its facial recognition software, which can accurately detect and tag individuals in photos. Facebook also uses FL to improve its news feeds by providing personalized content to users.

Microsoft: Microsoft is another company that utilizes FL for BI. Microsoft uses FL to develop its predictive analysis algorithms, which can accurately predict user behaviours and preferences. Microsoft also uses FL to improve its speech recognition software, which allows it to accurately respond to voice commands.

Uber: Uber is another company that relies heavily on FL for BI. Uber uses FL to develop its mapping algorithms, which can accurately predict the best routes for drivers. Uber also uses FL to develop its pricing algorithms, which enable it to set dynamic prices based on current demand.

8.8 ADVANTAGES AND DISADVANTAGES OF FEDERATED LEARNING FOR PREDICTIVE MAINTENANCE IN BUSINESS INTELLIGENCE

FL has the potential to revolutionize predictive maintenance in BI. In this new form of ML, multiple parties can work together to build models together while keeping the data secure and distributed. This approach has several advantages and disadvantages, which this article will discuss in detail.

Advantages:

1. **Increased privacy and security:** FL allows organizations to share data and models without having to send or store any of their sensitive information. This improves data privacy and security as data stays with the user, which reduces the risk of data leakage and malicious attacks.

2. **Reduced infrastructure costs:** By leveraging the existing infrastructure of multiple users, FL can reduce the need for organizations to invest in expensive infrastructure for data storage and computing.

3. **Increased model accuracy:** By leveraging data from multiple users, FL can increase the accuracy of predictive models. This is because it allows the model to be trained on a larger, more diverse set of data, which can lead to better predictive results.

4. **Faster model deployment:** FL can lead to faster model deployment, as users can quickly share their models with other users without the need to send any data. This reduces the time it takes to deploy models, which can be especially useful for businesses that need to make real-time decisions.

5. **Improved model personalization:** FL allows models to be personalized to individual users. This can be useful for businesses that need to make decisions based on individual user behaviours or preferences.

Disadvantages:

1. **Security and privacy issues:** FL can be vulnerable to data breaches as the data is stored and processed at the edge, which could be hacked. The data is also stored in multiple locations, so it is difficult to ensure its privacy and security. Additionally, different organizations may have different security standards and protocols, which may not be compatible with each other.

2. **Data quality and completeness issues:** While the data collected in FL is collected from multiple sources and locations, there is no guarantee that the data is accurate and of a high quality. This could lead to inaccurate insights and predictions.

3. **Time- and resource-intensive:** As FL involves multiple parties, it can be time- and resource-intensive to coordinate between all the players. Additionally, the data needs to be synchronized and properly structured before it can be used for predictive analytics.

4. **Collaboration issues:** Managing the collaboration between multiple organizations can be complex. There may be different levels of trust between the organizations, which can lead to disagreements and conflicts.

5. **Model performance issues:** As FL involves data from multiple sources, the performance of the model can vary depending on the quality and quantity of data from each source. This can make it difficult to accurately predict the outcomes.

8.9   CONCLUSION AND FUTURE DIRECTIONS

FL for BI has the potential to transform the predictive maintenance process in Industry 4.0. It offers a secure and privacy-preserving approach to training predictive models using data distributed across multiple sites, without transferring data to a central location. It can create robust and accurate predictive models for predictive maintenance while ensuring security and privacy. However, several challenges must be addressed to implement FL in predictive maintenance, such as establishing a robust communication infrastructure, ensuring data privacy and security, and developing scalable and robust models. Further research is required to investigate the potential of FL in predictive maintenance and to create secure and efficient solutions for real-world deployment. This article provides an overview of Industry 4.0 and predictive maintenance in Industry 4.0, as well as an introduction to FL. It discusses the challenges and potential solutions associated with implementing FL for predictive maintenance in BI. Case studies and examples of FL for BI are presented, and the advantages and disadvantages of FL for predictive maintenance in BI are examined.

In the future, further research is required to investigate the potential of FL in predictive maintenance and develop secure and efficient solutions that can be deployed in practical settings. To enhance the scalability and robustness of the models, novel techniques can be explored. Additionally, more effective communication protocols for distributed learning and advanced data privacy and security techniques can be developed. Furthermore, the potential applications of FL in other areas of BI, such as customer segmentation and recommendation systems, need to be studied. This will facilitate organizations to leverage the benefits of FL to improve their products and services.

REFERENCES

1. Zonta, T., Da Costa, C. A., da Rosa Righi, R., de Lima, M. J., da Trindade, E. S., & Li, G. P. (2020). Predictive maintenance in the industry 4.0: A systematic literature review. Computers & Industrial Engineering, 150, 106889.
2. Carvalho, T. P., Soares, F. A., Vita, R., Francisco, R. D. P., Basto, J. P., & Alcalá, S. G. (2019). A systematic literature review of machine learning methods applied to predictive maintenance. Computers & Industrial Engineering, 137, 106024.
3. Konečný, J., McMahan, B., & Ramage, D.. (2015). Federated optimization: Distributed optimization beyond the datacenter. arXiv preprint arXiv:1511.03575.
4. Hashemian, H. M. (2010). State-of-the-art predictive maintenance techniques. IEEE Transactions on Instrumentation and Measurement, 60(1), 226–236.
5. Li, T., Sahu, A. K., Talwalkar, A., & Smith, V. (2020). Federated learning: Challenges, methods, and future directions. IEEE Signal Processing Magazine, 37(3), 50–60.
6. Ullah, I., Hassan, U. U., & Ali, M. I. (2023). Multi-level federated learning for industry 4.0—A crowdsourcing approach. Procedia Computer Science, 217, 423–435.
7. Safri, H., Kandi, M. M., Miloudi, Y., Bortolaso, C., Trystram, D., & Desprez, F. (2022, May). A federated learning framework for IoT: Application to Industry 4.0. In 2022 22nd IEEE international symposium on cluster, cloud, and internet computing (CCGrid) (pp. 565–574). IEEE.
8. Kanagavelu, R., Li, Z., Samsudin, J., Hussain, S., Yang, F., Yang, Y., … & Cheah, M. (2021). Federated Learning for Advanced Manufacturing based on Industrial IoT Data Analytics. In: Implementing Industry 4.0: The Model Factory as the Key Enabler for the Future of Manufacturing (pp. 143–176). Springer International Publishing.
9. Kohl, L., Ansari, F., & Sihn, W. (2021). A Modular Federated Learning Architecture for Integration of AI-Enhanced Assistance in Industrial Maintenance. In Competence Development and Learning Assistance Systems for the Data-Driven Future (pp. 229–242). GITO. https://doi.org/10.30844/wgab_2021_14
10. Natanael, D., & Sutanto, H. (2022). machine learning application using cost-effective components for predictive maintenance in industry: A tube filling machine case study. Journal of Manufacturing and Materials Processing, 6(5), 108.
11. Jourdan, Z., Rainer, R. K., & Marshall, T. E. (2008). Business intelligence: An analysis of the literature. Information Systems Management, 25(2), 121–131.
12. Nguyen, D. C., Ding, M., Pham, Q. V., Pathirana, P. N., Le, L. B., Seneviratne, A., & Poor, H. V. (2021). Federated learning meets blockchain in edge computing: Opportunities and challenges. IEEE Internet of Things Journal, 8(16), 12806–12825.
13. Wang, G., Dang, C. X., & Zhou, Z. (2019, December). Measure contribution of participants in federated learning. In 2019 IEEE international conference on big data (Big Data) (pp. 2597–2604). IEEE.
14. Zhong, Z., Zhou, Y., Wu, D., Chen, X., Chen, M., Li, C., & Sheng, Q. Z. (2021, May). P-FedAvg: Parallelizing federated learning with theoretical guarantees. In IEEE INFOCOM 2021—IEEE conference on computer communications (pp. 1–10). IEEE.
15. Ziller, A., Trask, A., Lopardo, A., Szymkow, B., Wagner, B., Bluemke, E., … & Kaissis, G. (2021). Pysyft: A library for easy federated learning. Federated Learning Systems: Towards Next-Generation, AI, 111–139.
16. Zheng, H., Hu, H., & Han, Z. (2020). Preserving user privacy for machine learning: Local differential privacy or federated machine learning? IEEE Intelligent Systems, 35(4), 5–14.

17. Popescu, A. B., Taca, I. A., Nita, C. I., Vizitiu, A., Demeter, R., Suciu, C., & Itu, L. M. (2021). Privacy preserving classification of eeg data using machine learning and homomorphic encryption. Applied Sciences, 11(16), 7360.

18. Lacombe, A., Jetley, S., & Sebag, M.. (2021, June). EXtremely PRIvate supervised Learning. In Conférence d'APprentssage-CAP.

19. Sun, T., Li, D., & Wang, B.. (2022). Decentralized federated averaging. IEEE Transactions on Pattern Analysis and Machine Intelligence.

20. Anelli, V. W., Deldjoo, Y., Di Noia, T., Ferrara, A., & Narducci, F.. (2021). Federank: User controlled feedback with federated recommender systems. In Advances in Information Retrieval: 43rd European Conference on IR Research, ECIR 2021, Virtual Event, March 28–April 1, 2021, Proceedings, Part I 43 (pp. 32–47). Springer International Publishing.

21. Zhang, C., Liu, X., Zheng, X., Li, R., & Liu, H. (2020, March). Fenghuolun: A federated learning based edge computing platform for cyber-physical systems. In 2020 IEEE international conference on pervasive computing and communications workshops (PerCom Workshops) (pp. 1–4). IEEE.

22. Barga, R., Fontama, V., Tok, W. H., Barga, R., Fontama, V., & Tok, W. H.. (2015). Introducing Microsoft Azure machine learning. Predictive Analytics with Microsoft Azure Machine Learning, 21–43. Berkely, CA: Apress.

23. Chaudhary, K., Alam, M., Al-Rakhami, M. S., & Gumaei, A. (2021). Machine learning-based mathematical modelling for prediction of social media consumer behavior using big data analytics. Journal of Big Data, 8(1), 1–20.

24. Malhotra, S., Chaudhary, K., & Alam, M. (2022). Modeling the use of voice based assistant devices (VBADs): A machine learning base an exploratory study using cluster analysis and correspondence analysis. International Journal of Information Management Data Insights, 2(1), 100069.

25. Chaudhary, K., & Alam, M. (2022). Big Data Analytics: Applications in Business and Marketing. Auerbach Publications, New York.

26. Chaudhary, K., & Alam, M. (Eds.). (2022). Big Data Analytics: Digital Marketing and Decision-Making. CRC Press, New York.

27. Hasan, N., Chaudhary, K., & Alam, M. (2021). Unsupervised machine learning framework for early machine failure detection in an industry. Journal of Discrete Mathematical Sciences and Cryptography, 24(5), 1497–1508.

28. Ansari, M., & Alam, M. (2023). IoT-Cloud-Enabled Smart Framework for Real-World Applications. In Intelligent Systems and Applications: Select Proceedings of ICISA 2022 (pp. 87–105). Singapore: Springer Nature Singapore.

29. Ansari, M., & Alam, M. (2022). IoT-Cloud Enabled Statistical Analysis and Visualization of Air Pollution Data in India. In Proceedings of Data Analytics and Management: ICDAM 2021, Volume 2 (pp. 125–139). Springer Singapore. Jan Wyzykowski University, Poland.

30. Ali, S.A., Ansari, M., Alam, M. (2020). Resource Management Techniques for Cloud-Based IoT Environment. In: Alam, M., Shakil, K., Khan, S. (eds) Internet of Things (IoT). Springer, Cham. https://doi.org/10.1007/978-3-030-37468-6_4.

31. Ansari, M., Ali, S. A., & Alam, M. (2022). Internet of things (IoT) fusion with cloud computing: current research and future direction.

9 Role of IoT in Smart Cities

Proliferation and Challenges

Anupam Singh¹, Nitin Arora²,
and Thipendra P. Singh³
¹Computer Science and Engineering, Graphic Era
 Deemed to be University, Dehradun, India
²Electronics & Computer Discipline, Indian
 Institute of Technology, Roorkee, India
³School of Computer Science Engineering and
 Technology, Bennett University, Greater Noida, India

9.1 INTRODUCTION

9.1.1 SMART CITY

Many smart cities are designed to optimize city services and enhance the quality of life for citizens through the use of advanced technology and data analytics. There are several potential benefits and drawbacks associated with the development of smart cities. The benefits of smart city include improved efficiency: Smart city technology can help reduce waste, cut down on energy consumption, and optimize the use of resources. By leveraging data and automation, cities can improve transportation systems, reduce congestion, and improve public safety. Smart city technology can make urban living more comfortable and enjoyable. For example, citizens can use mobile apps to track public transportation, access city services, and report problems or issues. Smart city technology can create new jobs, attract businesses, and promote economic growth. By investing in smart city infrastructure, cities can attract high-tech businesses and foster innovation. Smart cities can leverage technology to reduce the environmental impact of urban living. For example, cities can use smart sensors to monitor and manage energy usage, water consumption, and waste management.

9.1.2 BENEFITS OF SMART CITY

Living in a smart city has several benefits, and knowing about them will help you balance these benefits against their drawbacks. Some of the benefits are as follows [1]:

- Improved transport services: Smart cities can encourage the use of sustainable transportation options, such as bikes, scooters, and electric vehicles.

DOI: 10.1201/9781032614083-9

By providing infrastructure and incentives for these modes of transportation, smart cities can reduce traffic congestion and promote environmental sustainability.

- Improved communiqué: However, it's important to note that there are potential privacy concerns associated with some of these technologies. For example, some citizens may be uncomfortable with the widespread use of body cameras or ALPR systems, as they can be seen as intrusive. It's important for smart cities to balance the need for public safety with citizens' right to privacy and ensure that these technologies are used responsibly and transparently.

- Effective government services: As mentioned earlier, smart cities can encourage the use of sustainable transportation options, such as bikes, scooters, and electric vehicles. By promoting these modes of transportation, smart cities can reduce the consumption of fossil fuels and promote environmental sustainability. Overall, smart cities can use technology to promote resource efficiency and sustainability, helping to reduce waste and conserve natural resources for future generations.

- More negligible environmental impact: Integrating energy-efficient buildings into smart cities promotes the use of renewable energy sources, improves air quality, and reduces dependence on fossil fuels. This will help reduce our ecological impact on the environment. Furthermore, ensuring equitable access to high-speed Internet and affordable devices is crucial for achieving digital equity. By providing free Wi-Fi in community hotspots, all residents of a city can enjoy equal opportunities.

- Opportunity for financial growth: Investing in smart cities can enhance regional and global competitiveness, attract new residents, and stimulate economic growth. By providing access to an open data policy, smart cities can facilitate the growth of information and other industries. With the aid of advanced technology, businesses can make informed decisions that promote economic development.

- Infrastructure improvement: Maintaining and extending the lifespan of aging infrastructure, such as roads, buildings, highways, and bridges, require significant investment. Nevertheless, by leveraging smart technology, cities can proactively identify and anticipate areas that are likely to lead to infrastructure issues.

- Jobs: A smart city can provide abundant job opportunities and attract numerous businesses, as everyone will have equal access to essential resources, such as transportation, Internet connectivity, and employment opportunities.

- Decrease in crime: Smart technology enables government officials to monitor citizen interactions closely, which can contribute to a decrease in crime rates. Furthermore, areas with higher unemployment rates often experience higher crime rates. By increasing job opportunities, smart cities can help reduce crime rates.

9.1.3   DRAWBACKS OF SMART CITY

Although smart cities have many advantages, it's crucial to acknowledge their drawbacks as well. According to [1], some of the drawbacks include the following:

- Restricted privacy: Since the establishment or the government would have the right to use safety cameras and advanced systems connected across several regions, it will be difficult for residents to maintain their identities. Facial recognition technology and comparable technologies will drastically alter the concept of privacy and personal space.
- Social command: Smart cities' security cameras allow those in positions of authority, whether government officials or businesses, to gather and centralize information. However, this also raises concerns about privacy and control over citizens' data, which could potentially be used to manipulate public opinion.
- Too much network trust: Because residents of these smart cities will be so dependent on electronics and networks, they may lose their independence and cognitive abilities. If these tools are not accessible, they would not be able to react correctly.
- Challenges in the pre-commerce phase: Despite the availability of funds, intelligent technologies will remain in the pre-commercial phase. These cities won't have the technical expertise or resources.
- Pre-training is necessary: If citizens don't understand the technology, they won't be able to utilize it effectively. Proper education and training are essential to ensure that students can apply technology in their daily lives. Although there may be some challenges, smart cities offer many benefits to society. A comparison of the benefits and drawbacks of smart cities can be found in Table 9.1.

9.1.4   IoT IN SMART CITIES CONCEPTS

As metropolitan areas experience a rapid increase in population density, there is a growing need for infrastructure and services to meet the needs of city dwellers. With

TABLE 9.1
Comparison Table for Smart City Benefits and Drawbacks

Benefits	Drawbacks
Stronger connection	Social control issues
Minimizing carbon footprint	Ongoing development
Effective government services	A challenge in the pre-commerce phase
Fewer crimes	A challenge in the pre-commerce phase
Better infrastructure	Building the business case for implementation might be challenging
More employment options	Overconfidence in the network
Improved communication	Limited privacy

the widespread adoption of Internet-enabled devices, such as sensors, actuators, and smartphones, the potential for business opportunities in the Internet of Things (IoT) has increased significantly [2–4]. The IoT prototype consists of interconnected self-configuring objects over a global network architecture. The IoT is primarily designed to improve the dependability, performance, and security of smart cities and their infrastructures, with a focus on real objects that are widely distributed and have limited storage and processing capacity [2]. This chapter reviews the IoT-based smart city.

9.1.5 MOTIVATIONS

Smart cities are now even smarter than they were in the past, thanks to recent developments in digital technologies. Many electrical parts in a smart city are used for numerous applications, including sensors for transportation systems and street cameras for surveillance. Additionally, this can lead to a rise in the use of specific mobile devices. As a result, it is essential to consider some concepts, including object attributes, contributors, incentives, and security laws [5]. Some of the essential characteristics of a smart city in 2020 are discussed in Ref. [6].

All applications of IoT in smart cities like smart media, smart education, smart home, and smart infrastructure can be collaborated in a domain and applied to a city to make it smart. Figure 9.1 depicts these elements, which play a vital role in our lives.

Devices in the IoT context can be combined based on location and assessed using an analytical system. Numerous ongoing initiatives involving monitoring bicycles, vehicles, public parking spaces, etc. can use sensor services to collect specific data. IoT infrastructure is used by numerous service domain applications to support operations related to noise and air pollution, vehicle mobility, and surveillance systems.

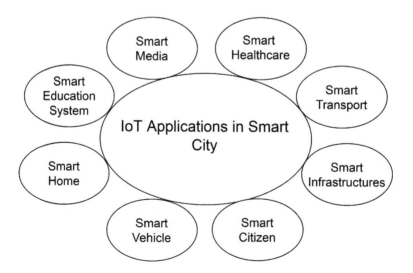

FIGURE 9.1   Taxonomy diagram of IoT applications.

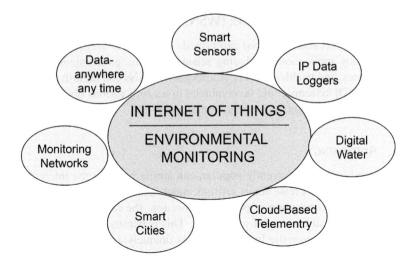

FIGURE 9.2 Environment monitoring.

IoT technology allows fresh insights and the acquisition of actionable information from vast streams of real-time data. The usage of IoT in smart cities also significantly reduces the amount of human labor required to control and monitor the system. One of the most inspiring and notable IoT applications is always thought of as smart city. The environmental risks we face are a severe topic of concern. Many monitoring and control systems can be set up using IoT to monitor essential aspects like air, water, and pollution. Figure 9.2 illustrates how IoT apps are used for intelligent environment monitoring.

9.2 IoT TECHNOLOGIES USED BY SMART CITIES

The Internet serves as the IoT's convergence point and is a broadband network that uses industry-standard communication protocols [7, 8]. The basic idea behind the IoT is the ubiquitous presence of objects that can be measured, deduced, understood, and can alter the environment. Accordingly, the advancement of numerous devices and communication technologies makes the IoT possible. Smart devices, such as mobile phones, and other items, such as food, appliances, landmarks, monuments, and works of art, are included in the IoT. These objects can work together to offer a common goal. One may argue that the IoT's most crucial aspect is how it affects people's daily lives [9].

The following discusses a few IoT-related technologies.

9.2.1 RADIO-FREQUENCY IDENTIFICATION (RFID)

In the context of the IoT, these systems made up of readers and tags are crucial. These technologies can automatically identify every involved object and provide a distinct digital identity so they can be connected to the network and to digital information and services [10].

9.2.2 Wireless Sensor Network (WSN)

Wireless sensor networks (WSNs) can provide a variety of useful data and can be used in various applications, including seismic sensing, government and environmental services, and health care [11]. Additionally, WSNs and radio-frequency identification (RFID) systems could be combined to achieve various objectives, such as gathering data on position, movement, temperature, etc.

9.2.3 Addressing

The IoT trend, which is currently popular, can similarly allow the interconnection of items and things to create smart settings, much like how the Internet can permit a tremendous interconnection of people. To this aim, the capacity to uniquely identify items is essential for the IoT to succeed. This is because operating a big group of connected things over the Internet requires uniquely addressing each object in the group. Along with the previously described uniqueness notion, dependability, scalability, and persistence signify the necessary conditions for creating a unique addressing scheme [12].

9.2.4 Middleware

Due to some problems with the heterogeneity of contributing elements, the limited capacity for storage and processing, and the wide variety of applications, the middleware is essential in connecting the objects to the application layer. The middleware's primary goal is to combine all associated devices' communication and operations effectively.

9.3 APPLICATIONS

The IoT uses the Internet to connect various devices. All of the gadgets that are accessible should be online in this regard to improve accessibility. To accomplish this goal, sensors can be developed at various locations for data collection and analysis to enhance utilization [13]. The following explains the primary goals in this field of study.

9.3.1 Smart Home

Smart cities can use data from sensors in smart houses to implement demand response (D.R.) programs. These programs encourage customers to reduce energy usage during times of high demand, helping to prevent power outages and reduce the need for additional power generation. By providing real-time data on energy usage and demand, smart cities can help customers make informed decisions about when and how they use energy. Smart cities can use sensors to monitor pollution levels in the air, water, and soil. This data can be used to identify sources of pollution and develop strategies to reduce it. Additionally, smart cities can use this data to notify customers when pollution levels reach a certain threshold, allowing them to take appropriate actions to protect their health. Smart cities can use data from sensors in smart houses to automate various aspects of daily life, such as lighting, heating, and security. For example, a smart home system can automatically adjust the temperature based on occupancy levels or turn off lights when a room is unoccupied. This can help to reduce energy usage and improve overall efficiency.

Overall, the use of sensors and data analytics in smart houses can help to promote energy efficiency, reduce pollution, and enhance the quality of life for residents. By providing real-time data and automating various aspects of daily life, smart cities can help customers make informed decisions about their energy usage and promote sustainable living.

9.3.2 SMART PARKING LOTS

By enabling smart parking, different cars' arrival and departure can be monitored for numerous parking lots dispersed throughout the city. As a result, smart parking lots ought to be created with the number of vehicles in each zone in mind. Additional parking lots that can accommodate more vehicles should also be built [14–17]. Accordingly, the information from smart parking lots can improve retailers' and car owners' daily lives in a smart city.

9.3.3 SYSTEM OF WATER AND WEATHER

Sensors can be employed by weather and water systems to provide important information, such as temperature, precipitation, wind speed, and pressure, which can enhance the efficiency of smart cities [18].

9.3.4 VEHICULAR TRAFFIC

Smart cities can greatly benefit from utilizing data collected by various sensors, such as those used to monitor weather and water systems. This data, which includes information on temperature, rainfall, wind speed, and pressure, can be used to improve the effectiveness of the city [19]. By conducting appropriate studies on this data, citizens and the government can gain valuable insights. Additionally, data on automotive traffic can be used by citizens to estimate arrival times at a particular location [20].

9.3.5 ENVIRONMENTAL POLLUTION

Data on vehicular traffic are among the most critical data sources. If its residents are ill, a city cannot be deemed intelligent. To do this, a smart city should keep an eye on environmental pollution and notify its residents, particularly those with medical issues, about it. A different module to collect noise and environmental data is also published in Refs. [2, 21]. There are many more applications discussed in Refs. [22–25].

9.3.6 Surveillance Apparatus

From the residents' perspective, security is the most crucial component of a smart city. The entire smart city should be constantly monitored for this purpose. However, it is pretty challenging to analyze the data and find crimes. New scenarios have been suggested in Ref. [2] to improve the security of the smart city.

9.4 CHALLENGES

This section addresses the typical issues brought on by implementing IoT-based smart cities. The idea of smart cities is quickly gaining traction because of IoT. Cisco believes there will be 50 billion smart connected devices on the market by 2020, bolstering bullish attitudes in the tech industry. The Indian government has ambitious plans to create 100 smart cities across the country. We will be on the right track toward establishing a fully functional smart city once it determines the environment and infrastructure within which it will operate. Better safety standards, lower levels of pollution, efficient energy use, and better urban lifestyles have drawn attention to what IoT can do to support the idea of smart cities. IoT solutions are adaptable and flexible enough to serve and drive a broad range of regional municipal and governmental goals. By way of illustration, let's look at one specific instance where the usage of sensors has the potential to significantly alter how various regional, state, or even national government departments collaborate. Then there is the idea of smart grids, which guarantee the best use of resources, prevent waste, and ensure that there are never any shortages of essential services like power and water supply. As a result, the potential of IoT for smart cities is thrilling both now and in the future.

9.4.1 IoT – Challenges

The idea of smart cities is quickly gaining traction because of IoT. Cisco believes there will be 50 billion smart connected devices on the market by 2020, bolstering positive attitudes in the tech industry. The Indian government has ambitious plans to create 100 smart cities nationwide. We will be on the right track toward establishing a fully functional smart city once it determines the environment and infrastructure within which it will operate. Improved safety standards, lower levels of pollution, efficient energy use, and better urban lifestyles have drawn attention to what IoT can do to support the idea of smart cities. IoT solutions are adaptable and flexible enough to serve and drive a broad range of regional municipal and governmental goals. By way of illustration, let's look at one specific instance where the usage of sensors has the potential to significantly alter how various regional, state, or even national government agencies collaborate. Then there is the idea of smart grids, which guarantee the best use of resources, prevent waste, and ensure that there are never any shortages of essential services like electricity and water supply. As a result, the potential of IoT for smart cities is thrilling both now and in the future.

9.4.2 Challenges with IoT Installation in Smart Cities

This section addresses the common issues created by implementing IoT-based smart cities. The following IoT restrictions must be taken into account by municipal planners to accomplish this objective using intelligent solutions:

1. Vulnerable to hacks

   Most connections with things will be made possible using RFID, which may be hacked. A hack-proof IoT ecosystem will ensure that the development of smart cities happens more quickly.

2. Security and privacy concerns

   In a smart city, everything will be connected, from your toaster and refrigerator to your T.V. and vehicle. This increases the possibility of exposing security and privacy vulnerabilities to hackers [26]. This danger can be significantly reduced by offering a secure access option. When all of the data is composed and analyzed on a single-IoT platform, the system is susceptible to various assaults. Furthermore, such a system is vulnerable to severe flaws; also, the multi-tenancy of this system might generate security concerns and data leaks [3].

3. Problems with interoperability

   Although the idea of open standards has been around for 25–30 years, nothing substantial has come. We observe a user choosing a side (consider Google and Apple in the instance of mobility) and then creating a complete ecosystem around this instead of using interoperable solutions. This interoperability restriction will also cause issues in the future. The number of tools, resources, and devices that may enable the value gained from IoT has surged due to continuous technological improvement. The construction of smart cities will consequently proceed at a faster rate as a result. Smart town planning and smart cities may deliver less traffic congestion and a more robust transportation ecology between two sites. However, this is only possible with active, long-term cooperation from infrastructure enablers and technological experts. Here, collaborations with IoT specialists and innovative I.T. suppliers will offer the fundamental building blocks required for the local town planner to realize their vision of the smart city.

4. Overcoming city merchant lock-in

   For IoT-enabled smart city solutions, the absence of an acceptable standard and an interoperable merchant ecology makes it complex for cities to execute a precise clarification without relying heavily on a solitary merchant. A nagging concern about merchant lock-in may influence future purchasing decisions for underlying infrastructure expansions and scalability without incurring high system integration costs. As a result, cities frequently hesitate to invest more money in smart infrastructure for cities, which hinders the market growth.

5. Overcome developer city lock-in

   The current APIs for accessing streaming data from IoT infrastructures and other sources may diverge substantially between locations, as may the ease of use of authentic information sources and primary information format.

This significantly decreases the benefits of economies of scale and makes it impossible for many developers and providers of IoT-based smart city services to arrange and function a facility designed for one urban context in another.

6. Meeting natural citizen needs

The sale pitch of significant skill suppliers, organization integrators, and the aspirations of home governments have long influenced the idea of smart cities. Instead of addressing everyday operational and public demands, early smart city models like Masdar or Songdo were designed from the top down as a scientific and market thrust. Other services frequently adopt the viewpoint of the city administration, which frequently differs from that of the residents. Although there are substantial cultural variations worldwide, there isn't much of a citizen's voice in the discussion concerning IoT instrumentation. Residents must take a significant part in the co-creation and proposal of smart city services if they benefit citizens significantly and are accepted by the public.

7. IoT infrastructure sharing for new business cases

It is challenging to allow IoT communications to recycle and accomplish the requisite economy of magnitude due to the IoT infrastructure's lack of interoperability and potent combination of specific applications and IoT platforms. It is more challenging to produce a meaningful return on investment because of the siloed business models that follow, such as one deployment for one particular service. Finding lesser uses for IoT deployments would open up new industry opportunities and lower the investment barrier. However, given the existing compartmentalized environment, this poses a significant issue. A trustworthy IoT data market is required between various IoT platforms to create prospects for additional revenue streams from IoT installations and increase the economic viability of numerous IoT deployments.

8. Calculating the social and economic advantages

IoT-based smart city solutions may frequently address the triple bottom line; thus, their effects reach well beyond economic gains (social, environmental, and economic). Even while decision-makers see benefits beyond economic considerations, it is difficult to quantify and evaluate the real-world impact of IoT actions in a city, such as cost savings and financial return on investment choices are made more challenging by the absence of a shared framework that also fully captures and monitors the socio-economic advantages of urban IoT.

9. Sharing more than just open data

Open data has mainly been used to construct the initial generation of smart city services. When not deemed sensitive, such data is typically shared, and the achievement of services built on top of it is frequently limited. Private Datasets, such as IoT-generated data, closed organizational data of firms, or citizen personal data, can provide more worth for richer smart city services but are either not provided for development or are not easily accessible.

As licensing models are poorly silent and implemented, organizations and people lack incentives, market confidence, and trust to share new datasets. For such a market, a crucial ecosystem base is still lacking. Also lacking are the future-proof market structures that would expand the financial feasibility of releasing data beyond conventional license arrangements.

10. Encouraging more agile policy making

The same principles-based adaptive policy-making for and by cities has not yet gotten much attention, although the potential of IoT to revolutionize several application areas by integrating information and sensor data into business operations in close to real-time. Policy decisions rely on educated guesses or commissioned research, which results in slow reactions or ill-informed choices. Due to the lack of near real-time simplicity of many city operations, agile policy-making for 21st century cities is still complicated, lacking approaches, and missing instruments for quick policy prototyping and subsequent effect evaluations.

11. Heterogeneity

The IoT structure has traditionally grown with distinct solutions in which each structure constituent is connected to the specific application environment. As a result, authorities must examine their goal scenarios, establish the computer gear and software necessary, and then combine these disparate substructures. The presence of such infrastructures and the supply of an appropriate cooperating scheme between them might be a tough challenge for the IoT structure.

12. Reliability

Some dependability difficulties have occurred in the IoT-based structure. For example, due to the vehicles' movement, contact with them is insufficiently dependable; also, many smart devices will pose specific dependability difficulties of collapse [27].

13. On a large scale

Several circumstances necessitate communications among many implanted devices, which may be spread across enormous areas. IoT systems provide a viable platform for analyzing and integrating data from various devices [3, 28–30]. However, such a massive volume of information needs appropriate storage and computational capabilities acquired rapidly, making conventional issues more challenging to overcome. On the other hand, deploying IoT devices might impact monitoring duties since these devices must deal with dynamics and communication delays.

14. Legal and societal implications

Based on the information given by the user, the IoT system may deliver a service. The service provider must adhere to several local and international rules in such instances. Furthermore, users should be sufficiently incentivized to engage in the given scenario and data collecting. It will be more expedient if users have the option of selecting and providing data that denotes an object [31]. Refs. [32, 33] address the application of IoT-based smart devices in health care using fog computing.

15. Sensor networks

Sensor networks are the majority of significant technology enabling IoT [34]. This expertise has the potential to influence the globe by enabling the measurement, inference, and comprehension of environmental indicators [5]. Recent technological advancements have given devices excellent efficiency and cheap cost for large-scale remote sensing applications [2].

Furthermore, cell phones are linked to various sensors, enabling a wide range of mobile applications in many areas of IoT. To that aim, the most difficult challenge is to handle the large-scale sensor information in terms of energy and network restrictions, as well as numerous uncertainties [35].

Even though the IoT can make it easier for responsive loads to participate in the system, D.R. adoption can still be constrained by various barriers. These obstacles are divided into three basic categories: consumer restrictions, IoT implementation in smart cities faces challenges. There are few objectives to make cities smarter.

Town planners must consider the following IoT restrictions and come up with clever solutions to accomplish the objectives: In a smart city, the chance of hacking is higher. So there is a need for secure infrastructure and everything will be connected, from your toaster and refrigerator to your T.V. and vehicle. This increases the possibility of leaving security and privacy vulnerabilities exposed to hackers. This risk can be significantly reduced by offering a secure access option. Although open standards have been discussed for the previous 25–30 years, little has come of them. In contrast to using interoperable solutions, we see users picking sides and building entire ecosystems around them (think of Google and Apple in the context of mobility) [36]. In the future, this interoperability constraint will also be problematic. With the ongoing technological advancements, there has been an increase in the number of tools, resources, and devices that can aid in maximizing the potential benefits of IoT. The construction of smart cities will consequently proceed at a faster rate as a result. Smart town planning and smart cities can deliver benefits like decreased traffic congestion and a more robust transit ecology between two sites.

However, this is only possible with active, long-term cooperation from infrastructure enablers and technological experts. Here, collaborations with IoT specialists and smart I.T. providers will offer the fundamental building blocks required for the local town planner to realize their vision of the smart city.

9.5   FUTURE DIRECTIONS

IoT and smart city infrastructure share many concepts and offer significant growth potential for businesses. However, there are several challenges that need to be addressed for the successful development of future IoT technologies in smart cities. The highest priority is given to sensor-oriented wireless networking technologies. One of the critical tasks in devices utilizing IoT technologies is providing suitably dispersed resources, ranging from low- to high-capacity processors. Additionally, intelligent planning, scheduling, and controlling technologies are necessary to handle the large computations and data transmissions resulting from adding more IoT-enabled devices.

As most of the generated data is unstructured or unusual, data management solutions are essential for handling the massive amounts of data. Intelligent data analysis and categorization tools should be developed and implemented. Furthermore, IoT technology services are currently delivered through independent specialized solutions focused on a particular setting. Therefore, reliable data processing and storage methods should be used with confidentiality, integrity, and privacy to connect to an IoT technology service.

9.5.1 Conclusion

The most recent research was studied to analyze IoT systems' many aspects and characteristics and the compelling reasons for adopting them. Because installing IoT infrastructures might open up a variety of opportunities, the top research reasons are given first, followed by a list of relevant applications. It details how they might be used to develop and improve daily tasks. In addition, the difficulties encountered when deploying the IoT system were extensively discussed. One of the most intriguing future developments is merging the IoT proposal with an erstwhile self-directed and intellectual system for creating an intelligent and broad application.

Furthermore, developing a method to address some of the most pressing issues, such as people's privacy rights, remains a priority. With its functionality and capabilities, the IoT should, in reality, use intelligent systems and sensors to protect the rights of smart city people. Though the present learning assessed the significance of IoT technology in the notion of a smart city, thorough conference and debate among experts in disciplines linked to smart cities and IoT technology must be ongoing to provide concrete action plans. Furthermore, professional panels of specialists in various study subjects, such as urban advances, information, message technology, transport, and ecological policy, should be formed.

REFERENCES

1. Kirimtat, A., Krejcar, O., Kertesz, A., & Tasgetiren, M. F. (2020). Future trends and current state of smart city concepts: A survey. IEEE Access, 8, 86448–86467.
2. Rathore, M. M., Ahmad, A., Paul, A., & Rho, S., Urban planning and building smart cities based on the internet of things using big data analytics. Computer Networks, 2016, DOI: 10.1016/j.comnet.2015.12.023.
3. Mora-Sánchez, O. B., López-Neri, E., Cedillo-Elias, E. J., Aceves-Martínez, E., & Larios, V. M. (2020). Validation of IoT infrastructure for the construction of smart cities solutions on living lab platform. IEEE Transactions on Engineering Management, 68(3), 899–908.
4. Arasteh, H., Hosseinnezhad, V., Loia, V., Tommasetti, A., Troisi, O., Shafie-khah, M., & Siano, P. (2016, June). IoT-based smart cities: A survey. In 2016 IEEE 16th international conference on environment and electrical engineering (EEEIC) (pp. 1–6). IEEE.
5. Botta, A., de Donato, W., Persico, V., & Pescapé, A. (2016). Integration of cloud computing and internet of things: A survey. Future Generation Computer Systems, 56, 684–700.
6. Kyriazis, D., Varvarigou, T., Rossi, A., White, D., & Cooper, J. (2013). Sustainable smart city IoT applications: heat and electricity management & Eco- conscious cruise control for public transportation. In IEEE 14th international symposium and workshops on world of wireless, mobile and multimedia networks (pp. 1–5).
7. Atzori, L., Iera, A., & Morabito, G. (2010). The internet of things: A survey. Computer Networks, 54, 2787–2805.
8. Bassi, A., & Horn, G. (2008). European Commission: Internet of Things in 2020: A Roadmap for the Future. Information Society and Media, Europe.
9. Evangelos, A. K., Nikolaos, D. T., & Anthony, C. B. (2011). Integrating RFIDs and smart objects into a unified internet of things architecture. Advances in Internet of Things, 1, 5–12.
10. Alamri, A., Ansari, W. S., Hassan, M. M., Hossain, M. S., Alelaiwi, A., & Hossain, M. A. (2013). A survey on sensor-cloud: Architecture, applications, and approaches. International Journal of Distributed Sensor Networks, 2013, 1–18.

11. Shafie-khah, M., Kheradmand, M., Javadi, S., Azenha, M., de Aguiar, J. L. B., Castro-Gomes, J., Siano, P., & Catalão, J. P. S. (2016). Optimal behavior of responsive residential demand considering hybrid phase change materials. Applied Energy, 163, 81–92.

12. Neyestani, N., Damavandi, M. Y., Shafie-khah, M., & Catalão, J. P. S. (2015). Modeling the PEV Traffic Pattern in an Urban Environment with Parking Lots and Charging Stations. In: PowerTech, IEEE Eindhoven, Eindhoven (pp. 1–6).

13. Yazdani-Damavandi, M., Moghaddam, M. P., Haghifam, M. R., Shafie-khah, M., & Catalão, S. (2016). Modeling operational behavior of plug-in electric Vehicles' parking lot in multienergy systems. IEEE Transactions on Smart Grid, 7, 124–135.

14. Singh, A., & Mahapatra, S. (2020). Network-Based Applications of Multimedia Big Data Computing in IoT Environment. In: Tanwar, S., Tyagi, S., Kumar, N. (eds) Multimedia Big Data Computing for IoT Applications. Intelligent Systems Reference Library, vol 163. Springer, Singapore.

15. Shafie-khah, M., Heydarian-Forushani, E., Golshan, M. E. H., Siano, P., Moghaddam, M. P., Sheikh-El-Eslami, M. K., & Catalão, J. P. S. (2016). Optimal trading of plug-in electric vehicle aggregation agents in a market environment for sustainability. Applied Energy, 162, 601–612.

16. Şerban, A. C., & Lytras, M. D. (2020). Artificial intelligence for smart renewable energy sector in Europe—Smart energy infrastructures for next generation smart cities. IEEE Access, 8, 77364–77377.

17. Brisimi, T. S., Cassandras, C. G., Osgood, C., Paschalidis, I. C., & Zhang, Y. (2016). Sensing and classifying roadway obstacles in smart cities: The street bump system. IEEE Access, 4, 1301–1312.

18. Sivrikaya, F., Ben-Sassi, N., Dang, X. T., Görür, O. C., & Kuster, C. (2019). Internet of smart city objects: A distributed framework for service discovery and composition. IEEE Access, 7, 14434–14454.

19. Cook, D. J., Duncan, G., Sprint, G., & Fritz, R. L. (2018). Using smart city technology to make healthcare smarter. Proceedings of the IEEE, 106(4), 708–722.

20. Morello, R., Mukhopadhyay, S. C., Liu, Z., Slomovitz, D., & Samantaray, S. R. (2017). Advances on sensing technologies for smart cities and power grids: A review. IEEE Sensors Journal, 17(23), 7596–7610.

21. Mishra, N., Singhal, P., & Kundu, S. (2020, December). Application of IoT products in smart cities of India. In 2020 9th international conference system modeling and advancement in research trends (SMART) (pp. 155–157). IEEE.

22. Chaudhari, S. S., & Bhole, V. Y. (2018, January). Solid waste collection as a service using IoT-solution for smart cities. In 2018 international conference on smart city and emerging technology (ICSCET) (pp. 1–5). IEEE.

23. Gupta, S. K., Vanjale, S., Rasal, S., & Vanjale, M. (2020, March). Securing IoT devices in smart city environments. In 2020 international conference on emerging smart computing and informatics (ESCI) (pp. 119–123). IEEE.

24. He, W., Yan, G., & Xu, L. D. (2014). "Developing vehicular data cloud services in the IoT environment. IEEE Transactions on Industrial Informatics, 10, 1587–1595.

25. ICT Regulation Toolkit, "Models for Infrastructure Sharing: Sweden's Stokab," Retrieved 2015-05-30.

26. Baxter, S. (2012-02-26), "Modest gains in first six months of Santa Cruz's predictive police program," Santa Cruz Sentinel. Retrieved 2015-05-26.

27. Wang, X. L., Wang, L., Bi, Z., Li, Y. Y., & Xu, Y. (2016). Cloud computing in human resource management (HRM) system for small and medium enterprises (SMEs). The International Journal of Advanced Manufacturing Technology, 84, 485–496.

28. Petrolo, R., Loscrì, V., & Mitton, N., Towards a smart city based on Cloud of Things. In Proceedings of the 2014 ACM international workshop on wireless and mobile technologies for smart cities, ACM, pp. 61–66, 2014.

29. Lazarescu, M. (2013). Design of a WSN platform for long-term environmental monitoring for IoT applications. IEEE Journal on Emerging and Selected Topics in Circuits and Systems, 3, 45–54.
30. Mitton, N., Papavassiliou, S., Puliafito, A., & Trivedi, K. S. (2012). Combining cloud and sensors in a smart city environment. EURASIP Journal on Wireless Communications and Networking, 1, 1–10.
31. Atkins, C., et al., A Cloud service for end-user participation concerning the Internet of Things. In International conference on signal-image technology & internet-based systems (SITIS), pp. 273–278, 2013.
32. Corsar, D., Edwards, P., Velaga, N., Nelson, J., & Pan, J., Short paper: addressing the challenges of semantic citizen-sensing. In 4th international workshop on semantic sensor networks, CEUR-WS pp. 90–95, 2011.
33. Zaslavsky, A., Perera, C., & Georgakopoulos, D., Sensing as a service and big data, 2013. ArXiv Preprint arXiv:1301.0159.
34. Mahapatra, S., & Singh, A. (2020). Application of IoT-Based Smart Devices in Health Care Using Fog Computing. In: Tanwar, S. (eds) Fog Data Analytics for IoT Applications. Studies in Big Data, vol 76. Springer, Singapore.
35. Ahatsham, N. A., & Singh, K. P. (2018). An approach towards real time smart vehicular system using internet of things. International Journal of Research in Engineering, IT and Social Sciences, ISSN, 2250-0588.
36. Shahare, V., Arora, N., Ahatsham, S. A., & Mouje, N. (2019). Smart home automation tool for energy conservation. International Journal of Recent Technology and Engineering, 8, 5312–5315.

10 AI-Based Planning of Business Management

Lakshay Agarwal[1], Naman Jain[1],
Niharika Singh[1], and Saurabh Kumar[2]

[1]University of Petroleum and Energy
Studies, Dehradun, India
[2]Sharda University, Greater Noida, India

10.1 INTRODUCTION

Artificial intelligence (AI) has been transforming businesses across various industries for several years now. The ability of AI-based systems to quickly and accurately analyze large datasets and identify patterns and trends that would otherwise be difficult or impossible for humans to detect has made them invaluable tools for businesses seeking to improve their operations and stay competitive.[1]

AI-based planning is one area where businesses can leverage the power of AI to improve their planning processes and make more informed decisions. AI-based planning refers to the use of AI and related technologies to enhance the process of planning, whether it is for financial forecasting, workforce management, supply chain planning, or other areas of the business.

The use of AI-based planning can bring a wide range of benefits to businesses. For example, it can help businesses to more accurately forecast demand for their products and services, enabling them to optimize their inventory and reduce the risk of stockouts. It can also help businesses to identify and mitigate risks, such as supply chain disruptions or changes in customer demand.[2,3]

One of the key advantages of AI-based planning is that it can help businesses to make decisions more quickly and with greater confidence. By automating the analysis of large datasets, businesses can get insights and recommendations that would take much longer to arrive at through manual analysis. This can help businesses to respond more quickly to changing market conditions and make decisions that are based on accurate, up-to-date information.

Despite the benefits of AI-based planning, there are also challenges associated with its implementation. One of the main challenges is the need for high-quality data. AI-based planning relies on large datasets to make accurate predictions and recommendations, and businesses must ensure that they have high-quality data to work with. This means investing in data collection, management, and analysis tools and processes to ensure that the data is accurate, reliable, and relevant (Figure 10.1).[4]

Another challenge is the need for expertise. AI-based planning systems require specialized knowledge and skills, and businesses must have the right talent in place to effectively implement and manage these systems. This might include data scientists, software engineers, and other technical experts who can design and develop

DOI: 10.1201/9781032614083-10

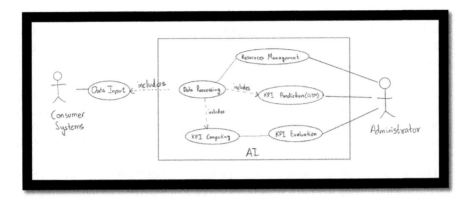

FIGURE 10.1   This is the UCD of a DSS (decision support system) based on AI.

AI-based planning systems, as well as business analysts who can interpret the data and make strategic decisions based on the insights provided by the AI system.

We will explore the benefits, challenges, and best practices associated with AI-based planning in business management. We will also provide case studies of businesses that have successfully implemented AI-based planning systems and outline the steps that businesses can take to effectively implement AI-based planning in their own organizations. By the end of this chapter, readers will have a better understanding of how AI-based planning can transform their business operations and enable them to make better, more informed decisions.

10.2   UNDERSTANDING AI-BASED PLANNING

AI-based planning is a rapidly growing field of study that involves the use of AI to develop and execute plans. This involves the use of algorithms, models, and other techniques to analyze and synthesize data, and to identify the best course of action in a given scenario. Understanding AI-based planning requires a deep understanding of the underlying technologies and techniques, as well as an understanding of the broader context in which these technologies are being applied.[5]

At its core, AI-based planning involves the use of AI algorithms to generate plans and execute them in a way that optimizes a specific set of objectives. These objectives may include factors, such as cost, efficiency, speed, or accuracy, depending on the specific application. The AI algorithms used in planning typically involve the use of machine learning, which allows the system to learn from experience and improve its performance over time.

One key challenge in AI-based planning is the need to balance conflicting objectives. For example, a system might need to optimize for cost while also ensuring a certain level of quality or reliability. This requires the development of sophisticated algorithms that can take into account multiple objectives and trade-offs and make decisions that balance these factors in a way that is optimal for the specific application.[6]

Another challenge in AI-based planning is the need to handle uncertainty and incomplete information. In many real-world applications, the system may not have complete information about the state of the world or may be uncertain about the outcomes of different actions. This requires the development of algorithms that can reason under uncertainty and make decisions that are robust to the presence of incomplete or uncertain information.

To address these challenges, AI-based planning systems typically involve the use of a range of techniques and technologies. These may include machine learning algorithms, such as decision trees, Bayesian networks, and reinforcement learning, as well as optimization techniques, such as linear programming and dynamic programming. The specific techniques used will depend on the nature of the application and the specific requirements of the system.

One important application of AI-based planning is in the field of robotics. Robots are increasingly being used in a wide range of applications, from manufacturing and logistics to healthcare and home automation. In many cases, these robots need to plan their actions in real-time, taking into account a range of factors, such as the position of objects in the environment, the presence of other agents, and the state of the robot itself. AI-based planning algorithms can be used to generate plans for robots that take into account these factors and optimize for a specific set of objectives.

Another important application of AI-based planning is in the field of transportation. With the increasing use of autonomous vehicles and the growing complexity of transportation systems, there is a growing need for AI-based planning systems that can optimize traffic flow, reduce congestion, and improve safety. AI-based planning algorithms can be used to generate plans for traffic management systems that take into account factors, such as traffic volume, road conditions, and weather, and optimize for a range of objectives, such as reducing travel time, minimizing emissions, and improving safety.

AI-based planning is a rapidly growing field of study that is having a significant impact on a wide range of applications. Understanding AI-based planning requires a deep understanding of the underlying technologies and techniques, as well as an understanding of the broader context in which these technologies are being applied. As AI-based planning continues to evolve and improve, it is likely to play an increasingly important role in a wide range of domains, from robotics and transportation to healthcare, finance, and beyond.[7]

10.3 ADVANTAGES OF AI-BASED PLANNING

There are several advantages to using AI-based planning in business management. One of the key advantages is that AI can help businesses make more informed decisions. By using AI algorithms to analyze data, businesses can identify patterns and trends that are not easily visible to humans. This can help businesses make decisions based on data-driven insights, rather than intuition or guesswork.

Another advantage of AI-based planning is that it can help businesses optimize their resources. By analyzing data on resource utilization, businesses can identify areas where resources can be better allocated. This can help businesses increase efficiency, reduce costs, and improve overall performance.[8]

AI-based planning can also help businesses with risk management. By analyzing data on potential risks, businesses can develop strategies to mitigate those risks. This can help businesses avoid costly mistakes and reduce their exposure to risk.

AI has become an integral part of modern-day business processes, including planning. AI-based planning refers to the use of machine learning algorithms to optimize various business processes. The advantages of AI-based planning are numerous, and this chapter will highlight some of the key benefits.

10.3.1 IMPROVED ACCURACY AND EFFICIENCY

One of the primary advantages of AI-based planning is improved accuracy and efficiency. Traditional planning methods rely on human decision-making, which can be subjective and prone to errors. On the other hand, AI algorithms can process vast amounts of data, analyze it, and make accurate predictions or recommendations. This means that businesses can make more informed decisions, leading to improved efficiency and productivity.[9]

10.3.2 COST SAVINGS

AI-based planning can lead to significant cost savings for businesses. For example, AI algorithms can optimize supply chain management, reducing the cost of transportation and inventory. Additionally, AI can analyze customer data to predict demand, which can help businesses avoid overproduction and wastage.[10]

10.3.3 INCREASED AGILITY AND FLEXIBILITY

AI-based planning can help businesses become more agile and flexible. For example, if market conditions change, AI algorithms can quickly analyze the data and recommend changes to the business strategy. This can help businesses stay ahead of the competition and adapt to changing market conditions.[11]

10.3.4 ENHANCED CUSTOMER EXPERIENCE

AI-based planning can also improve the customer experience. For example, AI algorithms can analyze customer data to provide personalized recommendations and offers. This can help businesses build stronger relationships with customers and increase customer loyalty.

10.3.5 BETTER RISK MANAGEMENT

AI-based planning can help businesses better manage risks. For example, AI algorithms can analyze data to identify potential risks and provide recommendations for mitigating those risks. This can help businesses avoid potential losses and minimize the impact of negative events.[12]

10.3.6 INCREASED INNOVATION

AI-based planning can also increase innovation in businesses. By analyzing data and identifying patterns, AI algorithms can identify new opportunities and potential areas for innovation. This can help businesses develop new products and services that meet the changing needs of their customers.

10.3.7 IMPROVED DECISION-MAKING

AI-based planning can help businesses make better decisions. By analyzing data and providing recommendations, AI algorithms can help businesses make more informed decisions, reducing the risk of making costly mistakes. Additionally, AI can provide real-time insights, allowing businesses to make decisions quickly and efficiently.

AI-based planning offers numerous advantages for businesses. From improved accuracy and efficiency to cost savings, increased agility and flexibility, enhanced customer experience, better risk management, increased innovation, and improved decision-making, the benefits of AI-based planning are clear. As businesses continue to adopt AI-based planning, they will be better positioned to compete in a rapidly changing business environment.[13]

10.4 APPLICATIONS OF AI-BASED PLANNING

AI-based planning can be used in a variety of applications in business management. One of the most common applications is forecasting. By analyzing historical data and current trends, businesses can use AI algorithms to make predictions about future outcomes. This can help businesses plan for different scenarios and make informed decisions.

AI-based planning can also be used for resource allocation. By analyzing data on resource utilization, businesses can identify areas where resources can be better allocated. This can help businesses increase efficiency, reduce costs, and improve overall performance.

Another application of AI-based planning is decision-making. By analyzing large amounts of data, businesses can identify patterns and trends that are not easily visible to humans. This can help businesses make more informed decisions based on data-driven insights.

AI-based planning can also be used in risk management. By analyzing data on potential risks, businesses can develop strategies to mitigate those risks. This can help businesses avoid costly mistakes and reduce their exposure to risk.

AI is a rapidly growing field, and AI-based planning is an essential component of AI. Planning is the process of determining the course of action to achieve a particular goal. AI-based planning is the application of AI to the process of planning. AI-based planning has many applications in various fields, such as healthcare, manufacturing, robotics, and transportation.[14]

10.4.1 HEALTHCARE

AI-based planning has several applications in healthcare. One of the main applications is the development of treatment plans for patients. AI-based planning can take into account a patient's medical history, symptoms, and test results to develop an

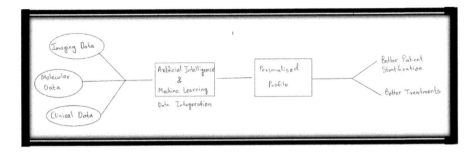

FIGURE 10.2 This diagram helps us to understand how AI can be used in analyzing various types of data for each patient and giving them treatment accordingly.

effective treatment plan. AI-based planning can also help doctors and nurses to manage patient care more effectively by predicting which patients are likely to require intensive care or other types of treatment (Figure 10.2).

10.4.2 MANUFACTURING

In manufacturing, AI-based planning can be used to optimize production schedules, reduce waste, and improve product quality. AI-based planning can be used to schedule the use of equipment, materials, and labor to ensure that products are produced efficiently and to the required quality standards. AI-based planning can also be used to identify and reduce bottlenecks in the manufacturing process.

10.4.3 ROBOTICS

AI-based planning is an essential component of robotics. AI-based planning can be used to control the movement of robots and to determine the best course of action for the robot to achieve its goals. AI-based planning can also be used to plan the trajectory of a robot's arm or to plan the movement of a robot through a complex environment.

10.4.4 TRANSPORTATION

AI-based planning has many applications in transportation. One of the main applications is the development of transportation schedules. AI-based planning can be used to optimize the use of vehicles and to minimize travel time. AI-based planning can also be used to plan the routes that vehicles take to minimize traffic congestion and to ensure that deliveries are made on time.

10.4.5 AGRICULTURE

AI-based planning has many applications in agriculture. One of the main applications is the development of irrigation schedules. AI-based planning can take into account soil moisture levels, weather conditions, and other factors to develop an irrigation schedule that optimizes water use and maximizes crop yields. AI-based planning can also be used to optimize the use of fertilizers and other inputs to maximize crop yields.

10.4.6 ENVIRONMENTAL MANAGEMENT

AI-based planning can be used to manage natural resources and to reduce environmental impacts. AI-based planning can be used to develop land-use plans that balance conservation and economic development. AI-based planning can also be used to develop plans to reduce greenhouse gas emissions and to manage waste disposal.

AI-based planning has many applications in various fields, such as healthcare, manufacturing, robotics, transportation, agriculture, and environmental management. AI-based planning can help to optimize processes, reduce waste, and improve efficiency. AI-based planning can also help to manage natural resources and to reduce environmental impacts. AI-based planning is a rapidly growing field, and it is expected to have even more applications in the future.

10.5   CHALLENGES OF AI-BASED PLANNING

While AI-based planning offers many advantages, it also presents some challenges. One of the key challenges is the quality of the data used in the analysis. AI algorithms require large amounts of data to be effective, and if the data is not of high quality, the analysis may be flawed. Additionally, there is a risk of bias in the analysis, which can lead to inaccurate results.

Another challenge of AI-based planning is the complexity of the algorithms used. Many AI algorithms are complex and difficult to understand, which can make it challenging for businesses to implement them effectively. Additionally, the algorithms may require significant computing power, which can be expensive.

There is also a risk of data privacy and security breaches when using AI-based planning. Businesses must ensure that the data used in the analysis is secure and that customer privacy is protected.

AI-based planning has numerous applications in business management, including strategic planning, resource allocation, risk management, and forecasting. However, the integration of AI-based planning into business management is not without challenges. This article explores some of the challenges faced by AI-based planning in business management.[15]

10.5.1 DATA QUALITY

The accuracy and effectiveness of AI-based planning rely heavily on the quality of the data used to train and develop the AI algorithms. Business managers face challenges with data collection, data storage, data quality, and data management. Poor data quality can lead to inaccurate plans, and the identification and remediation of these data quality issues can be time-consuming and costly.

10.5.2   LIMITED DOMAIN EXPERTISE

AI-based planning requires expertise in the business domain to develop effective plans. Managers must have knowledge and experience of the specific domain they are working in to ensure the accuracy and relevance of the plans. A lack of domain expertise can lead to ineffective planning, incorrect decision-making, and potentially costly mistakes.

10.5.3   DIFFICULTY IN INTERPRETING RESULTS

One of the main challenges of AI-based planning is the difficulty in interpreting the results. The output of the AI algorithms is often complex, and it can be challenging to understand how the plan was generated. This complexity can result in a lack of trust and confidence in the AI-based planning process, leading to reluctance to use it in decision-making.

10.5.4   BIAS IN THE DATA

AI-based planning relies on data to develop plans, and if the data is biased, the plans will be as well. Bias in the data can lead to inaccurate and unfair decision-making, which can have significant implications for the business. Bias can be introduced into the data in various ways, including through sampling, data collection, or data processing.

10.5.5   INTEGRATION WITH EXISTING BUSINESS SYSTEMS

AI-based planning must integrate with existing business systems to be effective. However, this integration can be challenging, and the AI-based planning system must be compatible with existing business systems. This compatibility requires a considerable investment in time, resources, and expertise.[16]

10.5.6   COST AND RESOURCES

The implementation of AI-based planning requires significant investment in resources, including hardware, software, and skilled personnel. Additionally, ongoing maintenance and upgrades can be expensive, making AI-based planning cost-prohibitive for some businesses.

10.5.7   REGULATORY AND ETHICAL CONSIDERATIONS

The use of AI-based planning in business management raises regulatory and ethical considerations. Businesses must comply with data protection regulations and ensure that the use of AI does not violate ethical standards. AI-based planning must be transparent, explainable, and accountable to avoid legal and ethical issues.

AI-based planning has numerous benefits for business management, including optimizing processes, reducing waste, and improving efficiency. However, the implementation of AI-based planning faces significant challenges, including data quality, limited domain expertise, difficulty in interpreting results, bias in the data, integration with existing business systems, cost and resources, and regulatory and ethical considerations. These challenges must be addressed to ensure the effective integration of AI-based planning into business management.[17]

10.6 BEST PRACTICES FOR AI-BASED PLANNING

AI-based planning has numerous applications in business management, including strategic planning, resource allocation, risk management, and forecasting. However, the integration of AI-based planning into business management is not without challenges. This chapter explores some of the challenges faced by AI-based planning in business management.[18]

10.6.1 DATA QUALITY

The accuracy and effectiveness of AI-based planning rely heavily on the quality of the data used to train and develop the AI algorithms. Business managers face challenges with data collection, data storage, data quality, and data management. Poor data quality can lead to inaccurate plans, and the identification and remediation of these data quality issues can be time-consuming and costly.

10.6.2 LIMITED DOMAIN EXPERTISE

AI-based planning requires expertise in the business domain to develop effective plans. Managers must have knowledge and experience of the specific domain they are working in to ensure the accuracy and relevance of the plans. A lack of domain expertise can lead to ineffective planning, incorrect decision-making, and potentially costly mistakes.

10.6.3 DIFFICULTY IN INTERPRETING RESULTS

One of the main challenges of AI-based planning is the difficulty in interpreting the results. The output of the AI algorithms is often complex, and it can be challenging to understand how the plan was generated. This complexity can result in a lack of trust and confidence in the AI-based planning process, leading to reluctance to use it in decision-making.

10.6.4 BIAS IN THE DATA

AI-based planning relies on data to develop plans, and if the data is biased, the plans will be as well. Bias in the data can lead to inaccurate and unfair decision-making, which can have significant implications for the business. Bias can be introduced into the data in various ways, including through sampling, data collection, or data processing.

10.6.5 Integration with Existing Business Systems

AI-based planning must integrate with existing business systems to be effective. However, this integration can be challenging, and the AI-based planning system must be compatible with existing business systems. This compatibility requires a considerable investment in time, resources, and expertise.

10.6.6 Cost and Resources

The implementation of AI-based planning requires significant investment in resources, including hardware, software, and skilled personnel. Additionally, ongoing maintenance and upgrades can be expensive, making AI-based planning cost-prohibitive for some businesses.

10.6.7 Regulatory and Ethical Considerations

The use of AI-based planning in business management raises regulatory and ethical considerations. Businesses must comply with data protection regulations and ensure that the use of AI does not violate ethical standards. AI-based planning must be transparent, explainable, and accountable to avoid legal and ethical issues.

AI-based planning has numerous benefits for business management, including optimizing processes, reducing waste, and improving efficiency. However, the implementation of AI-based planning faces significant challenges, including data quality, limited domain expertise, difficulty in interpreting results, bias in the data, integration with existing business systems, cost and resources, and regulatory and ethical considerations. These challenges must be addressed to ensure the effective integration of AI-based planning into business management.

10.7 ETHICAL CONSIDERATIONS FOR AI-BASED PLANNING IN BUSINESS MANAGEMENT

As AI-based planning becomes more prevalent in business management, it is important to consider the ethical implications of using these systems. While AI-based planning has the potential to improve decision-making and increase efficiency, it can also create ethical concerns related to bias, transparency, privacy, and accountability. In this chapter, we will explore some of the ethical considerations related to AI-based planning in business management and some best practices for addressing these concerns.[19]

One of the most significant ethical considerations related to AI-based planning is bias and discrimination. AI-based planning systems rely on large amounts of data to make decisions, and if the data used to train these systems is biased or if the algorithms themselves have inherent biases, the AI-based planning system may perpetuate existing biases and discrimination. For example, if an AI-based planning system is trained on historical data that reflects existing gender or racial biases, it may continue to make decisions that perpetuate these biases, even if they are not intentional.

To minimize bias and discrimination in AI-based planning systems, it is important to carefully consider the data used to train the system and to evaluate the algorithms used to make decisions. It may also be necessary to conduct regular audits of the AI-based planning system to identify and mitigate any bias that is discovered.

Transparency and explainability are also important ethical considerations related to AI-based planning. AI-based planning systems can be difficult to understand and explain, which can lead to mistrust and resistance. If stakeholders cannot understand how the AI-based planning system works and how it arrived at its recommendations, they may be less likely to trust and use the system.

To address these concerns, it is important to develop transparent and explainable AI algorithms. This can involve providing detailed documentation of the algorithms and the data used to train the system, as well as developing user-friendly interfaces that make it easy for stakeholders to understand the recommendations made by the AI-based planning system.[20]

Another ethical consideration related to AI-based planning is data privacy and security. AI-based planning systems rely on large amounts of data to make decisions, and if this data is not properly secured or if privacy regulations are not followed, it can lead to serious consequences for individuals and organizations. For example, if an AI-based planning system is used to make decisions about employee promotions, and this system is hacked, it may result in the exposure of sensitive employee data.

To address these concerns, it is important to ensure that data privacy and security measures are in place. This can involve using encryption to protect sensitive data, implementing access controls to limit who can access the data, and following privacy regulations such as GDPR and CCPA.

Accountability and responsibility are important ethical considerations related to AI-based planning. AI-based planning systems may make decisions that have significant impacts on business operations and outcomes, and it is important to establish clear lines of accountability and responsibility for the decisions made by the AI-based planning system. For example, if an AI-based planning system recommends that a particular product line be discontinued, it is important to identify who is responsible for making this decision and to ensure that this decision is properly communicated to stakeholders.

To address these concerns, it is important to establish clear lines of accountability and responsibility for the decisions made by the AI-based planning system. This can involve identifying who is responsible for making decisions based on the recommendations of the AI-based planning system and ensuring that these decision-makers are properly trained to understand the recommendations and the potential impacts of their decisions.

AI-based planning has the potential to revolutionize business management by improving decision-making and increasing efficiency. However, it is important to carefully consider the ethical implications of using these systems. By addressing concerns related to bias, transparency, privacy, and accountability, businesses can ensure that their AI-based planning systems are effective, fair, and trustworthy.[21]

10.8   FUTURE TRENDS AND DEVELOPMENTS IN AI-BASED PLANNING FOR BUSINESS MANAGEMENT

As AI-based planning becomes increasingly popular in the business world, it is important to consider the future trends and developments in this field. In this chapter, we will discuss some of the key areas where we can expect to see advancements and growth in the coming years.

One area where we can expect to see growth is in the use of machine learning algorithms in AI-based planning. Machine learning algorithms allow machines to learn from data and improve their performance over time, without being explicitly programmed. This technology is already being used in various areas of business management, such as marketing, supply chain management, and risk analysis, and we can expect to see even more applications in the future.[22]

Another area where we can expect to see growth is in the integration of AI-based planning with other technologies such as the Internet of Things (IoT). The IoT is a network of interconnected devices that can exchange data and perform tasks automatically. When combined with AI-based planning, the IoT can be used to gather data from a wide range of sources and use that data to optimize and improve business processes.

We can also expect to see advancements in the use of natural language processing (NLP) in AI-based planning. NLP is a subfield of AI that focuses on the interactions between computers and human language. By using NLP, machines can understand and respond to human language, making it easier for businesses to communicate with customers and stakeholders. In the context of planning, NLP can be used to analyze text-based data, such as customer feedback, reviews, and social media posts, providing valuable insights that can be used to improve business strategies.

The use of augmented reality (AR) and virtual reality (VR) technologies in AI-based planning is also expected to increase in the coming years. AR and VR allow users to interact with digital objects in the real world, providing a more immersive and engaging experience. In the context of planning, these technologies can be used to simulate different scenarios and test out different strategies in a safe and controlled environment.[23]

In addition to these advancements in technology, we can also expect to see a greater emphasis on collaboration and co-creation in AI-based planning. With the rise of digital platforms and social media, businesses can now collaborate and co-create with customers and other stakeholders to generate new ideas and improve existing products and services. This approach can help businesses to be more agile and responsive to changing market conditions, which is essential in today's fast-paced business environment.

Overall, the future of AI-based planning in business management looks promising. As technology continues to evolve and new applications are developed, we can expect to see even more innovative and effective uses of AI-based planning in the years to come. By staying up-to-date with the latest trends and developments, businesses can ensure that they are well positioned to take advantage of these new opportunities and stay ahead of the competition.

10.9   IMPLEMENTATION STRATEGIES FOR AI-BASED PLANNING IN BUSINESS MANAGEMENT

AI-based planning can revolutionize the way organizations plan and manage their operations. However, implementing such planning systems is not a straightforward process. The implementation requires a strategic approach, as there are several factors that organizations need to consider to ensure that the implementation is successful. In this chapter, we discuss some key implementation strategies for AI-based planning in business management.

1. Define clear objectives: The first step in implementing AI-based planning is to define clear objectives. Organizations should be clear on the business problem that they want to solve and the outcomes that they expect from the AI-based planning system. This clarity will ensure that the implementation team can focus on building the AI-based planning system that meets the organization's specific requirements.
2. Ensure data availability and quality: AI-based planning systems require large volumes of high-quality data to train the algorithms. Therefore, organizations need to ensure that data is available and of high quality. Data must be in a structured format to enable easy integration into the AI-based planning system. Data privacy and security concerns must also be addressed during the implementation.
3. Develop appropriate AI models: The development of AI models is a critical step in the implementation of AI-based planning systems. Organizations need to develop and select appropriate AI models that meet their specific requirements. There are various types of AI models, such as supervised, unsupervised, and reinforcement learning. The selection of the appropriate AI model depends on the nature of the data, the business problem, and the organization's objectives.
4. Define the planning process: The implementation team must define the planning process that the AI-based planning system will follow. The process must be structured and standardized to ensure consistency and accuracy. The planning process must be customized to fit the organization's specific requirements.
5. Train the implementation team: The implementation team must be trained on the AI-based planning system. The team must have the necessary skills to operate and maintain the system. This training will ensure that the system is implemented effectively and that it meets the organization's objectives.
6. Ensure continuous improvement: AI-based planning systems must be continuously improved to ensure that they remain relevant and effective. Organizations must continually monitor the system's performance and make improvements as necessary. This monitoring will ensure that the system meets the organization's objectives and delivers the expected outcomes.
7. Manage change: Implementing AI-based planning systems can be a significant change for an organization. Therefore, organizations must manage the change effectively. The implementation team must ensure that there is buy-in from all stakeholders, and the change is communicated effectively.

Implementing AI-based planning in business management requires a strategic approach. Organizations must be clear on their objectives, ensure data availability and quality, develop appropriate AI models, define the planning process, train the implementation team, ensure continuous improvement, and manage change effectively. By following these implementation strategies, organizations can effectively implement AI-based planning and gain a competitive advantage in their respective industries.[24]

10.10 CONCLUSION

In conclusion, AI-based planning is a powerful tool that can greatly enhance the efficiency and effectiveness of business management. Through the use of machine learning and data analysis, AI-based planning systems are capable of providing accurate and timely insights that can help businesses to make informed decisions and respond to changing circumstances more quickly.

However, as with any new technology, there are also challenges and ethical considerations to take into account when implementing AI-based planning systems. These include issues, such as data privacy, algorithmic bias, and the potential impact on jobs and human decision-making.

To ensure that AI-based planning is implemented in a responsible and effective manner, it is important to follow best practices for design and development, such as incorporating human oversight and transparency in decision-making processes. It is also important to consider the ethical implications of using AI in business management and to develop appropriate policies and guidelines to mitigate potential risks.

In terms of implementation strategies, there are several steps that businesses can take to successfully adopt and integrate AI-based planning into their operations. These include developing a clear understanding of business objectives and identifying specific use cases for AI-based planning, selecting appropriate data sources and tools, and ensuring that the necessary technical infrastructure and skills are in place.

Overall, AI-based planning has the potential to transform the way that businesses operate, providing significant benefits in terms of efficiency, accuracy, and decision-making. However, it is important to approach this technology with a critical and responsible mindset, taking into account the challenges and ethical considerations involved, and working towards the development of effective and sustainable AI-based planning systems.

REFERENCES

1. Brynjolfsson, E., & McAfee, A. (2014). The Second Machine Age: Work, Progress, and Prosperity in a Time of Brilliant Technologies. W.W. Norton & Company, 500 5th Ave, New York City.
2. Davenport, T. H., & Ronanki, R. (2018). Artificial intelligence for the real world. Harvard Business Review, 96(1), 108–116.
3. Fjeldstad, O. D., Snow, C. C., Miles, R. E., & Lettl, C. (2012). The architecture of collaboration. Strategic Management Journal, 33(6), 734–750.
4. Gartner. (2021). Gartner Top 10 Strategic Technology Trends for 2021.

5. Kshetri, N. (2018). Blockchain's roles in meeting key supply chain management objectives. International Journal of Information Management, 39, 80–89.
6. McAfee, A., & Brynjolfsson, E. (2017). Machine, Platform, Crowd: Harnessing Our Digital Future. WW Norton & Company, 500 5th Ave, New York City.
7. Melville, N. P., Kraemer, K. L., & Gurbaxani, V. (2004). Information technology and organizational performance: An integrative model of IT business value. MIS Quarterly, 28(2), 283–322.
8. Mithas, S., Ramasubbu, N., & Sambamurthy, V. (2011). How information management capability influences firm performance. MIS Quarterly, 35(1), 237–256.
9. Tushman, M. L., & O'Reilly, C. A. III (2002). Winning through Innovation: A Practical Guide to Leading Organizational Change and Renewal. Harvard Business Press, Boston, Massachusetts.
10. Wang, C., & Hu, Q. (2012). The impact of supply chain management practices on competitive advantage and organizational performance. Omega, 40(2), 131–143.
11. Gartner. (2021). 5 Best Practices for Planning With AI.
12. KPMG. (2019). The Future of Enterprise AI: How AI Can Help Organizations Grow and Scale.
13. McKinsey & Company. (2021). Artificial Intelligence: The Next Frontier in Business.
14. MIT Sloan Management Review. (2020). Making AI Work in Organizations.
15. PwC. (2019). 5 Best Practices for Implementing AI in Your Business.
16. IBM. (2021). AI in Planning and Decision-Making: 5 Best Practices.
17. McKinsey & Company. (2020). Five Building Blocks for Successful AI Strategies.
18. Goodfellow, I., Bengio, Y., & Courville, A. (2016). Deep Learning (Vol. 1). MIT Press, Cambridge, Massachusetts.
19. LeCun, Y., Bengio, Y., & Hinton, G. (2015). Deep Learning. Nature, 521(7553), 436–444.
20. Jordan, M. I., & Mitchell, T. M. (2015). Machine Learning: Trends, Perspectives, and Prospects. Science, 349(6245), 255–260.
21. Li, X., Liang, Y., & Li, H. (2019). Big Data-Driven Supply Chain Management: A Comprehensive Review and Future Directions. Annals of Operations Research, 283(1-2), 877–903.
22. Wang, C., & Liu, J. (2019). Supply chain finance for sustainable development of the logistics industry in China. Sustainability, 11(17), 4611.
23. Shen, L., & Zhang, J. (2019). Blockchain-based supply chain finance: A systematic review of literature, frameworks, and future research directions. International Journal of Information Management, 49, 366–382.
24. Katal, A., & Singh, N. (2022). Artificial Neural Network: Models, Applications, and Challenges. In: Tomar, R., Hina, M.D., Zitouni, R., Ramdane-Cherif, A. (eds) Innovative Trends in Computational Intelligence. EAI/Springer Innovations in Communication and Computing. Springer, Cham. https://doi.org/10.1007/978-3-030-78284-9_11

11 AI-Based Business Model Innovation in New Technologies

Niharika Singh[1], Charu Gupta[1], Prerana Chaha[1], and Thipendra P. Singh[2]
[1]University of Petroleum and Energy Studies, Dehradun, India
[2]Bennett University, Greater Noida, India

11.1 INTRODUCTION

Business models are being revolutionized by new technologies that disrupt industries around the world. Among the most important technological developments, artificial intelligence (AI) represents "interactive systems that perform certain tasks without any programming." Innovations in AI lead to disruptions in industries and businesses. Airbnb, Uber, Amazon, Netflix, Twitter, Apple, and many more businesses have used AI to reinvent their business models and strengthen their competitive advantages [27]. To be competitive and viable, top executives must adopt an inventive, entrepreneurial attitude and use AI to spread this mindset throughout their firms. The objective of AI in business is to identify cutting-edge research in the fields of AI and machine learning, as well as related areas like cryptography, cryptocurrency, and innovation, to develop a solution that has the greatest impact on the company's clients and industries (see Figure 11.1) [19, 31].

The core of the AI economy is controlled by businesses, and they steer innovation along a new axis while luring investors with their perfectly timed breakthroughs that promise a new frontier of efficiency. Online data analytics are integrated into business processes using a design pattern and framework known as continuous intelligence (CI), which is discussed more in the following section. The varied aspects of business model innovation would be much more intensely affected by the projected effects of AI technology [4]. To build a comprehensive understanding of how businesses, particularly those using AI technology, create value and carry out the necessary tasks, we aim to examine the likely effects of AI technology on business model innovation [1]. We seek to examine the likely effects of AI technology on the innovation of business models to develop a comprehensive understanding of how companies, particularly those adopting AI technology, gain a competitive advantage and carry out the required activities.

DOI: 10.1201/9781032614083-11

Data And Knowledge	**Learning From Experience**	**Reasoning and Planning**
Massive Data Understanding, Graphs Learning, Synthetic data, Knowledge representation	Reinforcement Learning, Learning from Data, Learning from Feedback	Domain Representation, Optimization, Reasoning under Uncertainity and Temporal constraint

Safe Human AI Interaction	**Multi Agent Systems**	**Secured and Private AI**
Agent Symbiosis, Ethics and Fairness, Explainability,Trusted AI	Multi Agent Simulation, Negotiation, Game And Behavior, Theory Mechanism Design	Privacy, Cryptography, Secure Mutl-Party Computation, Federated learning

Machine Vision and Language
Perception Image Understanding, Language Technologies

FIGURE 11.1   Artificial intelligence nucleus in the business domain (Samsung White Paper, 2020) [19].

11.2   BACKGROUND

11.2.1   WHAT IS AI?

The foundation of AI was, in fact, a computer capable of thinking like a human. John McCarthy established a research team and came up with the term "artificial intelligence" in 1956. The team embarked on the belief that every element of learning and every other trait of intelligence could be so perfectly characterized and emulated by a computer. Finding out how to program machines to use language, create abstractions and concepts, and solve challenging issues are examples of applications. While the original AI research program centered on the development of generalized AI (i.e., codes that could replicate human intelligence in the fullest possible way), the existing AI research wave is focused on narrow AI, i.e., AI that replicates some important aspects of human intelligence like the ability to recognize patterns and

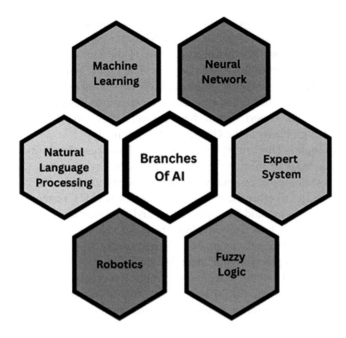

FIGURE 11.2 Six fundamental branches of AI.

linguistic representations [1]. Today's increased computer capacity has made it possible to develop several AI applications in a variety of industries. Machine learning is the key technology driving these applications of AI, with the majority of these applications focusing on automating repetitive tasks, image, and speech recognition, or translating languages. Numerous branches of AI are crucial to developing the breakthroughs required to automate and build resilient business models [1]. Figure 11.2 mentions these branches.

A brief description of all these branches is given as follows:

- **Machine learning**—Machine learning is a subfield of AI and computer science that focuses on using data and algorithms to mimic human learning processes and progressively increase accuracy [24].
- **Neural network**—The neural network is a subfield of AI that uses neurology and cognitive science to automate tasks (a part of biology that concerns the nerve and nervous system of the human brain) [14]. The purpose of a neural network is to encode brain neurons into a system or a machine, simulating the infinitely large number of neurons that make up the human brain [28]. A neural network is a collection of algorithms that mimic the workings of the human brain to find the fundamental connections among groups of data [8].
- **Expert system**—The first successful AI software model took into account expert systems. They were created for the first time in the 1970s, and their use then increased dramatically in the 1980s [14]. An expert system is a

computer program that simulates the decision-making abilities of a human expert and falls under the category of AI technology. It does this by applying reasoning and insight rules in terms of the user queries and drawing understanding from its knowledge base. The expert's information that has been gained in a knowledge base is wholly dependent on the efficacy of the expert system. The system increases in effectiveness as more data is gathered in it. The expert system, for instance, offers corrections for spelling and other problems in the Google Search Engine [8].

- **Fuzzy logic**—Their fuzzy logic provides appropriate flexibility for thinking that leads to mistakes and ambiguities of any condition [28]. In the actual world, we occasionally encounter a scenario where it is challenging to determine whether the condition is valid or not [17]. Fuzzy logic, to put it simply, is a method for representing and changing ambiguous information by gauging how likely the hypothesis is to be true [22]. Fuzzy logic is indeed utilized to make judgments about ideas that are inherently uncertain. Fuzzy logic is practical and adaptable for implementing machine learning techniques and helping to logically imitate human reasoning [15, 17].
- **Robotics**—This area of AI has become highly hot. Robotics design and construction is a fascinating area of research and development. Mechanical engineering, electrical engineering, computer science, and many other disciplines are all merged within the interdisciplinary field of robotics [15]. Robotics controls the creation, manufacture, operation, and application of robots. It deals with the management, intelligent outputs, and information transformation of computer systems [22].
- **Natural language processing (NLP)**—NLP is the area of computer science and AI that enables natural language interaction between computers and people [30]. It is a method for processing human languages computationally. It imitates human natural language to help computers read and comprehend data.

11.2.1.1   Types of AI Technology Development Approaches: Symbolic vs. Neural

Deep learning, also known as "deep neural networks," has recently been a dominant force in AI development methods thanks to its exceptional performance in the areas of voice and picture recognition, natural language processing, and prediction procedures. Deep neural networks, however, are not appropriate for all AI-related problems [4].

11.2.1.1.1   Symbolic AI

With symbolic AI, AI is trained like how the human brain learns. It develops internal symbolic representations of its reality as it learns to comprehend it.

In the cognitive and reasoning processes of humans, symbols are extremely important. To interact with ideas, we acquire both concrete and abstract knowledge. It is possible to formulate these laws in a manner that incorporates common knowledge.

The early AI pioneers believed that any aspect of learning or intelligence could be clearly characterized so that a machine could replicate it. As a result, symbolic AI gained prominence. To define and control symbols, scientists created tools.

These efforts led to the development of numerous computer science concepts and technologies. The foundation of symbolic AI programs is the development of declarative structures and behavior rules.

Figure 11.3 displays the Knowledge Graph search result for the query "Paris." Google's Knowledge Graph serves as an excellent example of a symbolic AI system that combines knowledge and reasoning techniques to improve search results. Keep in mind that there are 570 million entities and about 18 billion facts in the knowledge graph as of right now. Google Search Engine, Google Assistant, and Google Home voice questions are answered using data from the Knowledge Graph Graph and reasoning technologies [4].

The ideal applications of symbolic AI are for static issues; however, there are certain difficulties. Because symbolic AI systems rely on accumulating and comprehending intricate and implicit skills and knowledge, they are labor-intensive, difficult, and expensive to design. Additionally, because it is challenging to effectively

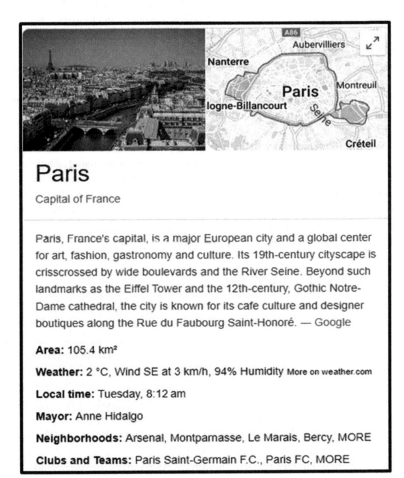

FIGURE 11.3 Google's Knowledge Graph produced the search result [4].

describe recognition knowledge, symbolic AI is not ideal for scenarios requiring recognition.

11.2.1.1.2 Neural AI

Machine learning has made a significant contribution to the fast rise of AI [32]. Strictly speaking, machine learning methods rely on patterns created from practice or sample data to increase learning performance on a particular job. To handle more complicated issues and learn in a way akin to neurons in the human brain, neural AI relies on an artificial neural network (ANN) or an aggregation of machine learning algorithms that operate in unison. It makes it possible for computers to gain knowledge implicitly from data [4].

In terms of technical classification, there are three categories for machine learning approaches: (1) supervised learning, which involves learning from correct responses (labeled data); (2) unsupervised learning, which is defined as discovering knowledge or information when presented with some raw data (unlabeled data); and (3) reinforcement learning, which describes how agents in an environment behave to maximize their rewards [20].

Deep neural networks have recently attracted a lot of interest and have found use in both industry and academia [4]. It is built on deeper layers of the ANN [32] as a component of machine learning, which enables it to learn from unprocessed data and handle more challenging problems. It has demonstrated exceptional performance in the areas of fraud detection, speech and image recognition, providing suggestions, and NLP [1].

As a result, top technology firms like Google and Facebook have shown groundbreaking advancements in speech and image recognition using deep learning. Machine learning algorithms are used by Netflix, Spotify, and Amazon to create customized suggestions. With a large amount of labeled data, neural AI has had success solving well-defined issues like vision and recognition. Given that it lacks human-like reasoning or thinking and requires a large amount of labeled data, neural AI may be critiqued for its current state of development.

11.2.2 DEFINING BUSINESS MODELS

The strategy a business uses to turn a profit is referred to as its business model. It lists any anticipated costs as well as the goods or services the company intends to sell, as well as its chosen target clientele. Both new and established businesses need strong business models. They aid young, developing businesses in luring capital, hiring talent, and inspiring management and staff [7].

A company's primary method of conducting business profitably is called its business model. Models typically include details, such as the goods or services the company intends to sell, its target markets, and any projected costs [7].

Numerous different business models exist, including those used by retailers, producers, fee-for-service businesses, and freemium service providers. Pricing and costs are a business model's two driving forces. As an investor, you should take into account whether the product being offered meets a genuine need in the market when assessing a business model.

A business model is a comprehensive strategy for running a company profitably in a particular industry. The value proposition is a key part of the business model. This is an explanation of the products or services a business provides and the reasons why customers or clients would find them appealing. Ideally, this description will set the product or service apart from those of its rivals [13].

A business model outlines how your organization expects to generate revenue. A business model typically explains four things [21]:

- What kind of goods or services a business will offer?
- The strategy it plans to use to market that good or service.
- What kinds of costs the business will incur?
- How the business anticipates making money?

11.2.3 ELEMENTS OF BUSINESS MODELS

- **Value proposition**

  It is an explanation of how your product or service satisfies customer needs. It should make it crystal clear why a customer would choose your business. The value proposition needs to be personalized and tailored to include the elimination of product searches, the elimination of price discovery costs, and the management of product delivery.

- **Revenue model**

  This section focuses on how you intend to profit from your company through sales and a strong return on investment. It might consist of affiliate revenue, sales revenue, transaction fees, subscription revenue, and advertising revenue. Naturally, the kind of income you generate depends on your particular business, but whatever your income strategy, it's critical to make it clear to both you and potential investors [2].

- **Market opportunity**

  The market space for your business should be mapped out, along with your target audience's size in total. It is justified to build a business around your services or goods if there is high demand among a sizable demographic. Additionally, the market opportunity makes it possible for you and others to comprehend the potential financial opportunities, and it's crucial to conduct enough research to have accurate financial projections [2].

- **Competitive environment**

  If you've established that you have a sizable target market, you should also make sure that there isn't a glut of your goods or services on the market. You might want to identify your rivals, for instance. Who in your market niche provides a comparable good or service? Then learn more about them, including their size. Learn about their market shares, the services they offer, and the prices they charge for the goods they sell.

- **Competitive advantage**

  You can work to set yourself apart from your competition by being aware of who they are, what they have to offer, and how much they charge. Determine your unique selling proposition (USP) first to persuade customers to choose your business. It might be offering a comparable good or service at a lower cost or having a distinctive corporate culture that appeals to customers [2].

- **Market strategy**

  Think of your target audience and how you can reach them with the most impact. Utilizing social media influencers, running a campaign on the social media network that best suits your company, and building a brand are all options [2].

- **Organization development**

  Organizing your business's operations is essential for preventing chaos and maintaining efficiency. Having organizational structures in place will help ensure that important work gets done. Additionally, you should have a process that outlines job duties at work so that employees can easily understand their responsibilities and work as efficiently as possible. Finally, as orders and support are delivered as quickly as possible, organizational development will have a direct impact on how satisfied your customers are [2].

- **Management team**

  This feature of the business model will outline the qualifications and experiences a company leader ought to look for. Regardless of whether your management team is present or not, you should think about what you need from them. When necessary, a strong team can alter the business model and the operation. A management team gains credibility with investors when they can pivot [2].

11.3   HOW TO CHOOSE A BUSINESS MODEL

The only recommendation made by the value migration framework is that businesses should focus on business model innovation to stay competitive. Of course, the circumstances under which business model innovation occurs are still unknown [1]. Business model change is an exploratory process in which components of the current business model are altered gradually [1]. From the perspective of established businesses, altering an existing business model can be challenging, and the choices that firms have tend to be constrained by the current features of the business model. As a result, as businesses adopt new business models, they may need to change the norms, behaviors, and organizational structures that govern value creation, delivery, and capture [1].

In this context, the phrase "institutional logic" has gained a lot of traction. The previous research on institutional logic is integrated by Thornton and Ocasio.

The theory states that investigation and experimentation are necessary to make changes to the current business model.

Business model innovation is fundamentally a learning process that takes the changing environment into account [1]. Even though testing out new business models is a common practice, it is crucial in the case of AI, a new field with many unanswered questions. Indeed, by assisting managers in choosing the best business model given the capabilities of the technology and the environmental constraints, experimentation helps businesses learn how the new technology functions and manages risks. To achieve this, the business might need to test the AI tool's utility in generating and seizing value. Importantly, this kind of testing might enable companies to learn about the technical properties of the technology and how employees, customers, and suppliers will react to a specific business model in which AI plays a significant role. Experimentation should take a long-term perspective and take into account the need to combine and test multiple initiatives for them to work together to produce value. For instance, a business may need to set up several sales and marketing initiatives and determine which ones can produce results quickly to enable AI tools to segment customers effectively [1].

11.4 WHAT IS BUSINESS INTELLIGENCE?

The process of taking large amounts of data, analyzing that data, and presenting a high-level set of reports that condense the essence of that data into the basis of business actions, enabling management to make fundamental daily business decisions [18]. Business intelligence (BI) combines business analytics with data mining, data visualization, data tools, infrastructure, and best practices to support organizations in making more data-driven decisions. In real life, you can tell if you have modern BI when you have a complete picture of the data in your company and use it to drive change, get rid of inefficiencies, and react quickly to supply or market changes [16].

Modern BI solutions place a high priority on governed data on reliable platforms, empowered business users, and speed to insight [5]. It's important to remember that this is a very contemporary definition of BI, and the term has a troubled past as a catchphrase. Traditional BI, complete with capital letters, first appeared as a method of information sharing between organizations in the 1960s. In 1989, the phrase "business intelligence" was introduced along with computer decision-making models. These programs continued to evolve, transforming data into insights before becoming a specific service solution from BI teams with IT-dependent support [11].

11.5 WHAT IS THE IMPACT OF AI ON BUSINESSES?

Many businesses want to use AI technology to boost productivity, reduce operating expenses, boost customer satisfaction, and increase revenue. Businesses can greatly benefit from using AI. However, great advantages also present great challenges.

Renew your products and business operations by using intelligent AI technologies like machine learning and natural language processing. One of the best ways to enhance your current business model is through this. AI has a big impact on how businesses operate. By implementing and integrating AI technology, you can automate, improve, and conserve time- and money-consuming traditional processes.

Your operational effectiveness and productivity standards will also increase thanks to AI. Making quicker and more logical business decisions is possible with the right AI business model. Additionally, using AI can improve customer insights, reduce human error, and personalize user experiences.

AI will undoubtedly have an impact on your company in the future. Although the negative impact is not immediately apparent, it could have a significant impact on how your company runs. It necessitates an open mind and a desire to seize new opportunities.

In the business world, AI is fundamentally altering many industries. AI opens up entirely new possibilities with its capacity to recognize patterns and spot anomalies in massive amounts of digital data in business processes. Once trained, it can easily handle a variety of daily tasks [9].

The advent of AI frees staff members from mundane, low-complexity tasks so they can concentrate on solving more difficult technical issues or enhancing customer service [9].

11.5.1 AI AS A GENERAL-PURPOSE TECHNOLOGY

The argument that AI is an example of a general-purpose technology is where the literature that studies AI's impact on businesses and economic outcomes more generally (or GPT) starts. Bresnahan and Trajtenberg, who first described GPT as a pervasive technology that attracted complementary innovations and was open to further advancements, are credited with the idea. They gave numerous instances of GPTs, like the steam engine, electricity, and computers, which had a significant economic impact. Most industries experience an increase in business productivity due to GPTs, and by fostering additional complementary innovations or enabling companies to take advantage of economies of scale, these complementary innovations further the positive impact of GPTs on productivity [1].

The description of AI provided by Bresnahan and Trajtenberg appears to be accurate. Machine learning in general, according to Agrawal, Gans, and Goldfarb, is particularly well suited for automating tasks where prediction matters, and it can be applied to the majority of tasks currently carried out by humans. Additionally, AI systems that incorporate machine learning can develop over time. It's interesting to note that an algorithm, rather than a software engineer, can lead the process of improvement. For instance, machine learning algorithms can, even without supervision, determine which functions are best for connecting inputs and outputs. Additionally, machines can exchange knowledge and learn from one another. Thanks to the availability of cloud computing, once a machine develops a skill in one location, it can be replicated across digital networks. And finally, innovations that are complementary to machine learning systems can be sparked. Machine learning can aid engineers in creating a wider range of new applications that can improve the capabilities of current machine learning algorithms [1].

11.5.2 THE EFFECT OF AI ON COMPANIES AND OVERALL ECONOMIC RESULTS

The majority of economic research on AI has concentrated on the potential effects of robotics on existing jobs and, consequently, on economic growth. The key papers in this area are those by Zeira, Acemoglu, Autor, and Restrepo, which discuss the effects of automation on tasks, productivity, and work, and those by Aghion et al., which concentrate on the relationship between economic growth and automation. The incentives for introducing AI are related to cost savings, and automation is assumed to be exogenous.

11.5.3 THE LABOR MARKET AND AUTOMATION

According to Acemoglu and Restrepo's model, automation will replace workers in certain tasks. It's interesting to note that in this model, high-skill tasks are also replaced with routine ones. Because of this, employment in equilibrium will be significantly lower, all else being equal, even though labor productivity is rising [1]. In the model, there are a few CS factors at play: as the economy grows and productivity among the current workforce rises, so does demand for jobs whose duties cannot be automated. Additionally, as automation rises, capital investment rises as well, creating a demand for labor in fields like robotics and engineering. Last but not least, automation will lead to the creation of new jobs that will support robots and their upkeep (for instance). Importantly, it is important to keep in mind that the adjustment will be expensive because workers will need to look for new jobs and undergo retraining, even if there are factors that could slow down the displacement effect of AI on labor. The adoption of AI at the firm level as well as employee decisions about education and training will determine the speed of adjustment, which is endogenous.

11.5.4　WHAT EFFECT DOES AUTOMATION HAVE ON ECONOMIC EXPANSION?

The positive impact of automation on growth may be limited by the fact that industries with relatively slow productivity growth may see increases in their size, according to research on the subject by Aghion et al. This phenomenon has been compared to Baumol's "cost disease," which describes how industries with slow productivity growth may expand in size even though they do not grow as quickly as other industries with fast productivity growth. Sectors with slow productivity growth slowdown economic growth when Baumol's observation is used in models where automation causes fast productivity growth. Consequently, the labor share is still significant even if the extent of automation is pervasive. There are no models that concentrate on other varieties of AI and how they affect business operations. In reality, the analysis of automation and its effects on productivity growth and, through those channels, on economic growth, is what drives the majority of our understanding of the impact of AI on economic outcomes [1].

Companies may use AI to enhance the customer experience or provide services that are more in line with what customers want. Although the effects of these alternative uses of AI on productivity and, ultimately, economic growth are not fully understood, doing so will require an understanding of how AI shapes business models and how existing players are still able to generate value through AI. However, studying business models makes sense in economic models where disruption from innovation forces incumbents to come up with new survival strategies. The mechanisms used by incumbents to create value may no longer be appropriate as new entrants adopt fundamentally different business models that depend on the creative uses of AI. There are numerous instances where, due to AI, well-known newcomers such as Uber and Airbnb operate differently than market leaders and eventually take over their respective industry sectors. How should incumbents respond? [1]

Business model innovation is the main tool incumbents can use to counteract the negative effects of value migration, according to several authors. Our main argument here is that business model innovation is not just about introducing new products or new procedures in the context of AI-driven value migration. However, it necessitates a thorough rethinking of the value creation and value capture mechanisms that link the various parts of the existing business model. To help businesses (and organizations in general) rebuild their business logic, this section's goal is to identify various patterns of business model innovation. Before introducing the idea of industry-level value migration, we will first define the concept of the business model and its elements. Finally, we'll present an analysis framework for business model innovation and a taxonomy that compiles the various business model innovation subtypes that we can see in practice [1].

11.6   BUSINESS MODELS INNOVATION AND AI

Only recently has the introduction of new technologies been investigated as a factor driving business model innovation, and very few papers have so far examined the role of technology. Technology and business model innovation classification efforts have developed along two axes. On the one hand, some researchers contend that incorporating technology into a company and improving performance are mutually beneficial. However, some authors believe that the idea of a business model can exist independently of technology.

This allows us to pinpoint four ways in which AI can alter various aspects of business models (Figure 11.4). We start with a small change before making the business model drastically different, which calls for changing every component of the business model [1]. Importantly, these four models can be used by businesses and are not mutually exclusive.

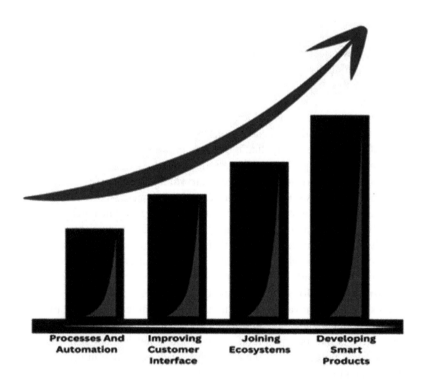

FIGURE 11.4   Four AI-driven models.

Additionally, business model innovation will be examined in the context of established businesses that, in response to the advent of AI, prefer to rearrange the components that make up their business model. In other words, we are not concerned with the newcomers' business plans. In general, we also want to distinguish between incremental business model innovation and radical business model innovation [1].

11.6.1 AUTOMATION AND PROCESSES

In this situation, businesses primarily use AI to enhance internal operations without altering the overall business architecture. The company's main objective is to become more efficient, and it achieves this by automating processes. For instance, the use of bots can streamline relationships with suppliers. In general, this kind of business model innovation places a focus on automating current processes to take advantage of the company's current expertise and resources. The best example is in the automotive sector, where companies like Jaguar Land Rover and BMW have been using robots on their assembly lines for some time [3].

In this instance, improved machine connectivity, a more productive workforce, and open management all contribute to value creation. The key to value capture and value delivery to customers is the effective use of internal resources [3]. Finally, value capture is fueled by resource and process efficiency improvements [1].

11.6.2 ENHANCING CUSTOMER INTERACTION

The use of AI helps businesses better comprehend their clients' needs. The main technologies here are virtual reality and bots, which follow the initial investment in automation in that they enable them to profit from the growing efficiency of their internal processes. Segmentation (based on data analysis) and the ensuing growth of long-term relationships with customers facilitate the delivery of value [1]. Additionally, digital distribution methods can boost consumer sales.

The extensive use of data gathered by bots allows for the creation of new services as consumer needs are quickly determined. Finally, new services create fresh revenue streams that let companies profit. Examples include supermarkets and major retailers that segment customers and personalize offers based on their traits and preferences using data obtained from loyalty cards. Other instances include the use of AI by KFC and Spotify to enhance their customer relationships [3].

11.6.3 ADHERING TO ECOSYSTEMS

AI makes it easier to build virtual marketplaces that let companies develop new services and build new value networks. In these instances, AI enables the integration of information and assets from numerous organizations and companies into networks that enable the delivery of new services or products to customers or other businesses [3].

Utilizing real-time data on production, sales, and the availability of new services, this business model creates value. Delivering the new services that are inextricably linked to the platform's presence ensures value delivery to all the network's

businesses. Last but not least, value capture is ensured by the revenue streams produced by the new services. A prime example of such an ecosystem is the virtual
marketplace that Amazon supports [3].

11.6.4 THE CREATION OF SMART PRODUCTS

AI enables them to create and market a variety of products and services, enabling
businesses to diversify or widen their market. The creation of AI-powered products,
which are a key mechanism for value creation, is the focus. Due to AI, it is significant
that customers participate in the process of creating value and that there is a direct
connection between the company and its clients. Smart products and innovative services that go along with them create value for delivery, whereas the value for capture
is created by new revenue streams connected to new products [3]. All smart home or
car products use AI and frequently engage with customers to provide services that
are catered to their needs [1].

11.7 THE BENEFITS OF BUSINESS INTELLIGENCE

11.7.1 FAST AND ACCURATE REPORTING

Employees can monitor KPIs using a variety of data sources, including financial,
operational, and sales data, using pre-built templates or custom reports. For businesses to take quick action, these reports are created in real-time using the most
pertinent data. The majority of reports include simple-to-read visuals like graphs,
tables, and charts. Some BI software reports are interactive, allowing users to experiment with various parameters or gain access to information more quickly [5].

11.7.2 VALUABLE BUSINESS INSIGHTS

Employees can monitor KPIs using a variety of data sources, including financial, operational, and sales data, using pre-built templates or custom reports. For
businesses to take quick action, these reports are created in real-time using the
most pertinent data. The majority of reports include simple-to-read visuals like
graphs, tables, and charts. Some BI software reports are interactive, allowing
users to experiment with various parameters or gain access to information more
quickly [5].

11.7.3 COMPETITIVE ANALYSIS

A competitive advantage in and of itself is the capacity to manage and manipulate
a large amount of data. Additionally, using BI software makes it simple to perform
budgeting, planning, and forecasting, which goes far beyond standard analysis and is
a very effective way to stay one step ahead of the competition. Businesses can also
monitor the sales and marketing results of their rivals to develop their product and
service differentiation strategies [6].

11.7.4   BETTER DATA QUALITY

Data is rarely perfect, and there are numerous ways for discrepancies and inaccuracies to surface, especially when using a poorly constructed "database" [29]. Businesses that take the time to gather, update, and produce high-quality data typically have greater success. Companies can combine various data sources using BI software to get a more comprehensive picture of their business's state [5].

11.7.5   INCREASED CUSTOMER SATISFACTION

Businesses can better understand customer patterns and behavior with the aid of BI software. The majority of businesses collect customer feedback in real-time, and this data can aid in both customer retention and acquisition. These tools may also assist businesses in identifying purchasing trends, which aids customer service representatives in anticipating needs and providing better service [6].

11.7.6   IDENTIFYING MARKET TRENDS

Businesses can gain a competitive edge, significantly impact long-term profitability, and gain a comprehensive understanding of what is going on by identifying new opportunities and developing a strategy with supporting data. By examining customer information and market conditions and identifying business issues, employees can use internal and external market data to identify new sales trends [12].

11.7.7   INCREASED OPERATIONAL EFFICIENCY

To improve a company's overall organization and free up managers and staff to concentrate on creating accurate and timely reports, BI tools combine multiple data sources. Employees can concentrate on their short- and long-term goals and assess the effects of their decisions when they have access to current and accurate information [6].

11.7.8   IMPROVED, ACCURATE DECISIONS

Companies must make decisions as quickly as possible because their rivals operate in a fast-paced environment. Inaccuracies and delays could cost businesses customers and revenue [23]. Organizations can take advantage of available data to optimize time to decision by providing information to the appropriate stakeholders at the appropriate time.

11.7.9   INCREASED REVENUE

Any business should aim to increase its revenue. The purpose of this website is to provide information about upcoming events and to provide a forum for people to share their experiences. Revenue is more likely to rise when businesses pay attention to their clients, keep an eye on their rivals, and enhance their processes [5].

11.7.10 LOWER MARGINS

For the majority of businesses, profit margins are another issue. Luckily, BI tools can identify inefficiencies and support margin expansion. Aggregated sales data gives businesses a better understanding of their customers and enables sales teams to create better spending plans [25].

11.8 DEVELOPING A BUSINESS MODEL BASED ON AI

Business model innovation is characterized as a significant shift in the company's operations and value generation, often resulting in an increase in firm performance. A business model represents an activity system or a collection of interconnected activities that cross firm boundaries [4]. Many industries, including technology/ media, consumer goods, financial services, health care, industrial, energy, the public sector, and others, have benefited from AI's promotion of business model innovation. More than 3,000 corporate executives were surveyed, and the results showed that 84 percent of them believed AI would help their organizations gain or maintain a competitive advantage, and 75 percent said AI would help them expand into new markets and initiatives. What factors should we take into account in this situation as we construct or reinvent our business model using AI?

By using lessons learned from his leadership of Google Brain and Baidu AI, Andrew Ng published an AI playbook to revolutionize businesses using AI. The five steps listed and the concerns we think need to be raised for each step are discussed below. The discussion in this section provides more context for how the actual cases in the preceding section exemplify the role of business model innovation [10].

The important components that make up an AI virtuous cycle that produces better products, more users, and more data are to implement pilot projects to gather momentum, build an internal AI team, offer widespread AI training, and build an AI strategy [4]. The issues and debates are summarized in Figure 11.5.

11.9 CONCLUSION

The current study makes two contributions to both academia and practice. Secondly, this study made an effort to explain how AI technology catalyzes new business model development. Additional research is required to connect developing technology to novel business models. Second, this study clarifies the auxiliary elements influencing business model innovation spurred by new technology. We share insights on these unforeseen variables in our case study and the following debate on the development of AI-based business model innovation [4]. Many of those elements, though, need to be properly listed and quantitatively evaluated for further research. Data analytics and AI advancements will continue to present benefits and pose challenges to delivery systems [26].

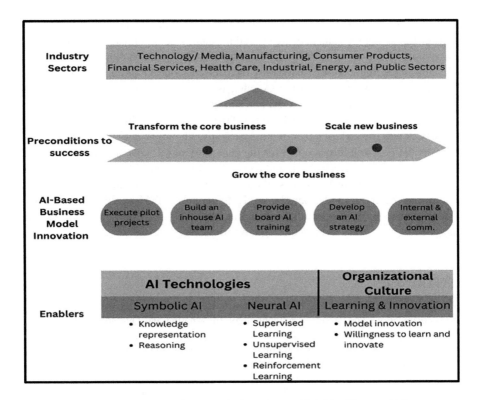

FIGURE 11.5 Developing a business model based on artificial intelligence (AI).

Successful leaders must develop fresh, creative strategies for utilizing these developments to alter their businesses and spur expansion. Many business executives will discover that these innovations drive them in ways they had never imagined [26]. Focusing on a company's core capabilities and business strategy is still essential, but it can be difficult for executives to remain open to and support innovations that change the business model of the organization [4].

"Make Your Smart Pivot to the New" is an article that Accenture recently published. They explain in it how "C-level executives recognize that clinging to their legacy businesses will jeopardize the future health of their organization." The authors go on to say that three prerequisites—transforming the core business, growing the core business, and scaling new businesses—pave the way for success. As organizations must concentrate most of their effort on the business producing the greatest profits, we think that for many businesses, reforming and expanding the core business will take precedence over developing a new business [4].

In addition, as the preceding part of establishing an AI-based business model mentioned, the organizational culture probably has a significant impact. According to the literature, organizational characteristics are crucial in determining how business model innovation happens. Contextual elements, including organizational design, organizational culture, and organizational values, are regularly brought up in discussions [4].

Major pivots call for a certain amount of freedom to take chances and expose a new lens or frame. Senior managers are crucial in shaping an organization's culture; thus, they must set an example of innovation and a commitment to constantly learn and develop. They might start by educating themselves about AI and how it can improve the company's systems and business model, as well as promoting and rewarding staff members who become experts in AI and start internal pilot projects [4].

Further research is necessary because of the limitations of this study. The primary drawback was the lack of cases in our case study. The idiosyncrasies of various sectors should be taken into account for the generality of our conclusions, even though we did a thorough investigation and close observation to disclose both general and unique components of the issues. Future research must also include examples of many new business model paradigms. In the context of AI-based business model innovation, many delivery models, including platforms, SaaS (software as a service), and PaaS (platform as a service), might be considered [4].

REFERENCES

1. Sena, V., & Nocker, M. (2021). AI and business models: The good, the bad and the ugly. Foundations and Trends® in Technology, Information and Operations Management, 14(4), 324–397. ISSN 1571-9545.
2. Couturier, L. (2022). 8 Key Elements Of A Business Model that You Should Understand. From startupmindset.com: https://startupmindset.com/8-key-elements-of-a-business-model-that-you-should-understand/
3. Tirakyan, V. (2021, August 25). A Checklist For Selecting The Right Business Model For Your Startup.
4. Jaehun, L., Taewon, S., Daniel, R., & Melissa, B. (2019). Emerging technology and business model innovation: The case of artificial intelligence. Journal of Open Innovation: Technology, Market, and Complexity, 5(3), 44. https://doi.org/10.3390/joitmc5030044
5. British University of Egypt. Business Intelligence: A Complete Overview March 2016. From tableau.com: https://www.tableau.com/learn/articles/business-intelligence
6. Mantissa College (2020, June). Here Are 10 Key Benefits of Business Intelligence Software. From mastersindatascience.org: https://www.mastersindatascience.org/resources/benefits-of-business-intelligence/
7. Carol, M. K. (2022, August 1). How Companies Make Money. From investopedia.com: https://www.investopedia.com/terms/b/businessmodel.asp#:~:text=The%20term%20business%20model%20refers,both%20new%20and%20established%20businesses
8. Tyagi, N. (2021, January 23). 6 Major Branches of Artificial Intelligence (AI). From analyticssteps.com: https://www.analyticssteps.com/blogs/6-major-branches-artificial-intelligence-ai
9. Khmara, A. (2022, March 18). The Impact of Artificial Intelligence (AI) on Business; From itchronicles.com: https://itchronicles.com/artificial-intelligence/the-impact-of-artificial-intelligence-ai-on-business/#:~:text=The%20impact%20of%20AI%20on%20your%20business%20is%20huge%20as,technologies%20to%20make%20business%20decisions
10. Ng, Y. (2018). AI Transformation Playbook. Available online: https://landing.ai/ai-transformation-playbook/ (accessed on 3 May 2019).
11. What is Business Intelligence? From ibm.com: https://www.ibm.com/topics/business-intelligence

12. The College of Westchester (2020, June). Here Are 10 Key Benefits of Business Intelligence Software. From mastersindatascience.org: https://www.mastersindatascience.org/resources/benefits-of-business-intelligence/
13. Kriss, R., & Murphy, R. (2022, July 15). Far Eastern University. What Is a Business Model? From nerdwallet.com: https://www.nerdwallet.com/article/small-business/what-is-a-business-model
14. Tyagi, N. (2021, January 23). Asia Pacific University College of Technology and Innovation (UCTI). 6 Major Branches of Artificial Intelligence (AI). From analyticssteps.com: https://www.analyticssteps.com/blogs/6-major-branches-artificial-intelligence-ai
15. Tyagi, N. (2021, January 23). Asia Pacific University College of Technology and Innovation (UCTI). 6 Major Branches of Artificial Intelligence (AI). From analyticssteps.com: https://www.analyticssteps.com/blogs/6-major-branches-artificial-intelligence-ai
16. University of Salford. Business Intelligence: A Complete Overview. From tableau.com: https://www.tableau.com/learn/articles/business-intelligence
17. Tyagi, N. (2021, January 23). 6 Major Branches of Artificial Intelligence (AI). From analyticssteps.com: https://www.analyticssteps.com/blogs/6-major-branches-artificial-intelligence-ai
18. Ferkoun, M. (2014, August 20). Cloud Computing and Business Intelligence. From ibm.com: https://www.ibm.com/blogs/cloud-computing/2014/08/20/cloud-computing-business-intelligence/
19. Mishra, S., & Tripathi, R. (2021, July). AI business model: An integrative business approach. Journal of Innovation and Entrepreneurship. From researchgate.net: https://www.researchgate.net/publication/352932586_AI_business_model_an_integrative_business_approach
20. Schalkoff, R. J. (1997). Artificial Neural Networks, vol 1. McGraw-Hill, New York, NY.
21. Kriss, R., & Murphy, R. (2022, July 15). What Is a Business Model? From nerdwallet.com: https://www.nerdwallet.com/article/small-business/what-is-a-business-model
22. Central Queensland University. 6 Major Branches of Artificial Intelligence (AI). From analyticssteps.com: https://www.analyticssteps.com/blogs/6-major-branches-artificial-intelligence-ai
23. University of Hertfordshire. Benefits of Business Intelligence Software. From mastersindatascience.org: https://www.mastersindatascience.org/resources/benefits-of-business-intelligence/
24. Jefferson, I. C., Ryndel, A., Jeffrey, S. S., & Princess Marie, B. M. (2021, December). Machine Learning Estimation for Course Enrollment Using Logistic Regression. Batangas State University.
25. Savannah State University. Benefits of Business Intelligence. From mastersindatascience.org: https://www.mastersindatascience.org/resources/benefits-of-business-intelligence/
26. Foss, N. J., & Saebi, T. (2017). Fifteen years of research on business model innovation: How far have we come, and where should we go. Journal of Management, 43, 200–227.
27. Boitnott, J. 7 Innovative Companies Using A.I. to Distrust Their Industries, 15th March 2016. Available online: https://www.inc.com/john-boitnott/7-innovative-companies-using-ai-to-disrupt-their-industries.html (accessed on 1 June 2019).
28. Tyagi, N. (2021, January 23). 6 Major Branches of Artificial Intelligence (AI). From analyticssteps.com: https://www.analyticssteps.com/blogs/6-major-branches-artificial-intelligence-ai
29. National School of Business Management NSBM, Sri Lanka. Benefits of Business Intelligence, June 2020. From mastersindatascience.org: https://www.mastersindatascience.org/resources/benefits-of-business-intelligence/

30. Sena, V., & Nocker, M. (2021). AI and Business Models: The Good, The Bad and The Ugly. Foundations and Trends® in Technology, Information and Operations Management.
31. René, S., & Reinhard, A. (2023). Responsible Artificial Intelligence, Challenges for Sustainable Management. Springer Professional "Wirtschaft+Technik", Springer Professional "Technik", Springer Professional "Wirtschaft".
32. Katal, A., & Singh, N. (2022). Artificial Neural Network: Models, Applications, and Challenges. In: Tomar, R., Hina, M. D., Zitouni, R., Ramdane-Cherif, A. (eds) Innovative Trends in Computational Intelligence. EAI/Springer Innovations in Communication and Computing. Springer, Cham. https://doi.org/10.1007/978-3-030-78284-9_11

12 Cloud Computing
Storage Management, Security, and Privacy

Taran Singh Bharati
Department of Computer Science, Jamia
Millia Islamia, New Delhi, India

12.1 INTRODUCTION

Cloud environment keeps cloud provider, consumer, auditor, broker, and carrier, cloud computing is on-demand resource sharing on internet. It provides various things to be hired on internet such as platform, storage, computing power, or services. Because so many reasons like lack of infrastructure, security, and convenience, people can migrate their data to client so that they can access it from anywhere and there is no need to own the storage and other infrastructure needed to perform the tasks. It creates a virtual environment for users that they have enormous resources in enormous capacity, available on demand all the times [8]. Cloud computing shares the service and characteristics models; service model – Saas, Paas, and Iaas; characteristics model – resource pooling, network access, on-demand self-services, measured service, and rapid elasticity [1]. The nature of clod can be classified as public cloud – which are scalable for on demand resources but they are not reliable; private cloud – they are good and customizable for the organization but have some security issues; hybrid cloud – they are faster, effective, and cost-effective but suffer from integrity challenges of data.

12.2 SECURITY, PRIVACY, AND THREATS

Security is the feeling of being secure means our data must be safe, integral, and confidential. Only indented people can access, use, and modify it. Threat is a feeling of being leaked, modified, misused, and replayed. Therefore, threats always give the feeling, a scaring of being insecure for the activities which compromise the security of the system. Vulnerabilities in web applications are unnoticed capture and unaware identification, lack of breach response, lack of control and transparency, unauthorized disclosure and loss of governance, profiling and tracking, unforeseen inference, outdated or incorrect personal data. Threats can be viewed as follows [2, 9, 10]:

i. **Security Threats:** Eavesdropping, spoofing, man-in-the-middle, replay attacks.
ii. **Physical Threat:** Device capturing, node damaging, side-channel attack.

DOI: 10.1201/9781032614083-12

iii. **Data Threats:** Threat during retrieval from devices, transfer, storage, deployment of unauthorized device, key compromisation, and the crypto-graphic protocols.

iv. **Service Threats:** Unidentified and unauthorized access, identity theft, service hijacking, insecure, or compromising interface API.

v. **Other Threats:** Malicious insider, shared technology issues, abusing cloud computing.

vi. **Anomaly Detection:** Unusual abnormal activities are identified to measure the system's security.

vii. **Vendor Lock-in:** It is the minion time which a contractor cannot leave the system.

12.2.1 Location-Based Security and Privacy

The security of the cloud can be enhanced by using the location of the user also. The location is provided in mobile devices with the help of GPS sensors connected to centralized servers. The mobile devices are connected to the cloud securely. They send their locations in the form of encrypted messages to the cloud. Similarly cloud also shares its information through encrypted messages to prevent the attacks on the locations. Data segregation and protection, threat and vulnerability management, identity and access management, physical and personal security, data leak prevention on cloud, session hijacking, availability of services and data on cloud, application security, incident response arrangement are also proposed [4, 5], as shown in Figures 12.1–12.3.

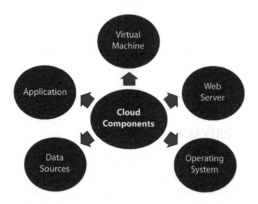

FIGURE 12.1   Cloud components.

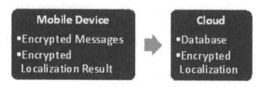

FIGURE 12.2   Privacy-preserving localization architecture.

FIGURE 12.3 Mobile cloud computing architecture.

The location-based security and privacy are used by social media also [3]; Facebook – it tracks the users to know the location of the user to let other know, check in certain places, tag it on the images meant for location serve up ads; Google apps – they track the user's location by their permission to offer some localized services, scenery, food, monuments, ads, etc.; Instagram – location is collected by the posts of the users. If users tag location on the photo, it records the location from those photographs; Snapchat – it allows other users to know the location of other users in real time; therefore, it is a security and privacy concern of individuals; Uber – it tracks the users even if she is not using the application after 5 minutes; after ride competition, this location record is removed. Nowadays, this feature is removed by the company. Other factors, such as load balancing, concurrency, network, operating system, database, memory management, resource management, transaction management, and virtualization, affect the cloud security and it keeps many security concerns such as:

i. **Loss of Control on the Data:** Once data is stored on the cloud, the client loses its control. Therefore, a strict mechanism to prevent the mishandling of this data may be settled.
ii. **Multi-tenancy:** There are so many resources which are shared among many users; therefore, each user's data must be protected.
iii. **Service Agreements:** There must be a clear agreement between the users and cloud for using the specified services to hold a strong trust between them.
iv. **Server Downtime:** It must be kept minimum for better utility of the resources and better efficiency of the overall system.
v. **Backup:** Data must be restored in as soon as possible when there is a system failure or system crash so that the clients' work should not hamper.
vi. **Data Redundancy:** Cloud should maintain the authentic data to be verified against so many copies of the same data in network.

12.3 DATA STORAGE ISSUE

Data of many users and many organizations comes from cloud to be stored; therefore, it deserves to be handled properly. This big data available on cloud needs better management in the sense of its storing, accessing, security, privacy, integrity, and availability for its seamless and flawless working. Same copy of the data is seen at several servers so that the data can be made available quickly to the users. If one source fails to provide data, data can be provided from other servers and work should not affect. Therefore, this duplication or multiplicity of the data creates a lot of problems in terms of memory space as well as management and maintenance.

Therefore, we need a technique to minimize the redundancy of the data. The duplicity is found at client, server, file, etc. sides [6, 10, 11, 17].

Storage Security: It must be ensured by data encryption. Despite storing user's plain data, user must first encrypt its own data before sending it to the cloud; thereafter, cloud should also encrypt the data once again before finally storing it to storage. Any good cryptosystem like RSA and IDEA may be used for encryption.

Duplication Technique: They suggest keeping only one copy of each data and removing other copies. And redundant file data is pointed to the original data copy. Hence, there would be several links to the same data copy. As per the survey, 80% data can be saved by removing the duplicity. Additionally with the help of good compression, again data size can be reduced to save the memory space of the system. Some related existing work on the duplicity is proposed:

i. Duplicity by popularity: Despite assigning equal security to all file, security can be inserted on the basis of their popularity. Files are seen in one of two categories. A threshold is decided to see if file is popular or not. This security can be fixed at block and file level as necessary.
ii. Proof of traceability, ownership, and possession is required when data is owned by middle party.
iii. Legality of the data owned at cloud as per the law enforcement agencies.

Auto Encryption and Decryption: This can be an idea to be applied before sending data to the cloud and taking data from cloud to user, a device which performs both encryption and decryption but one at a time is installed between user and cloud. This will reduce the burden of doing encryptions and decryptions separately each time and the same can be visualized in Figure 12.4 [7, 14, 16]:

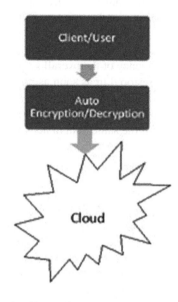

FIGURE 12.4   Auto encryption/decryption in uploading/downloading to cloud.

12.4   PROPOSED SOLUTIONS

A. In order to hide the identity of some attributes, following techniques are proposed to be used [13, 15]:

    i. **K-Anonymity**: It is used to hide the privacy of the users by dispersion techniques so that private attribute and correct identification of individual can be avoided.

    ii. **Transformation**: User's location is modified to thwart location identification by two transformations; by non-cryptographic protocols for getting the strong security and privacy, and spatial transformation to modify the location by the geometric transformations.

    iii. **Dummy Location**: Some fake locations are conveyed to protect the location of the user.

    iv. **Mix Zones**: These are areas where mobile devices are not allowed to update their current locations to the server.

    v. **Jurisdiction Area of Cloud**: This is an area which is decided for each cloud for offering and maintaining the services.

    vi. **Denial of Services and Distributed Denial of Services (DDoS)**: It is an attack in which authorized clients would not be to use services. It may be launched by single or by multiple servers. It consumes the system resources for no useful work.

    vii. **Privilege Elevation**: A person who has no right but manages to get the access of the system to harm or destroy the system.

    viii. **Spoofing**: It is used to hide the message to gain the access to get the personal data, launch the malware, and infect the data files.

    ix. **Tampering**: It is the modification of the data to hamper the operations. It affects the XML poisoning and able to change the commands. Ransomware is also one kind of tampering ion disclosure

    x. **Repudiation and Information Disclosure**: User must not deny latter and information must not be leaked from the virtual system. No disclosure information is expected, neither from insider nor outsider.

    xi. **Digital Signature**: It is a method to secure and authenticate the data on the cloud; for better results, can it be used in combination with other cryptosystems like Diffie-Hellman (D-H) and AES.

B. **Users' Registration with Cloud**: We assume that (KR, KU) is the key pair having KR as its private component and KU as its public component. We also assume that E_k is already shared between trusted third party (TPA) and user.

$$\text{User} \rightarrow \text{Third party: } E_k\,(id, cloud, nonce)$$

$$\text{Third party} \rightarrow \text{user} \| cloud: \; E[KU_u \| id \| E_{uc})] \| E\left(k, \left[E_{uc}, nonce\right]\right)$$

$$\text{User} \rightarrow \text{Cloud: } E_{uc}\,(Data)$$

C. **Analysis**: Here only user is registered for authentication to the TPA but user's data is vulnerable in the cloud means this data can be read at cloud. Data storage with security:

$$User \rightarrow Cloud : E_{uc}(data)$$

D. **Billing**: The subscription is decided on the basis of volume of data, variety of data, frequency of accessing, and time period for which data is to be retained on cloud.
E. **Mirroring of Data Servers**: Mirror images of servers are deployed. So that if one server faces some issues, the same data can be made available from other servers to get the fault tolerance.
F. **Location of Servers**: Several servers must be kept at several places on the earth so that local data can be stored in nearby located servers. It will save time and other overheads to reduce the efforts and cost of overall system. This may lead to the originality (or first copy) issue. If the same data is available at several servers, then which data copy is authentic needs to be clarified. For managing all these activities, storage management is required.

12.5   CLOUD APPLICATIONS

A lot of data is generated and the same may be needed at any time by people so it is not feasible to bring your data from the data in storage in home. That is why people want their data available whenever they need it and convenient, quickly, and at low cost. This is made possible by the cloud. Therefore, cloud has applications in various fields some of them are listed as follows:

i. **Healthcare**: To share the numbers of healthcare resources, like technology, expertise, and discussions, for better service offerings.
ii. **Basis for IoT and Big Data Analysis**: It is the basic technology which enables working of IoT and Bigdata operations.
iii. **QoS Parameters**: Cloud somehow improves the QoS parameters, i.e. performance, internet connectivity, and network delay are some of the examples.
iv. **In Education**: In the remote areas, we can provide the state of the art resources to students, farmers, and educators through a cloud. That will be more beneficial with fewer efforts and less costs. We can record video lectures with more expertise and the same can be shared with people in remote areas.
v. **Smart City**: To improve the lifestyle of common people, in terms of inter-actions, services, infrastructures, and accessibility to handle the day-to-day difficulties.
vi. **Smart Homes**: Smart objects in homes can be connected to cloud and they can be controlled or navigated from anywhere via cloud.
vii. **Smart Surveillance**: Video surveillance for see if work is going fine or not via cloud from anywhere in the world.

viii. **Smart Energy and Smart Grid**: This enhanced the ICT capabilities to automate and control the tools efficiently for efficient energy management.

ix. **Smart Mobility**: It automatically updates and manages the flaws of items from departure to arrival.

x. **Environment Monitoring**: The information is linked to sensors and actuators to get the real-time information such as water, electricity, air quality and gas concentration, soil humidity monitoring, and lightening conditions.

12.6 CONCLUSIONS

Cloud offers a variety of services conveniently, easily accessible at reasonable prices. People need not to own their all requisite infrastructure to work on. The cloud services are provided by the company on demand. Many people store their important data; therefore, management, security, billing, availability of data, authenticity of data, etc. are so many issues. This chapter discusses these issues and challenges and at the same, it proposes feasible solutions to them.

CONFLICT OF INTEREST

This chapter has no any conflict with anyone in any matter.

ACKNOWLEDGMENT

For this research work, the author has not received any financial support from any organization.

CONTRIBUTOR BIOGRAPHY

Dr. Taran Singh Bharati earned B.Tech, ME, and PhD in Computer Science. He possesses more than 22 years of teaching and research experience and he has served in many Engineering Colleges/Institutions at different capacities. His area of interests includes Security, Database, Machine Learning, and Theoretical Computer Science. He may be contacted on taran4100@gmail.com.

REFERENCES

1. Ahmed, I. (2019). "A Brief Review: Security Issues in Cloud Computing and Their Solutions," *Telkomnika*, *17*(6), 2812–2817.
2. Tabrizchi, H., & Kuchaki Rafsanjani, M. (2020). "A Survey on Security Challenges in Cloud Computing: Issues, Threats, and Solutions," *The Journal of Supercomputing*, *76*(12), 9493–9532.
3. A Almusaylim, Z., & Jhanjhi, N. Z. (2020). "Comprehensive Review: Privacy Protection of User in Location-Aware Services of Mobile Cloud Computing," *Wireless Personal Communications*, *111*(1), 541–564.
4. Ari, A. A. A., Ngangmo, O. K., Titouna, C., Thiare, O., Mohamadou, A., & Gueroui, A. M. (2020). "Enabling Privacy and Security in Cloud of Things: Architecture, Applications, Security & Privacy Challenges," *Applied Computing and Informatics*, *16*(1), 1–23.
5. Fatima, S., & Ahmad, S. (2019). "An Exhaustive Review on Security Issues in Cloud Computing," *KSII Transactions on Internet and Information Systems (TIIS)*, *13*(6), 3219–3237.
6. Prajapati, P., & Shah, P. (2020). "A Review on Secure Data Duplication: Cloud Storage Security Issue," *Journal of King Saud University-Computer and Information Sciences*, 34(7), 3996–4007.
7. Tajammul, M., & Parveen, R. (2020). "Auto Encryption Algorithm for Uploading Data on Cloud Storage," *International Journal of Information Technology*, *12*(3), 831–837.
8. Hussein, A. A. (2021). "Data Migration Need, Strategy, Challenges, Methodology, Categories, Risks, Uses With Cloud Computing, and Improvements in Its Using With Cloud Using Suggested Proposed Model (DMig 1)," *Journal of Information Security*, *12*(01), 79.
9. Rajkumar, K., & Dhanakoti, V. (2020, March). Methodological survey to improve the secure data storage in cloud computing. In *2020 International Conference on Emerging Smart Computing and Informatics (ESCI)* (pp. 313–317). IEEE.
10. Shen, J., Yang, H., Vijayakumar, P., & Kumar, N. (2021). "A Privacy-Preserving and Untraceable Group Data Sharing Scheme in Cloud Computing," *IEEE Transactions on Dependable and Secure Computing*, 19(4), 2198–2210.
11. Lu, X., Pan, Z., & Xian, H. (2020). "An Efficient and Secure Data Sharing Scheme for Mobile Devices in Cloud Computing," *Journal of Cloud Computing*, *9*(1), 1–13.
12. Singh, D. P., Kaushik, P., Jain, M., Tiwari, V., & Rajpoot, S. (2021, February). Data Storage Security Issues in Cloud Computing. In *2021 International Conference on Innovative Practices in Technology and Management (ICIPTM)* (pp. 216–220). IEEE.
13. Bharati, T. S. (2020). "Challenges, Issues, Security and Privacy of Big Data," *International Journal of Scientific & Technology Research (IJSTR)*, *9*(2), pp 1482–1486, ISSN 2277 8616.
14. Bharati, T. S. (2019). "Internet of Things (IoT): A Critical Review," *International Journal of Scientific & Technology Research (IJSTR)*, *8*(9), pp 227–232, ISSN 2277 8616.
15. Bharati, T. S. (July-Aug, 2018). "MANETs and Its' Security," *International Journal of Computer Networks and Wireless Communication (IJCNWC)*, *8*(4), 166–171, ISSN 2250 3501.
16. Bharati, T. S. (2015). "Enhanced Intrusion Detection System for Mobile Adhoc Networks Using Mobile Agents With No Manager," *International Journal of Computer Applications*, *111*(10), 33–35, New York, USA, ISSN 0975 887.
17. Sadeeq, M. M., Abdulkareem, N. M., Zeebaree, S. R., Ahmed, D. M., Sami, A. S., & Zebari, R. R. (2021, March 15). "IoT and Cloud Computing Issues, Challenges and Opportunities: A Review," *Qubahan Academic Journal*, *1*(2), 1–7.

13 Social Media Marketing and Online Impulse Buying Behaviour
An Analysis through Website Quality as Moderator

Manoj Bansal[1], Satinder Kumar[2],
and Ary Soro Utami[3]
[1]University School for Graduate Studies (USGS),
 Chaudhary Devi Lal University, Sirsa, Haryana, India
[2]School of Management Studies, Punjabi
 University, Patiala, Punjab, India
[3]Alumnus of UNISULLA, Semarang, Indonesia

13.1 INTRODUCTION

Social media presents new intriguing possibilities for customer and marketer interaction (Miller and Lammas, 2010). Programs for social media marketing (SMM) promotion are designed to put in more effort at centres or places where members of your organization can interact with customers for the benefit of the brand (Evans, 2010). In recent years, the businesses have been actively present on social media platforms like Facebook and Twitter and have coordinated their efforts with more conventional strategies to maximize impact. Recently, marketers and researchers have been giving SMM campaigns a lot of thought (Ibrahim et al., 2020). Every aspect of indulgence brands' SMM has a bearing on consumer interactions and purchasing behaviour, but entertainment has a greater impact on a wider range of variables than any other aspect (Kim and Ko, 2010). The main reason why people use social media affects how they perceive and respond to brand SMM efforts (SMMEs) (Yazdanparast et al., 2016). The reputations of brands and the two components of brand equity, primarily brand recognition and brand image, are significantly and favourably impacted by SMMEs (Godey et al., 2016). The five elements of the observable SMM exercises of the indulgent design businesses are entertainment, engagement, trend, personalization, and word of mouth. These aspects have a positive impact on value equity, partnership value, and brand value (Kim and Ko, 2012).

Consumer analysts have studied impulsive purchasing for almost 50 years (Rook and Fisher, 1995). Literature on the concept of impulse buying (IB) shows that 60% of purchases are made on IB behaviour (IBB) (Amos et al., 2014). When an impulse purchase was linked to a US $1 donation, the rate of impulse purchases increased from around 2% to almost 9% (Jeffrey and Hodge, 2007).

This positive correlation between website quality (WQ) and online IB (OIB) suggests that users are more likely to shop online and are consequently more likely to make impulsive purchases at online stores when users have a positive impact on WQ in terms of usability, navigation, and website security. There is a positive correlation between WQ and online motivation purchasing, indicating that when customers are influenced by WQ, they make rash purchases at online stores (Godara, 2019). According to a study, WQ significantly and favourably influenced users' OIB behaviour (OIBB), with sales promotion tools and credit card usage acting as moderators. Purchases were influenced by commercial progress and design awareness. The study didn't find any proof that the quality of a website actually drove sales (Akram et al., 2018). Instead, they discovered that WQ appeared to serve as a cleanliness factor that would call for deal advancement to improve the site's acceptable quality plan in order to stimulate IB (Wiranata and Hananto, 2020). OIBB significantly influences the content of websites (Akram et al., 2018).

Customers' apparent utilitarian and gluttonous motivation to browse online audits enhances their browsing behaviour. Perusing strongly affects consumers' desire to buy, which in turn affects how they choose to make purchases (Zhang et al., 2018). Government regulations and WQ have an impact on online motivation to buy (Hayu, 2019). To increase organic intake, experts in online marketing are urged to review their strategies for managing existing customers by creating sites with social learning tools that are more user-friendly and aesthetically pleasing (Tariq et al., 2019). When deal advancement and WQ worked together, it could significantly affect IB (Wiranata and Hananto, 2020). When normative evaluations are favourable, there should be a strong correlation between consumers' IB tendencies and their OIBB; however, when a negative normative level is crossed, there should be a weaker correlation between consumers' trait tendencies and their IBB (Rook and Fisher, 1995).

By examining the relationship between SMM and OIB through the moderating effect of WQ, this study aims to fill a gap in the literature. This study also aims to determine how SMM factors affect OIB more specifically. In particular, this analysis could provide important insights that online merchants represent in their efforts to comprehend and improve customers' online drive purchasing practices. Three research questions were investigated:

1. What impact does SMM have on online impulse purchases?
2. How does the quality of a website impact online impulse purchases?
3. How does WQ moderate between SMM and OIB?

13.2   LITERATURE REVIEW

13.2.1   SOCIAL MEDIA MARKETING

SMM initiatives are designed to put more effort into focusing on or creating places where members of your organisation can interact with customers for the benefit of the brand (Evans, 2010). Social media platforms are fantastic tools for building relationships with customers (De Vries et al., 2012). The context of the content modifies how users view social media advertising (Shahbaznezhad et al., 2021).

Five pillars support the apparent web-based media advertising efforts of luxury fashion firms: entertainment, engagement, trend, customization, and word of mouth. SMM has positive, inherent effects on value, partnership value, and brand value (Kim and Ko, 2012). Destinations on social networking sites have a significant impact on respondents' perceptions of online advertisements and how to reach different types of audiences to increase the effectiveness of online advertising (Vinerean et al., 2013).

Many have come to the conclusion that social media is an effective tool for increasing customer loyalty as a result of its widespread use (Pütter, 2017). Companies have started involving their customers in the planning stages through blogs and other online media tools (Saravanakumar and SuganthaLakshmi, 2012).

13.2.2 ONLINE IMPULSE BUYING

Situational association factors have the most grounded relationship with IB (Amos et al., 2014). The atmosphere of the store has influenced IB through demand and positive impact (Mohan et al., 2013). Customers' propensity to buy and desire to buy are positively correlated with their motivation to buy (Parsad et al., 2017). Shopping pleasure is benefited by innovation's practicality and usefulness (Fataron, 2019). Customers under pressure displayed a higher propensity to make purchases online (Moran, 2015). Web-based media ads' perceived personalization had a significant impact on perceived novelty, relevance, and esteem-building (Dodoo and Wu, 2019). In a situation where no specific object has been mentioned, neuroticism and extraversion have a positive impact on causing impulsive behaviour (Parsad et al., 2019). While all of the motivating factors include potential offers that drive online pulse purchases and give customers some sort of use or satisfaction, the majority of the hygienic factors relate to how online stores are laid up (Yi-Shih Lo et al., 2016). According to research by Liao et al. (2009), the sales marketing strategy and its connections to product demand have a significant impact on reminder IB (Liao et al., 2009). The relationship between website content and OIB is significantly moderated by the sales promotion, which has a significant impact on online purchase behaviour (Akram et al., 2018). The SOR model's applicability in the context of OIBB and its demonstration is of significant benefits of two-dimensional virtual atmospheric signal design and navigation (Floh and Madlberger, 2013). Age is the most significant demographic indicator for IBB, with gender and educational attainment playing much smaller roles (Akram et al., 2016).

13.2.3 WEBSITE QUALITY

The diversification of SMM has been greatly aided by the WQ. The WQ encourages customers to make online purchases. There is a gap in the literature that suggests WQ should act as a moderator between SMM and OIB.

Website usability, aesthetic appeal, and item accessibility are important online cues for triggering impulse purchases (Liu et al., 2013). Usability and value of innovations contribute to consumers' delight in a continuous cycle, and consumers' satisfaction shed light on the factors that motivate their impulsive purchases (Fataron, 2019).

Since it actually assumed a part as a cleanliness factor, part of WQ was still basic at the time. An important factor influencing motivation to buy from its distinctive drivers is the flow experience. Trust and confidence are frequently fundamental to incentive purchasing, just as flow familiarity plays a significant role in influencing IB away from its initial drivers. For the purchase of incentives, trust is essential because perceived utility is not (Wu et al., 2016). To manage current customers, online marketers should review their strategies and build websites with social learning systems that make customers more approachable and outgoing, pushing natural admission (Tariq et al., 2019). Customers would support a website if they believed it ensured a high level of ethical concern sustainability, such as adhering to privacy policies by explicitly mentioning them and adequately describing products and services (Yang et al., 2009). Credit cards have a significant impact on OIB, promotional advertising has a positive effect on OIB, and it serves as a powerful moderator in the interaction between website content and OIB (Akram et al., 2018).

13.3 HYPOTHESIS DEVELOPMENT

13.3.1 SOCIAL MEDIA MARKETING

The most successful marketers will be those who use Facebook or other online platforms to cater to and respond to the needs of the new generation, as they will gain their trust and dependability in purchasing a particular brand (Radzi et al., 2018). Despite the fact that impulse purchases are more prevalent offline than online, social media has a significant impact on both, according to Aragoncillo and Orus (2018). Every asset included in the SMM of indulgence brands has a bearing on consumer interactions and purchasing behaviour, but entertainment has a greater influence on a wider range of variables than any other asset (Kim and Ko, 2010). According to Manthiou et al. (2016), SMMEs have a significant positive effect on brand equity's two pillars of brand recognition and brand image. Five elements of the obvious SMM activities of indulgence design companies include entertainment, engagement, trend, customization, and word of mouth. They significantly enhance brand value, partnership value, and value equity (see Figure 13.1) (Kim and Ko, 2012).

It is therefore presumably factual: H1: SMM positively influences OIB.

13.3.2 WEBSITE QUALITY

The study examined the moderating effects of sales promotion, credit card use, as well as the effect of WQ on OIBB. Study found that WQ was significantly impacted by OIB (Akram et al., 2018).

The findings of this investigation confirmed that business growth and product awareness influenced consumer demand. It is not found as evidence that the quality of a website directly influenced consumer behaviour. The developers found that WQ seemed to be a cleanliness factor that would require advancement to improve the site's acceptable quality plan to energies OIB (Wiranata and Hananto, 2020). This study presented experimental findings that examined the effects of WQ and governmental restrictions on specific college students' drive-buying behaviours at Brawijaya Malang University.

The findings demonstrated that the frequency of impulsive purchases made by people while shopping online was influenced by both the content of the websites themselves and governmental regulations (Hayu et al., 2020). Consumers are

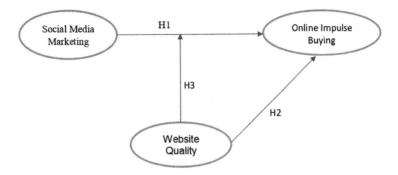

FIGURE 13.1   Empirical model.

increasingly serving as key storytellers for brands thanks to the current dynamic networks of clients and goods created by social networking and the quick exchange of brand interactions in those networks (Gensler et al., 2013)

So, it is assumed that

H2: WQ positively affects OIB;
H3: WQ moderates between SMM and OIB.

This research consists of gender, educational qualification, occupation, and income per month as demographic respondents (Table 13.1).

TABLE 13.1

Demographic Respondents

	Respondents	Percentage
Gender		
Male	230	39
Female	364	61
Educational Qualification		
Graduation	196	33
Post-Graduation	296	50
Doctorate	102	17
Occupation		
Student	388	65
Salaried Employee	158	27
Self-Employed	48	8
Income Per Month		
Up to 30,000	242	41
30,001–50,000	191	32
Above 50,000	161	27
Total	594	100

Female participants accounted for 61% of the total respondents. In terms of educational qualification, most of the respondents had a post-graduated education as much as 50%. Respondents' occupation is dominated by student, amounting to 65%. Meanwhile, in terms of income per month, majority respondents earn up to 30,000 (41%).

13.4   RESEARCH METHOD

13.4.1   Data Gathering, Population, and Sample

Using the snowball sampling technique, data were collected from the three Indian states of Haryana, Punjab, and Chandigarh for current research. Those respondents were taken who were using social media and buying products with the help of SMM. The selection of respondents was quite tough, and to identify the respondents who were using social media to buy products impulsively, a referral method was used. Seven hundred and sixty-six questionnaires were distributed for data collection purposes. One hundred and twenty questionnaires were refused because respondents were not casual shoppers and never bought anything impulsively. Fifty-two surveys were deleted during the data cleaning procedure due to missing data management criteria (Hair et al., 2014). Finally, 594 respondents were considered to be eligible for the survey.

13.4.2   Measurement of Variable

To measure the intended items and collection of data, a standardized survey instrument was used to evaluate hypotheses. Two scales were used in this study: a nominal scale and a 7-point Likert scale (from 1 strongly disagree to 7 strongly agree). All of the items are from prior studies; there are 9 in the IBB (Rook and Fisher, 1995), 11 in the SMM (Kim and Ko, 2010), and 36 in the WQ (Loiacono et al., 2007), making 56 items in total.

13.4.3   Hypotheses Testing

As per partial least square (PLS)-SEM requirements, two main assessments are required; the measurement model and bootstrapping (Hair et al., 2017).

This study's research model was assessed using PLS-SEM with SmartPLS software. The approach in variance-based PLS uses fewer constraints than covariance-based PLS (Chin et al., 2003). The PLS-SEM model evaluated both outer and inner measurement-structural models at the same time. In the PLS-SEM method, the predictor variable is converted into an orthogonal component called PLS. Therefore, this method also addresses the problem that often occurs in multivariate regression analysis, namely multicollinearity. There are two main stages in implementing the PLS model: validity and reliability testing of the inner model and hypothesis testing of the outer model. At the initial stage, confirmatory factor analysis is used to determine inner model evaluation. Therefore, hypothesis testing is done through the outer model test via the path coefficient.

The problem that often occurs in research using a questionnaire is the common method bias (CMB) or common method variance (Schwarz et al., 2017). Self-response in collecting data from individual data sources leads to the level of covariance among the questionnaire items (Podsakoff et al., 2012). CMB testing that occurs between variables uses the most reliable approach (Kock, 2015), with full collinearity evaluation through SmartPLS. If a model is said to be free from any CMB, its VIF of all indicators and variance should be less than 3.3 (Table 13.2).

TABLE 13.2
Measurement Model Test Results

Variables	Indicators	Convergent Validity		Internal Consistency Reliability		
		Outer Loadings	AVE	CR	Cr.α	VIF
		>0.70	>0.70	>0.7	>0.7	<3.3
OIB	OIB1	0.811	0.574	0.923	0.904	
	OIB2	0.830				
	OIB3	0.783				
	OIB4	0.771				
	OIB5	0.744				
	OIB6	0.722				
	OIB7	0.511				
	OIB8	0.822				
	OIB9	0.777				
Moderating effect	SMM * WQ --> OIB	1.703	1.000	1.000	1.000	1.477
SMM	SMM1	0.822	0.694	0.961	0.956	1.570
	SMM10	0.806				
	SMM11	0.771				
	SMM2	0.866				
	SMM3	0.811				
	SMM4	0.862				
	SMM5	0.827				
	SMM6	0.833				
	SMM7	0.821				
	SMM8	0.879				
	SMM9	0.861				
Website quality	WQ1	0.853	0.723	0.989	0.989	1.801
	WQ10	0.824				
	WQ11	0.811				
	WQ12	0.569				
	WQ13	0.883				
	WQ14	0.845				
	WQ15	0.876				
	WQ16	0.890				

(Continued)

TABLE 13.2   (Continued)
Measurement Model Test Results

		Convergent Validity		Internal Consistency Reliability		
		Outer Loadings	AVE	CR	Cr.α	VIF
Variables	Indicators	>0.70	>0.70	>0.7	>0.7	<3.3
	WQ17	0.875				
	WQ18	0.917				
	WQ19	0.888				
	WQ2	0.812				
	WQ20	0.895				
	WQ21	0.885				
	WQ22	0.917				
	WQ23	0.928				
	WQ24	0.938				
	WQ25	0.917				
	WQ26	0.860				
	WQ27	0.811				
	WQ28	0.851				
	WQ29	0.868				
	WQ3	0.853				
	WQ30	0.932				
	WQ31	0.885				
	WQ32	0.898				
	WQ33	0.809				
	WQ34	0.884				
	WQ35	0.824				
	WQ4	0.828				
	WQ5	0.840				
	WQ6	0.853				
	WQ7	0.736				
	WQ8	0.728				
	WQ9	0.668				
	WQ36	0.856				

Source: SmartPLS Output

13.4.4 MEASUREMENT MODEL

Estimating the model is the first step before measuring model evaluation. Cronbach's alpha and composite reliability are used for model testing.

If the indicator reliability of the outer loading for each item is greater than 0.5, the results of the outer model assessment are considered adequate (Hair et al., 2010). All of the variables used in this study had an average value greater than 0.50. Between

TABLE 13.3

Fornell–Larcker Criterion and HTMT

Variables	Moderating Effect 1	OIB	SMM	WQ
Moderating effect 1	**1.000**	0.508	0.455	0.551
OIB	−0.486	**0.758**	0.509	0.474
SMM	−0.444	0.492	**0.833**	0.597
WQ	−0.548	0.464	0.584	**0.851**

Source: SmartPLS Output

Note: Bold diagonal (AVE root) to bottom values is Fornell–Larcker Criterion; up of bold diagonal values is HTMT

0.40 and 0.60, 0.60 and 0.80, and 0.80 and 1.00, respectively, are considered to be moderate, high, and excellent levels of reliability by Cronbach's alpha (Hair et al., 2010). The model is regarded as having convergent validity if the composite stability is greater than zero and the AVE (average variance extracted) of the computation model is less than zero (Fornell and Larcker, 1981). In order to test discriminant validity, this study followed the advice of Henseler et al. (2016) and used a matrix of Fornell–Larcker and HTMT. The Fornell–Larcker matrix is displayed in Table 13.3 with AVE root square values (diagonal) higher than all other values and an HTMT value greater than 1. As a result, the discriminatory validity of the measurement model was established.

The outer loading is higher than 0.7, according to the PLS [SEM PLS] models Algorithm results. The results of the PLS-SEM model's algorithm show that the outer loading is greater than −0.7. These findings show that the indicators for all variables are reliable. The validity and reliability of the model are demonstrated in Table 13.2.

Fornell and Larcker (1981) state that discriminant validity may be confirmed if the square root of the AVE for the latent variable is greater than the correlation between individual latent variables. As can be seen in Table 13.3, the HTMT values are all less than 1, which are consistent with the Fornell–Larcker criterion.

13.4.5 STRUCTURAL MODEL

Table 13.4 shows coefficients of determination values that were used to evaluate how well an exogenous variable (SMM) explains a set of dependent variables (OIB). A model is expected to have a value of R^2 between 0 and 1. The R^2 value owing by an

TABLE 13.4

Determination Coefficient

Variable	R^2	Adj R^2
OIB	0.343	0.340

Source: SmartPLS Output

TABLE 13.5

Path Coefficient

Hypothesis	B_{coef}	SD	$t_{-statistic}$	p_{-value}	f^2	Results
H1: SMM -> OIB	0.282	0.027	7.287	0.000	0.077	Supported
H2: WQ -> OIB	0.145	0.039	2.876	0.004	0.018	Supported
H3: WQ * SMM --> OIB	−0.165	0.050	6.059	0.000	0.082	Supported

Source: SmartPLS Output

endogenous variable indicates its ability/power to forecast the formula. The R-square (R^2) values of 0.75, 0.50, and 0.25 (Hair et al., 2017) indicate that the endogenous variables in the model have high, medium, and low predictive ability.

The predictive power of the model is low (0.343) when using OIB as an endogenous variable. Assuming a rate of 34.3% of online impulsive buying, it is reasonable to assume that SMM can anticipate these actions. Meanwhile, the other is impacted by factors that are beyond the scope of this study.

Table 13.5 demonstrates the inner model analysis. The analysis' output displayed the path coefficient along with its level of significance. The coefficient of beta/"path"(β) indicates the power of the effect among latent variables. This assessment is comparable to using regression coefficients. The significance of each coefficient was examined via the use of bootstrapping methods and a similar indicator-weight analysis.

All hypotheses were supported, despite the low values of the coefficients of determination (Table 13.5). All hypotheses, H1, H2, and H3, are supported by the path coefficient's evidence of a substantial influence of SMM and WQ on OIB.

There are several categories of path coefficient suggested by Diamantopoulos et al. (2005); less than 0.30 results in medium (effects), 0.30–0.60 results in strong (effects), and more than 0.60 results in very strong (effects). A moderately positive and statistically significant relationship between SMM and impulsive online purchases was reported ($\beta_{coef} = 0.282$; $t > 1.96$; $p < 0.05$). There is a moderate, positive, and statistically significant relationship between the quality of a website and impulsive buying made online ($\beta_{coef} = 0.145$; $t > 1.96$; $p < 0.05$). Therefore, H1 and H2 indicate the data's empirical support. Furthermore, the findings of H3 support the importance of WQ in moderating the association between SMM and OIB. The moderating effect denotes an interplay between an extrinsic variable (determinate) and a moderator variable to influence an endogenous variable (Baron and Kenny, 1986; Henseler and Fassott, 2010). WQ is the moderator variable of interaction between SMM and OIB ($\beta_{coef} = -0.165$; $t_{statistic} > 1.96$; $p_{value} < 0.05$). The findings indicate that WQ has a moderate, negative, and substantial mediating impact on the interaction between SMM and OIB. The effect degree of f^2 shows that SMM has a weak impact on OIB, with parameters (0.02 = small; 0.15 = medium; and 0.35 = large) (Baron and Kenny, 1986). The f^2 in Table 13.5 shows that SMM and WQ have a weak effect on OIB (0.077 and 0.018). These results show effect of SMM on OIBB at the bottom of high and low degrees of WQ.

In terms of the moderating effect, f^2 explains how much the moderating variable (WQ) helps to explain the endogenous variable (OIB). The f^2 value classifications (0.005, 0.010, and 0.025) represent more practical low, moderate, and high effect size standards, respectively (Hair et al., 2017). Table 13.5 illustrates that WQ, as a moderator in the interplay between SMM and OIB, offers a high measuring impact with a value of f^2 0.082.

13.5 DISCUSSIONS

The relationship between SMM, OIB, and WQ is hypothesized and put to the test while considering a moderating effect. Results showed that SMM has a positive impact on OIB.

These findings support the notion that SMM is a crucial campaign to increase OIB. Additionally, the quality of a website has a moderate impact between SMM and OIB and a direct impact on OIB. These findings suggested that attractive website content will aid in boosting OIB. In addition to this, WQ improves the bond between SMM and OIBB. These findings provide intriguing theoretical and practical insights into the function of SMM in improving the OIBB. In the case of OIB, WQ also plays a crucial and significant role in luring in new clients.

13.5.1 THEORETICAL IMPLICATIONS

The study's findings made some significant theoretical inferences, which help to explain why SMM has such a strong favourable impact on OIB. Marketers are searching for novel ways to target consumers and create the OIB. SMM is a strategy used by marketers to target customers and influence OIB. The online audience is a booming industry in every country; however, due to its globalized nature, some segmentation is necessary. This is especially crucial because WQ acts as a moderator between the two and there is almost no existing literature on how SMM influences OIB.

The study found a significant, direct relationship between SMM and OIB, as predicted in H1. H1 was therefore supported. These findings demonstrate that SMM triggers consumer interest in OIB.

SMM activities had a positive impact on purchase aim and brand equity, according to a study by Yadav and Rahman (2017), which supports the nomological validity of the scale. Similar and convincing evidence that the local Bangladeshi fashion industry's SMMEs are successful in forging customer connections and preferences in the context of online buying was discovered in a different study (Wang et al., 2019). Similar results were found in another study by Dodoo and Wu (2019), which suggested that advertising personalization directly affects the OIB tendency and that perceived significance had a significant impact on it. Ibrahim et al.'s (2020) study found a connection between a company's brand value and its use of social media for marketing.

The study also discovered a significant relationship between WQ and OIB, which is consistent with H2.

The analysis shows that SMM users engage in OIB and that WQ facilitates these customers' impulsive purchases. This research is strikingly similar to that of Turkyilmaz et al. (2015), which offered crucial insights into website architecture for all e-commerce businesses looking to increase the likelihood that their customers will make impulse purchases. Although the findings of one study by Wiranata and Hananto (2020) differ, they found that website efficiency had no impact on impulsive buying but that sales promotion and fashion awareness did. The importance of WQ nevertheless persisted because it served as a hygienic factor. Instinctive purchases increase when website content works in concert with a marketing campaign. Another study by Godara and Kumar Bishnoi (2019) came to the same conclusion that there are numerous qualities of a high-quality website, including task-related cues like accessibility, stability, and a lack of download delay that specifically help a customer achieve his shopping target and mood-related cues like visual appeal that help the consumer achieve his shopping goal and make shopping enjoyable. As a result, various website attributes have a direct or indirect impact on OIB.

H3 suggests that WQ moderates the interaction between SMM and OIB. This study's findings are similar to those of Wu et al.'s (2016) study, which found that Internet users frequently make impulsive purchases and use website devices. This is in line with the findings of Turkyilmaz et al. (2015), who showed that customers' pleasurable online shopping experiences led them to make impulsive purchases.

We find that social attractiveness mediates the relationship between consumers' attitudes and their impulsive online purchases, and that website personality plays a moderating role in this mediated interaction, which is in line with earlier research by Tariq et al. (2019). The results showed that full moderation in a committed relationship was statistically significant. The tone and atmosphere of the website also limit the influence of social appeal as a moderating factor. According to the findings, online marketers should reconsider how they interact with their current customers, including incorporating social learning techniques, enhancing user-friendliness, and using more aesthetically pleasing layouts.

As a theoretical contribution, the research expands on our understanding of some comparable structures that haven't been thoroughly covered in earlier literature relating to SMM and OIB. As a result, our main theoretical contribution is an enhanced understanding of the interaction between SMM and OIB, with moderating effects from WQ.

13.5.2 MANAGEMENT IMPLICATIONS

There are several practical implications for online advertisements, retailers, and marketers in addition to the aforementioned theoretical ones. Online marketers must first provide customers with the social media content they requested. Marketers spend a lot of money creating advertising content that encourages consumers to buy their products. Therefore, social media content needs to be interesting and informative in order to persuade users to buy products. Marketers need to pay attention to how SMM is being incorporated into their strategies. By providing consumers with the best engagement opportunities, trustworthy product information, individualized product reviews, and fashionable goods, marketers can use social media to entice customers. All e-marketers aim to provide consumers with the greatest possible benefit; this study would give them a useful perspective on customers' experiences that improves the interaction between e-marketing practitioners and current and potential customers.

Second, WQ has an impact on and is beneficial for enhancing OIB. When a customer saw an advertisement on social media, they dutifully followed the website. The results of the study show that website content strengthens SMM ads and OIB, so marketers must add compelling content that encourages customers to buy more quickly. The first and most important factor is usefulness, which also includes response time, customized website correspondence, user interest in the website, and informational fit to mission. The second aspect of a consistent website is ease of use (easiness of comprehension, intuitive operations), which has an impact on online impulse purchases. The third crucial factor in impulsive online shopping is website entertainment, which includes the website's aesthetic appeal. Fourth, complementary relationships and online impulse purchases frequently have an effect. The findings indicated that online merchants should create efficient websites to increase OIB.

13.6 CONCLUSIONS

SMM is a strategy that gives customers a place to make online purchases through social media campaigns. Customers who use social media platforms like Facebook, WhatsApp, and Instagram. can buy products from online retailers who advertise their products there. All of these elements could encourage customers to make impulsive purchases online. SMM offers a powerful platform for business and marketing strategies. It is simple to buy a product because personal information is readily available on social media. Social media has helped to create OIB, where a customer sees an online advertisement and purchases a product without considering its need or benefits. It has a significant impact on marketers' ability to increase sales.

The majority of brands today, particularly those in the fashion and electronics sectors, advertise their goods on social media. A person can easily buy a product by using the company website. Due to the factors mentioned above, customers occasionally make impulsive purchases, The evolving technological era of marketing has led to an increase in activity on social networks like Facebook, YouTube, Linkedin, and Twitter, all of which have given users a platform to connect with one another and engage in OIB. The assumption that SMM is a useful tool for customer targeting has been influenced by the growing use of SMM for online product purchases.

13.7 LIMITATIONS AND FUTURE RESEARCH

This study has some shortcomings, such as the fact that India, a developing nation, served as the site for it. The adoption of SMM for OIB in other nations may not be accurately reflected in the findings. Second, the variables used for measurement are few; more variables need to be used for additional research. The model can be expanded in future research by including more variables. Finally, since this study used a cross-sectional design, it should be noted that data was collected at a specific time and that future studies of a similar nature might employ a cross-sectional design over a range of time periods. The product categories were not covered in this research, but that only provides more room for future research.

REFERENCES

Akram, U., Hui, P., Kaleem Khan, M., Tanveer, Y., Mehmood, K., & Ahmad, W. (2018). How website quality affects online impulse buying: Moderating effects of sales promotion and credit card use, *Asia Pacific Journal of Marketing and Logistics, 30*(1), 235–256.

Akram, U., Khan, M. K., Hashim, M., Hui, P., Kaleem Khan, M., & Rasheed, S. (2016). Impact of store atmosphere on impulse buying behaviour: Moderating effect of demographic variables, *International Journal of U-and e-Service, 9*(7), 43–60.

Amos, C., Holmes, G. R., & Keneson, W. C. (2014). A meta-analysis of consumer impulse buying, *Journal of Retailing and Consumer Services, 21*(2), 86–97.

Aragoncillo, L., & Orus, C. (2018). Impulse buying behaviour: An online-offline comparative and the impact of social media, *Spanish Journal of Marketing, 22*(1), 42–62.

Baron, R., & Kenny, D. (1986). The moderator-mediator variable distinction in social psychological research: Conceptual, strategic, and statistical considerations, *Journal of Personality and Social Psychology, 51*, 1173–1182.

Chin, W., Marcolin, B. L., & Newsted, P. R. (2003). A partial least squares latent variable modeling approach for measuring interaction effects: Results from a Monte Carlo simulation study and an electronic-mail emotion/adoption study, *Information Systems Research, 14*(2), 189–217.

De Vries, L., Gensler, S., & Leeflang, P. S. (2012). Popularity of brand posts on brand fan pages: An investigation of the effects of social media marketing, *Journal of Interactive Marketing, 26*(2), 83–91.

Diamantopoulos, A., Riefler, P., & Roth, K. (2005). The problem of measurement model misspecification in behavioral and organizational research and some recommended solutions, *Journal of Applied Psychology, 90*, 710–730.

Dodoo, N. A., & Wu, L. (2019). Exploring the anteceding impact of personalised social media advertising on online impulse buying tendency, *International Journal of Internet Marketing and Advertising, 13*(1), 73–95.

Fataron, Z. A. (2019). online impulse buying behaviour: Case study on users of tokopedia, *Journal of Digital Marketing and Halal Industry, 1*(1), 47–60.

Floh, A., & Madlberger, M. (2013). The role of atmospheric cues in online impulse-buying behavior, *Electronic Commerce Research and Applications, 12*(6), 425–439.

Fornell, C., & Larcker, D. F. (1981). Evaluating structural equation models with unobservable variables and measurement error, *Journal of Marketing Research, 18*(1), 39–50.

Gensler, S., Völckner, F., Liu-Thompkins, Y., & Wiertz, C. (2013). Managing brands in the social media environment, *Journal of Interactive Marketing, 27*(4), 242–256.

Godara, S. (2019). A study on influence of website quality on online impulse buying behavior of Indian consumers, *Journal of the Gujarat Research Society, 21*(10), 1497–1511.

Godey, B. et al. (2016). 'Social media marketing efforts of luxury brands: Influence on brand equity and consumer behavior', *Journal of Business Research, 69*(12), pp. 5833–5841. Available at: https://doi.org/10.1016/j.jbusres.2016.04.181.

Hayu, R., Surachman, S., Rofiq, A., & Rahayu, M. (2020). The effect of website quality and government regulations on online impulse buying behavior, *Management Science Letters, 10*(5), 961–968.

Hayu, R. S. (2019). Smart digital content marketing, strategi membidik konsumen millennial Indonesia, *JMK (Jurnal Manajemen dan Kewirausahaan), 4*(1), 61–69.

Henseler, J., Ringle, C., & Sarstedt, M. (2016). Testing measurement invariance of composites using partial least squares, *International Marketing Review, 33*, 405–431.

Ibrahim, B., Aljarah, A., & Ababneh, B. (2020). Do social media marketing activities enhance consumer perception of brands? A meta-analytic examination, *Journal of Promotion Management*, 26(4), 544–568.

Jeffrey, S. A., & Hodge, R. (2007). Factors influencing impulse buying during an online purchase, *Electronic Commerce Research*, 7(3–4), 367–379.

Kim, A. J., & Ko, E. (2010). Impacts of luxury fashion brand's social media marketing on customer relationship and purchase intention, *Journal of Global Fashion Marketing*, 1(3), 164–171.

Kim, A. J., & Ko, E. (2012). Do social media marketing activities enhance customer equity? An empirical study of luxury fashion brand, *Journal of Business Research*, 65(10), 1480–1486.

Kock, N. (2015). Common method bias in PLS-SEM: A full collinearity assessment approach, *International Journal of E-Collaboration*, 11(4), 1–10.

Liao, S. L., Shen, Y. C., & Chu, C. H. (2009). The effects of sales promotion strategy, product appeal and consumer traits on reminder impulse buying behaviour, *International Journal of Consumer Studies*, 33(3), 274–284.

Liu, Y., Li, H., & Hu, F. (2013). Website attributes in urging online impulse purchase: An empirical investigation on consumer perceptions. *Decision support systems*, 55(3), 829–837.

Loiacono, E. T., Watson, R. T., & Goodhue, D. L. (2007). WebQual: An instrument for consumer evaluation of web sites, *International Journal of Electronic Commerce*, 11(3), 51–87.

Miller, R., & Lammas, N. (2010). Social media and its implications for viral marketing, *Asia Pacific Public Relations Journal*, 11(1), 1–9.

Mohan, G., Sivakumaran, B., & Sharma, P. (2013). Impact of store environment on impulse buying behavior, *European Journal of Marketing*, 47(10), 1711–1732.

Moran, B. (2015). Effect of stress, materialism and external stimuli on online impulse buying. *Journal of Research for Consumers*, (27), 26–51. http://www.jrconsumers.com/Consumer_Articles/issue_27/Issue27-ConsumerArticle-Kwak8-12.pdf

Parsad, C., Prashar, S., & Tata, V. S. (2017). Understanding nature of store ambiance and individual impulse buying tendency on impulsive purchasing behaviour: An emerging market perspective, *Decision*, 44(4), 297–311.

Parsad, C., Prashar, S., & Vijay, T. S. (2019). Comparing between product-specific and general impulse buying tendency: Does shoppers' personality influence their impulse buying tendency? *Asian Academy of Management Journal*, 24(2), 41–61.

Podsakoff, P. M., MacKenzie, S. B., & Podsakoff, N. P. (2012). Sources of method bias in social science research and recommendations on how to control it, *Annual Review of Psychology*, 63, 539–569.

Pütter, M. (2017). The impact of social media on consumer buying intention, *Journal of International Business Research and Marketing*, 3(1), 7–13. https://doi.org/10.18775/jibrm.1849-8558.2015.31.3001

Radzi, N. A. A., Harun, A., Ramayah, T., Kassim, A. W. M., & Lily, J. (2018). Benefits of Facebook fan/brand page marketing and its influence on relationship commitment among Generation Y: Empirical evidence from Malaysia, *Telematics and Informatics*, 35(7), 1980–1993.

Rook, D. W., & Fisher, R. J. (1995). Normative influences on impulsive buying behavior, *Journal of Consumer Research*, 22(3), 305–313.

Saravanakumar, M., & SuganthaLakshmi, T. (2012). Social media marketing, *Life Science Journal*, 9(4), 4444–4451.

Schwarz, A. T., Rizzuto, C., Carraher-Wolverton, J., Roldhan, L., & Barrrea-Barrera, R. (2017). Examining the impact and detection of the 'urban legend' of common method bias, *The ACM Sigmis Database: The Database for Advances in Information Systems*, 48(4), 93–119.

Shahbaznezhad, H., Dolan, R., & Rashidirad, M. (2021). The role of social media content format and platform in users' engagement behavior, *Journal of Interactive Marketing*, *53*, 47–65.

Tariq, A., Wang, C., Tanveer, Y., Akram, U., & Bilal, M. (2019). Online impulse buying of organic food: A moderated (website personality) mediation (social appeal) process, *International Journal of Information Systems and Change Management*, *11*(1), 3–24.

Turkyilmaz, C. A., Erdem, S. and Uslu, A. (2015). The effects of personality traits and website quality on online impulse buying, *Procedia – Social and Behavioral Sciences*, *175*, 98–105. https://doi.org/https://doi.org/10.1016/j.sbspro.2015.01.1179

Vinerean, S., Cetina, I., Dumitrescu, L., & Tichindelean, M. (2013). The effects of social media marketing on online consumer behavior, *International Journal of Business and Management*, *8*(14), 66.

Wang, C., Tanveer, Y., Akram, U., & Bilal, M. (2019). Online impulse buying of organic food: A moderated (website personality) mediation (social appeal) process, *International Journal of Information Systems and Change Management*, *11*(1), 3–24.

Wiranata, A. T., & Hananto, A. (2020). Do website quality, fashion consciousness, and sales promotion increase impulse buying behavior of e-commerce buyers? *Indonesian Journal of Business and Entrepreneurship*, *6*(1), 74–74.

Wu, L., Chen, K. W., & Chiu, M. L. (2016). Defining key drivers of online impulse purchasing: A perspective of both impulse shoppers and system users, *International Journal of Information Management*, *36*(3), 284–296.

Yang, M. H., Lin, B., Chandlrees, N., & Chao, H. Y. (2009). The effect of perceived ethical performance of shopping websites on consumer trust, *Journal of Computer Information Systems*, *50*(1), 15–24.

Yadav, M., & Rahman, Z. (2017). Measuring consumer perception of social media marketing activities in e-commerce industry: Scale development & validation, *Telematics and Informatics*, *34*(7), 1294–1307.

Yazdanparast, A., Joseph, M., & Muniz, F. (2016). Consumer based brand equity in the 21st century: An examination of the role of social media marketing, *Young Consumers*, *17*(3), 243–255.

Yi-Shih Lo, L., Lin, S.-W., & Hsu, L.-Y. (2016). Motivation for online impulse buying: A two-factor theory perspective, *International Journal of Information Management*, *36*(151), 759–772.

Zhang, K. Z., Xu, H., Zhao, S., & Yu, Y. (2018). Online reviews and impulse buying behavior: The role of browsing and impulsiveness, *Internet Research*, *28*(3), 522–543.

BOOKS & PRECEEDINGS

Evans, D. (2010). *Social Media Marketing: The Next Generation of Business Engagement*. John Wiley & Sons, Indiana.

Hair, J. F., Black, W. C., Babin, B. J., & Anderson, R. E. (2010). *Multivariate Data Analysis* (7th Ed.). Pearson, New York.

Hair, J. F., et al. (2014). Partial least squares structural equation modeling (PLS-SEM), *European Business Review*, *26*(2), 106–121. https://doi.org/10.1108/EBR-10-2013-0128

Hair, J. F., Hult, T. M., & Sarstedt, M. (2017). *A Primer on Partial Least Squares Structural Equation Modeling (PLS-SEM)* (2nd Ed.). SAGE Publicstion, Inc, Los Angeles, London, New Delhi, Singapore, Washington, DC, Melbourne.

Henseler, J., & Fassott, G. (2010). Testing moderating effects in PLS path models: An illustration of available procedures. In W. Esposito Vinzi, J. Chin, J. Henseler, & H. Wang (Eds.), *Handbook of Partial Least Square* (pp. 713–735). Springer, Heidelberg.

14 Effect of Blockchain Technology on the Future of E-Commerce in India

Chhavi Sharma and Supriya Kamna
Department of Commerce, Shivaji College,
University of Delhi, Delhi, India

14.1 INTRODUCTION

The concept of blockchain was visualized in the year 1991. At that time, e-documents were increasing. People had just started accepting digital records. At that time, Haber and Stornetta (1990, August) had shown their concern for 'Time-Stamp a Digital Document'. In modern days, we have options of digitally signing a document and geotagging a picture but at that time, things were not possible. In 2014, blockchain technology found a new revolution. People started discussing the future of blockchain beyond the scope of currency. Few believe that this is the time when blockchain 2.0 has started. Cryptocurrency, decentralization, and distributed ledger made Blockchain technology unique and robust.

Blockchain is a system where data is saved in the form of blocks. The benefits of blockchain lie in the code. The more complex code represents more automation. That is how the blockchain develops the self-executing and smart contract. Blockchain is a database innovation that deals with the help of the Internet. No central server holds command over the database. The information is saved as a ledger or a library of sections on the blockchain.

Blockchain is a concern for everyone in the business world. The use of blockchain technology will simplify business operations. As the technology is new, the risk of adoption is always there. Yet it has changed many businesses. The technology that blockchain uses helps business security. Healthcare electronics security food products and many more businesses on the e-commerce platform will be helped by the ledger technology used by blockchain. Arora et al. (2019) raised these concerns in their paper 'Blockchain Technology Transforms E-Commerce for Enterprises'. Moreover, Kumar et al. (2020) focused on a rating-based consensus process called Proof of Accomplishment (PoA) in there research paper. They have studied the Ethereum network. They have emphasized PRODCHAIN in e-commerce products and services. It helped in increasing the traceability of the product. Their work helped us to understand the use of blockchain technology in supply chain management.

This work will help the researchers to gain knowledge about the blockchain implications for supply chain possibilities in future developments for society.

DOI: 10.1201/9781032614083-14

	Traditional Commerce	E-commerce	Blockchain Based E-commerce
1	Business Happens Face to Face. A bond between buyer and sellers developed	Online Sales and purchases happen. Buyers never know the sellers. No social bonding	Buyer and seller will not meet but the country of origin /Manufacturer will be known to the buyer. It will reduce the issue of Bondage labor of Chain/ Blood Diamond of Africa etc.
2	Limited to geographic location	Potential to sell across the world. International Payments are regulated under international laws.	This type of trade marketplace is global and no intervention of banks and crypto payments can be made.
3	Payments and Delivery fraud are less.	The risk of fraud is higher than in traditional commerce	Fraud is almost not possible. As each traction has a previous Hash and Ledger can't be tempered.
4	Instant delivery of Goods	Delivery takes time	Delivery takes time but the package is traceable
5	Businesses are limited to Business hours	Businesses are beyond Business hours. (24X7). Limitation of payment time by banks.	Businesses are beyond Business hours. (24X7). No dependence on banks in trade

FIGURE 14.1   Comparison of Traditional Commerce, E-commerce, and Blockchain-Based E-Commerce[a]

[a] Researcher's' Observation based upon literature

Blockchain technology will eliminate the problems in e-commerce. In India, cryptocurrency is not able to get legal tender. But once it gets, the payments will be far safer than even. With the help of blockchain technology, the tracking of merchandise will become easy. Loss of package will almost become impossible once the blockchain technology is implemented correctly (Figure 14.1).

It can be said that the future of blockchain will be opening a new horizon for e-commerce. Not only this but surely customers will also be having a new product range. NFT (non-fungible tokens), e-real state, and properties in metaverse will be introducing a completely new product line. The different aspects related to blockchain-based e-commerce can never be decided with mere debate. Also, the blockchain model is in the process of development at this stage, so collecting real-time experiences from consumers cannot be discussed. So, the researcher tried to gather the onion of software developers and IT professionals about the future of blockchain-based e-commerce. The researcher has defined the research problem as **'Effect of BlockChain Technology upon the future of E-commerce in India'**.

14.2   RESEARCH METHODOLOGY

Because researchers typically choose a postulate to study a phenomenon and define the construct using similar criteria, this study is distinctive in and of itself. Making the research methodology explicit will aid in making the study thorough and well-organized.

14.2.1   Objectives of the Study

- To study the scope of blockchain technology in e-commerce
- To study the blockchain technology-based e-commerce structure
- To study the new product types that may be available exclusively due to blockchain technology in the e-commerce

14.2.1.1   Population

This research considers software developers and IT professionals as the population. Those who have an interest and involvement in blockchain technology.

14.2.1.2   Sample Location

Delhi NCR.

14.2.1.3   Sampling Method

The researcher has used blockchain technology-related interest groups as the population. The convenience sampling method is used for the sample section. To eliminate the cost and complexity of the sample selection, the researcher has used non-parametric sampling. The acceptable margin of error can be assumed as 5%. The margin of error is the amount of error that you can tolerate. If 90% of respondents answer yes, while 10% answer no, you may be able to tolerate a larger amount of error than if the respondents are split 50–50 or 45–55. A lower margin of error requires a larger sample size. In Delhi NCR, the number of respondents (software developers and IT professionals) can be tentatively considered 20,000.

14.2.1.4   Response Distribution

If you ask a random sample of ten people and if they like donuts and nine of them respond positively, your conclusion about the general population will differ from what it would be if five responded positively and five negatively. The most cautious assumption is to set the response distribution at 50%. Beam is taken into account for the current sampling at 50%. Thus, 377 will be the required sample size for a 95% level of confidence (Raosoft, Inc. Sample Size Calculator).

The primary methods used by the researcher to choose the respondent were email and referrals used to secure their consent. People were questioned about their involvement with cryptocurrency, e-commerce, and blockchain technology. They are also asked to express their opinions on the potential for blockchain-based e-commerce in India. Few specific goals account for the majority of the response. The most frequent predictions made by respondents were an increase in tradability, an improvement in quality, the prevention of fraud, and secure online shopping. Additionally, they predicted that we might soon see a new line of NFT products, including e-flats (e-space) and VR-based offices and schools (metaverse). The researcher used all of these responses to create a questionnaire to gauge public opinion on the potential for blockchain-based e-commerce.

14.2.1.5 KMO and Bartlett's Test

We should move forward with exploratory factor analysis if the Kaiser–Meyer–Olkin (KMO) Measure of Sampling Adequacy is equal to or greater than 0.60; this indicates that the sample used was suitable (Figure 14.2). We should move forward with the exploratory factor analysis if Bartlett's test of sphericity is significant (p 0.05). By having a KMO value of 0.871 and a Bartlett's Test value of 0.000, the current sample meets both criteria. The Initial Eigenvalues are displayed in Figure 14.3. Only components with Total Initial Eigenvalues greater than 1 should be considered.

KMO and Bartlett's Test		
Kaiser-Meyer-Olkin Measure of Sampling Adequacy.		.871
Bartlett's Test of Sphericity	Approx. Chi-Square	2695.123
	Df	300
	Sig.	.000

FIGURE 14.2   KMO and Bartlett's Test

	Total Variance Explained						
	Initial Eigenvalues			Extraction Sums of Squared Loadings			Rotation Sums of Squared Loadings
Component	Total	% of Variance	Cumulative %	Total	% of Variance	Cumulative %	Total
1	8.552	34.209	34.209	8.552	34.209	34.209	4.969
2	3.580	14.322	48.530	3.580	14.322	48.530	5.429
3	1.939	7.756	56.286	1.939	7.756	56.286	5.276
4	1.291	5.162	61.449	1.291	5.162	61.449	3.691
5	1.122	4.486	65.935	1.122	4.486	65.935	4.271
6	.909	3.635	69.570				
7	.867	3.469	73.039				
8	.759	3.035	76.074				
9	.630	2.520	78.594				
10	.623	2.494	81.087				
11	.567	2.267	83.355				
12	.507	2.028	85.383				
13	.484	1.935	87.318				
14	.431	1.722	89.040				
15	.406	1.624	90.664				
16	.345	1.381	92.044				
17	.319	1.275	93.319				
18	.286	1.142	94.461				
19	.280	1.119	95.580				
20	.253	1.012	96.593				
21	.224	.897	97.489				
22	.199	.796	98.285				
23	.194	.776	99.062				
24	.131	.522	99.584				
25	.104	.416	100.000				
Extraction Method: Principal Component Analysis.							
when components are correlated, sums of squared loadings cannot be added to obtain a total variance.							

FIGURE 14.3   Total Variance Explained Table

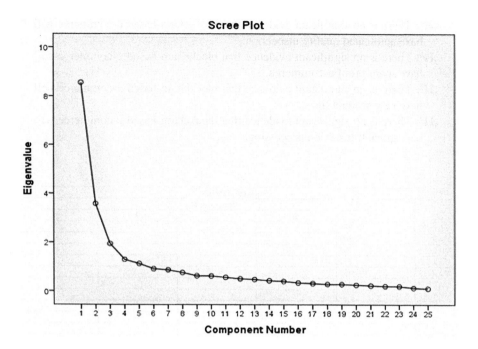

FIGURE 14.4   Scree plot.

Five components in our case have Total Initial Eigenvalues that are higher than 1. These five factors account for 65.93% of the variance. We can therefore infer that there are two factors. But we also need to consider the Scree storyline.

Scree plot shows that we have five factors (Figure 14.4). Figure 14.5 shows factor weights. The five factors have a mix of negative and positive components.

Figure 14.6 shows that there is no strong correlation between factors which is good for our analysis.

Based on the components selected from the opinion of respondents, the extracted factors can be named:

1. Automated tradability
2. Automated quality inspection
3. Scam-proof e-commerce
4. New product lines
5. Quick transaction processing

Based upon the literature review, objective, research gap, and FA (PCA and EFA), the following hypotheses are developed:

$_1H^0$: There is no significant evidence that blockchain-based e-commerce will have automated tradability.

$_2$H^0: There is no significant evidence that blockchain-based e-commerce will have automated quality inspection.

$_3$H^0: There is no significant evidence that blockchain-based e-commerce will have scam-proof e-commerce.

$_4$H^0: There is no significant evidence that blockchain-based e-commerce will have new product lines.

$_5$H^0: There is no significant evidence that blockchain-based e-commerce will have quick transaction processing.

Pattern Matrix[a]					
	Component				
	1	2	3	4	5
VAR008	.849				
VAR015	.809				
VAR019	.788				
VAR020	.672				
VAR012	.480				
VAR023	.458			.408	
VAR013		.894			
VAR007		.802			
VAR016		.796			
VAR014		.786			
VAR018		.770			
VAR010		.712			
VAR004			.859		
VAR006			.777		
VAR002			.738		
VAR001			-.718		
VAR005			-.649		
VAR003			-.460		
VAR021				.779	
VAR022				.642	
VAR011				.450	
VAR025				-.442	
VAR017					-.784
VAR009					-.725
VAR024					.598

Extraction Method: Principal Component Analysis.
Rotation Method: Oblimin with Kaiser Normalization.
a. Rotation converged in 13 iterations.

FIGURE 14.5   Pattern Matrix

Component Correlation Matrix					
Component	1	2	3	4	5
1	1.000	-.109	.192	.304	-.378
2	-.109	1.000	-.388	-.109	.278
3	.192	-.388	1.000	.236	-.312
4	.304	-.109	.236	1.000	-.209
5	-.378	.278	-.312	-.209	1.000

Extraction Method: Principal Component Analysis.
Rotation Method: Oblimin with Kaiser Normalization.

FIGURE 14.6   Component Correlation Matrix

The consistency of Cronbach's Alpha has been used to help with the questionnaire's test. Cronbach's Alpha has a value of 0.696. A score greater than 0.600 is regarded as favourable for the questionnaire. SPSS will be used for both data collection and analysis. IBM's SPSS is a feature-rich software package for calculations. It uses a drop-down menu and is user-centric. A Wilcoxon signed-rank test with one sample will be used by the researcher. When the data cannot be assumed to be normally distributed, a non-parametric alternative to a one-sample t-test is the one-sample Wilcoxon signed-rank test. It is used to ascertain whether the sample's median is equal to a standard value that is well known (in our case, the midpoint of the 1–5 scale, 2.5, which is the theoretical value).

In statistics, we can define the corresponding *null hypothesis* (*H0*) as follows:

$H0{:}m{=}m0$

The corresponding *alternative hypotheses* (*Ha*) are as follows:

$Ha{:}m{\neq}m0$ (different)

14.3   DATA ANALYSIS AND INTERPRETATION

1. $_1H^0$: There is no significant evidence that blockchain-based e-commerce will have automated tradability.

Total N	377
Test statistics	53,213.500
Standard error	1,982.247
Standard test statistics	10.363
Asymptotic Sig. (2-side test)	0.000

The observed median is greater than the fictitious mean, according to a sample Wilcoxon test. Positive test statistics are present. This also supports the testing of the hypotheses. There is strong evidence that blockchain-based e-commerce will have automated trading because the sig value (p) is 0.000 (less than 0.05), and the null hypothesis will therefore be rejected (Figures 14.7 and 14.8).

Hypothesis Test Summary

	Null Hypothesis	Test	Sig.	Decision
1	The median of Automated_tradability equals 2.500.	One-Sample Wilcoxon Signed Rank Test	.000	Reject the null hypothesis.

Asymptotic significances are displayed. The significance level is .05.

FIGURE 14.7   Hypothesis test summary.

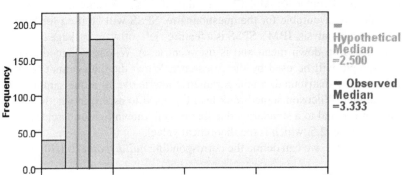

FIGURE 14.8   One-Sample Wilcoxon signed-rank test.

2. $_2$**H^0:** There is no significant evidence that blockchain-based e-commerce will have automated quality inspection.

Total N	377
Test statistics	60,643.500
Standard error	1,999.753
Standard test statistics	13.962
Asymptotic Sig. (2-side test)	0.000

The observed median is greater than the fictitious mean, according to a sample Wilcoxon test. Positive test statistics are present. This also supports the testing of the hypotheses. There is strong evidence that blockchain-based e-commerce will have automated quality inspection because the sig value (p) is 0.000 (less than 0.05), rejecting the null hypothesis (Figures 14.9 and 14.10).

Hypothesis Test Summary

	Null Hypothesis	Test	Sig.	Decision
1	The median of Automated_Quality_Inspection equals 2.500.	One-Sample Wilcoxon Signed Rank Test	.000	Reject the null hypothesis.

Asymptotic significances are displayed. The significance level is .05.

FIGURE 14.9   Hypothesis test summary.

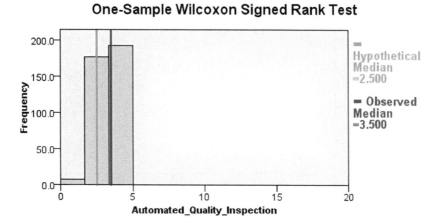

FIGURE 14.10   One-Sample Wilcoxon signed-rank test.

3. ₃**H⁰**: There is no significant evidence that blockchain-based e-commerce will have scam-proof e-commerce.

Total N	377
Test statistics	61,703.00
Standard error	1,982.832
Standard test statistics	15.750
Asymptotic Sig. (2-side test)	0.000

The observed median is greater than the fictitious mean, according to a sample Wilcoxon test. Positive test statistics are present. This also supports the testing of the hypotheses. The null hypothesis will be rejected because the sig value (p) is 0.000 (less than 0.05), indicating that there is strong evidence that blockchain-based e-commerce will feature scam-proof transactions (Figures 14.11 and 14.12).

Hypothesis Test Summary

	Null Hypothesis	Test	Sig.	Decision
1	The median of Scam_Proof_E_commerce equals 2.500.	One-Sample Wilcoxon Signed Rank Test	.000	Reject the null hypothesis.

Asymptotic significances are displayed. The significance level is .05.

FIGURE 14.11   Hypothesis test summary.

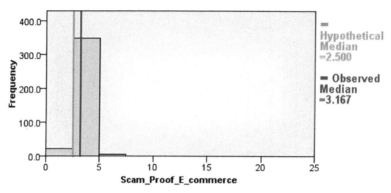

FIGURE 14.12   One-Sample Wilcoxon signed-rank test.

4. ₄**H⁰:** There is no significant evidence that blockchain-based e-commerce will have new product lines.

Total N	377
Test statistics	47,945.500
Standard error	1,683.772
Standard test statistics	12.841
Asymptotic Sig. (2-side test)	0.000

The observed median is greater than the fictitious mean, according to a sample Wilcoxon test. Positive test statistics are present. This also supports the testing of the hypotheses. There is strong evidence that blockchain-based e-commerce will offer new product lines because the sig value (p) is 0.000 (less than 0.05), rejecting the null hypothesis (Figures 14.13 and 14.14).

Hypothesis Test Summary

	Null Hypothesis	Test	Sig.	Decision
1	The median of New_Product_lines equals 2.500.	One-Sample Wilcoxon Signed Rank Test	.000	Reject the null hypothesis.

Asymptotic significances are displayed. The significance level is .05.

FIGURE 14.13   Hypothesis test summary.

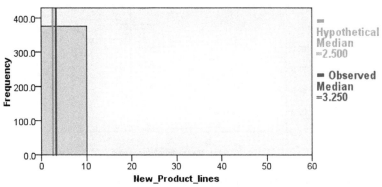

FIGURE 14.14   One-sample Wilcoxon signed-rank test.

5. $_5$**H^0:** There is no significant evidence that blockchain-based e-commerce will have quick transaction processing.

Total N	377
Test statistics	63,025.500
Standard error	2,112.312
Standard test statistics	12.971
Asymptotic Sig. (2-side test)	0.000

The observed median is greater than the fictitious mean, according to a sample Wilcoxon test. Positive test statistics are present. This also supports the testing of the hypotheses. The null hypothesis will be rejected because the sig value (p) is 0.000 (less than 0.05), and it can therefore be stated that 'There is substantial evidence that blockchain-based e-commerce will have Quick transaction Processing' (Figures 14.15 and 14.16).

Hypothesis Test Summary

	Null Hypothesis	Test	Sig.	Decision
1	The median of Quick_transaction_Processing equals 2.500.	One-Sample Wilcoxon Signed Rank Test	.000	Reject the null hypothesis.

Asymptotic significances are displayed. The significance level is .05.

FIGURE 14.15   Hypothesis test summary.

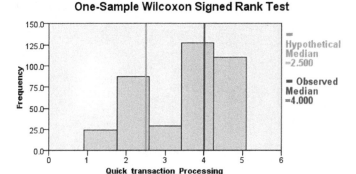

FIGURE 14.16   One-Sample Wilcoxon signed-rank test.

14.3.1 Implications

The researcher can interpret future e-commerce in addition to the statistical intervention of the respondents' onions. Blockchain is a ledger-based technology that extends beyond cryptocurrencies like Bitcoin. Blockchain also provides e-commerce features that make it possible for buyers and sellers to engage in seamless online buying and selling. E-commerce and blockchain have a direct relationship. Offering enormous advantages, its growth has numerous effects on the e-commerce sector, some of which are listed later. Smart contracts, which are computer programmes that automate operations based on predetermined criteria, are introduced by blockchain technology. Since smart contracts are stored on blockchains, e-commerce-related activities can be easily automated thanks to them. By lowering the cost of hiring staff, they can aid in the growth of an online store. Smart contracts can also facilitate inventory management, enabling online retailers to keep track of their stock levels. When online retailers employ blockchain technology to run their operations, they can immediately offer their customers redeemable loyalty points once they meet certain purchase thresholds. These reward points may also be applied to various e-commerce platforms, as part of a collaborative effort, or alternatively, assuming a parent association has numerous e-commerce websites. Customers can now benefit from tailored offers and restrictions from online businesses thanks to technology as well. These incentive programmes can assist online retailers in gaining loyal customers and expanding the appeal and advantages of their products.

A dependable supply and appropriation chain can help online retailers achieve their specific business goals and objectives. This is due to the inventory network's ability to let business owners know what products are on the way and when they will arrive. It aids company owners in assessing the types of goods suppliers are providing. These business owners have the option of preventing suppliers from trading items and ensuring that the process is honest and transparent when they use blockchain technology to track their inventory. Blockchain enables e-commerce businesses to quickly integrate stock control, exchange processing, marketing content, and other authoritative processes. By not overspending on services that support these operations or hiring IT support staff to oversee the operations, they save money.

According to estimates, there are more than 100 million cryptocurrency users worldwide, showing that there is a sizable global market for this technology. Due to the inaccessibility of certain countries or payment methods in particular areas, a business may now enter new markets thanks to cryptocurrency.

It is amazing how cryptocurrency enables online trade in underdeveloped nations. The peer-to-peer mechanism that cryptocurrencies offer means that people and other clients in such countries don't need to bother with an intermediary to handle their payments. Furthermore, blockchain technology enables online merchants to profit from the marketplace's growing consumer base, enabling trade to support both the buyer's and seller's ends.

14.4   CONCLUSION

This chapter aims to predict the direction of e-commerce. Blockchains enable all activities permitted by current trading systems and are faster and less expensive than current trading systems. We can only democratize the economy now that the future is here by increasing the transparency of finance and trade. By using the strength of financial institutions, blockchain technology aims to give users control over their transactions. An effective economic ecosystem for customers and online retailers is created by blockchain technologies and e-commerce platforms. Online retailers are finding new ways to serve their customers as they quickly integrate distributed ledger technology into their business processes. They now have a powerful tool to enhance their customers' experiences thanks to the blockchain. Here are some additional e-commerce market opportunities that blockchain technologies will bring about. Blockchain technology in e-commerce is intriguing because it has advantages for both buyers and sellers. It lowers costs associated with inventory management and payment processing while providing cost-effective solutions to problems with financial security and cyber threats. Cartridges make it simple for e-commerce businesses to combine other commercial activities with inventory management, payment processing, product descriptions, and images.

This analysis aims to predict the long-term success of e-commerce. With the help of a survey of a specialized group, the research assistant attempted to gather important factors. Blockchain technology offers an exciting business opportunity in terms of transparency, dependability, and price reductions. It also presents numerous threats to companies that are unable to raise the value of their customers. Due to the unique benefits of blockchain in e-commerce, it is now crucial for the company to use it for its overall development. Those vendors who adopted transparency in their business exchanges and successfully managed client data claim that blockchain technology is beneficial. It also includes crypto exchanges and aids in reducing reliance on paper-based inheritance systems. E-commerce is becoming a popular front for the business endeavours of vendors from all over the world. Blockchain technology is now in use as the foundation for online payments and sales. Blockchains facilitate all activities that current commerce systems permit, in addition to being quicker and more affordable.

The innovative aspect of blockchain technology in e-commerce is that it benefits both consumers and retailers. It provides practical answers to problems with financial security and cyberthreats. Additionally, it lowers the costs associated with processing payments and managing inventories. Blockchains make it simple for e-commerce companies to combine traditional business activities with inventory control, payment processing, product descriptions, and product images. In exchange, they receive a discount on the cost of operating the systems that support these operations or the cost of employing IT support personnel. Similar to Bitcoin, cryptocurrencies slug down the transaction fees that banks charge to facilitate transactions. Blockchain technology makes it simple for e-commerce companies to combine different business activities with inventory management, payment methods, product descriptions, and images. However, it's wonderful that blockchain technology is enabling online trade between third-world nations. Customers in these nations don't require a middleman to process their payment requests thanks to Bitcoin's peer-to-peer network. Additionally, these technologies are opening doors for online merchants to tap into the consumer markets in developing nations.

REFERENCES

Arora, A., Sharma, M., & Bhaskaran, S. (2019, November). Blockchain Technology Transforms E-Commerce for Enterprises. In *International Conference on Recent Developments in Science, Engineering and Technology* (pp. 26–34). Springer, Singapore.

Bulsara, H. P., & Vaghela, P. S. (2020). Blockchain technology for e-commerce industry, *International Journal of Advanced Science and Technology*, *29*(5), 3793–3798.

Chang, Y. W., Lin, K. P., & Shen, C. Y. (2019, March). Blockchain technology for e-marketplace. In *2019 IEEE International Conference on Pervasive Computing and Communications Workshops (PerCom Workshops)* (pp. 429–430). IEEE.

Garg, S., Gupta, S., & Gupta, B. (2022). Impacts of Blockchain on Digital Marketing. In *Intelligent Sustainable Systems* (pp. 209–217). Springer, Singapore.

Haber, S., & Stornetta, W. S. (1990, August). How to Time-Stamp a Digital Document. In *Conference on the Theory and Application of Cryptography* (pp. 437–455). Springer, Berlin, Heidelberg.

Hueber, O. (2018). The blockchain and the sidechain innovations for the electronic commerce beyond the Bitcoin's framework, *International Journal of Transitions and Innovation Systems*, *6*(1), 88–102.

Ismanto, L., Ar, H. S., Fajar, A. N., & Bachtiar, S. (2019, July). Blockchain as E-Commerce Platform in Indonesia. In *Journal of Physics: Conference Series* (Vol. 1179, No. 1, p. 012114). IOP Publishing.

Jiang, Y., Wang, C., Wang, Y., & Gao, L. (2019, February). A Privacy-Preserving e-Commerce System based on the Blockchain Technology. In *2019 IEEE International Workshop on Blockchain Oriented Software Engineering (IWBOSE)* (pp. 50–55). IEEE.

Kumar, G., Saha, R., Buchanan, W. J., Geetha, G., Thomas, R., Rai, M. K., ... & Alazab, M. (2020). Decentralized accessibility of e-commerce products through blockchain technology, *Sustainable Cities and Society*, *62*, 102361.

Lahkani, M. J., Wang, S., Urbański, M., & Egorova, M. (2020). Sustainable B2B e-commerce and blockchain-based supply chain finance, *Sustainability*, *12*(10), 3968.

Liu, C., Xiao, Y., Javangula, V., Hu, Q., Wang, S., & Cheng, X. (2018). Normachain: A blockchain-based normalized autonomous transaction settlement system for IoT-based e-commerce, *IEEE Internet of Things Journal*, *6*(3), 4680–4693.

Mohdhar, A., & Shaalan, K. (2021). The Future of e-Commerce Systems: 2030 and Beyond. In *Recent Advances in Technology Acceptance Models and Theories* (pp. 311–330). Springer, Cham.

Roy, U. K., & Tang, W. (2021). Transformation the Business of eCommerce Through Blockchain. In *International Conference on Human-Computer Interaction* (pp. 85–91). Springer, Cham.

15 Assessing the Usage of Various Data Mining Techniques for Analysis of Online Social Networks

Sushma Malik[1], Deepti Gupta[1],
and Anamika Rana[2]
[1]Institute of Innovation in Technology
and Management, Delhi, India
[2]Maharaja Surajmal Institute, Delhi, India

15.1 INTRODUCTION

By the end of the 20th century, the use of the internet had grown enormously and changed the social life of the internet user. Internet has brought great communication platform by introducing social networking sites (SNS) and these sites are also called the online social networks (OSN). Basically, these sites are online communities that are created by users with common interest and activities, similar backgrounds and mutual friendships [1]. SNS are web-based design sites that help the user to upload the data in different format like in text, images, videos, remark about the products, and share their views on their activities with other online users. SNSs have reached an incredible number of users. These websites are used by millions of users as a novel communication tool and real time dynamic data source on which users can communicate with other active users on these sites besides geographical location [2, 3]. SNS is commonly used for information sharing, posting the reviews of the products, sharing online photos, advertisements and opinion or sentiment expression. Number of users become interested in and relaying on the social networks for information in real time. SNS allows users to express their opinion on the activity and it may be positive or negative. Consumers' opinion of products, which is shared on social platform, plays a significant role for the number of organizations [4]. Social networks act as a communication platform where a number of users are interacting and sharing information with other users through personalized user profiles [5, 6].

Facebook become the market leader with 2740 million monthly active users and 2291 million monthly active users in YouTube. On social microblogging site like Twitter, it has reached 253 million monthly active users [7, 8].

Social networks play vital role in several business activities like invention of new products, promotion of products, customer services, marketing research, publicity and communication with workers [9]. Social networking sites have vital role in disaster management by spreading emergency information to the affected community

DOI: 10.1201/9781032614083-15

by disaster. Social media data is used to extract the critical information to develop alleviation plan on pre- and post-disaster time [10].

For studying the connections and exposing the relations among nodes in a network, a new area called social network analysis (SNA) has evolved. SNA is an imperative and valuable tool which is used to extract the knowledge from enormous and unregulated form of data [11].

Social network analysis, generally defined as mapping, determines the relationship and flow of data among users, groups of users, organizations or other information processing entities. Earlier SNA was basically used for exploratory of individual and social group structure and behaviors but now it's used in complex domains like commerce, economy, banking, health and many more [12]. Social networks term was first used by John A. Barnes who examined the relation between people living in Norway. Social networks are structures that consist of nodes with which individuals, groups and organizations are linked to each other by common values, vision and thoughts. After establishing the social networks successfully, it influences the social processes by accessing user information. In development process, social networks can affect policies, strategies, projects and partnerships, including their designs, implementations and results [13, 14]. Sentimental analysis is the mechanism to identify the opinion of the user which may be positive or negative and it is basically used where users provide the data in the form of reviews like on social networking sites, blogs etc. [15]. The analogy of social networks with graphs is presented in Section 15.2 followed by discussion over some important properties of graph in Section 15.3. The review of all the DM techniques and corresponding proposed approaches for analysis of social networks has been introduced in tabular format in Section 15.4 of the paper that follows the various research problems and challenges involved in Sections 15.5 and 15.6, respectively.

15.2 REPRESENTATION OF SOCIAL NETWORKS AS GRAPHS

A social network is similar to a graph consisting of finite count of vertices and ties among those vertices. These ties or relations can be professional, personal or acquainted in nature, which can represent flow of goods, services, information or emotions over them [16]. Social networks analysts use two kinds of tools from mathematics to represent information about patterns of ties among social actors: graphs and matrices [17]. Further, a social networks can be a directed graph like Twitter where several people follow an individual or an undirected graph like Facebook where a tie or link amid two vertices signifies a mutual or reciprocal relationship. Also, a distinction can be made between weighted and unweighted graphs. The weight of an edge or tie is a function of frequency of interaction, exchange of services, intimacy and emotional intensity [18].

15.3 PROPERTIES OF SOCIAL NETWORKS

The arrangement of nodes and connections in a social network resembles a graph where various individuals are tied together through social relationships among them [19]. The author [20] discussed about the static and the changing properties of weighted and unweighted graphs. Static properties describe the structure of the snapshot of a graph, whereas the dynamic properties help to study the evolvement of graph over time. One of the interesting static property of graph was discovered by [21] popularly named small world phenomena or the six degrees of separation. The study of the network properties has found its applications in detecting frauds in online auction networks [22], improving recommendation systems and analyzing the network value of customers by various marketing companies.

15.3.1 DIAMETER

For a static graph, the maximum distance amid any two nodes where distance is nothing but the minimum count of hops from one node to another on a path irrespective of directionality is basically the diameter of a graph [20]. Also, some literature in reference to social networks have defined diameter to be average shortest path or sometimes the longest shortest path between connected nodes [17].

15.3.2 NAVIGABILITY

According to author in [23], social networks have a very interesting property of search ability. They presented a model that defines a class of searchable networks, which can be applied to various search problems in social networks like finding the location of data files in a peer-to-peer network or the information in case of distributed databases.

15.3.3 CLUSTERING COEFFICIENT

For a node u in a set of vertices V, clustering coefficient is described as the probability of having an edge between two adjacent neighbors of u. Or in other way round, it can be expressed as two persons having a mutual friend in a network. The extent of connection among neighbors of a node is measured by the coefficient of clustering [24].

15.3.4 RECIPROCITY

It can be considered an important network level statistical measure, which is basically the probability of having mutual connections or bidirectional arrows in a directed graph. The measure of reciprocity can be figured out by dividing the number of mutual connections with the total count of connections in a network [16]. A mutual edge or connection is where an edge exists from vertices a to b and b to a. For an undirected graph, this reciprocity measure is having its value equal to 1 as all the nodes are symmetric in nature. Life is all about give and take relationship [25].

15.3.5 CENTRALITY AND POWER

The power of a social networks is actually a crucial property [18].

15.4   DATA MINING TECHNIQUES FOR SOCIAL NETWORK ANALYSIS

Various techniques of data mining are used in the social network analysis. Some techniques are listed in Table 15.1.

TABLE 15.1

Data Mining Techniques for Social Network Analysis

Approach/Definition	Tool/Technique/Experiment	Author/Year
Graph theoretic/A social network can be observed and modeled as a graph where the people in graph are treated as nodes and links or connections between them as edges. It can be a directed graph in the case of influencer-follower relationship like Instagram or an undirected graph like Facebook depicting a friendship link between the two.	Clustering-based churn prediction model Taking into consideration the competition in telecommunication sector, the author proposed a churn prediction model based on graph theory and clustering. Firstly, a network call graph is created using one month CDR data. Next, the data is preprocessed by eliminating non-valid MSISDNs. Nine different metrics are split into three categories: directed, undirected and articulation point metrics. Some statistical approaches give three clusters for undirected and four clusters for directed metrics. Ward's minimum variance method is later used for clustering of standardized sample data.	[26, 27]
Community Detection/A community is a smaller group in a large network where nodes generally have something common among them like interests, profession and religion. It is crucial to identify communities to model the dynamism of domain to which they belong.	Borgia clustering based on gravitational clustering algorithm leader follower algorithm (LFA) and fast leader-follower algorithm (FLFA) based on sequential community graph	[28] [29]
	Each actor or node is represented by affinity of best friend, best common friend affinity and influence matrix. Each actor is assigned a social value based on its degree in the network. LFA and FLFA algorithms based on sequential community graph model were proposed to disclose intersecting communities and their performance and accuracy is assessed using F1-score and runtime against some previously proposed algorithms-modularity optimization, CESNA and BigClam on several graphs: Prime Number graph, Culture Show 2010, Culture Show 2011, Les Misérables and IMDB graph.	[30] [31] [32] [33]

(Continued)

TABLE 15.1 (Continued)
Data Mining Techniques for Social Network Analysis

Approach/Definition	Tool/Technique/Experiment	Author/Year
Recommender system/It is a type of information refining system that provides customized content and services to users according to their preferences from explosive amount of randomly and frequently generated data.	Collaborative filtering content based	[34]
	A user-based collaborative filtering model is generated to recommend best and needed research papers to researchers to save their time and effort. The dataset taken here consists of userid, paperid and the ratings given by users to respective papers. A content-based filtering recommender system Movie Genome is proposed by author to recommend movies on the grounds of various content descriptors that are block level and I-vector audio features, aesthetic and deep learning visual features and genre and tags metadata features.	[35] [36] [37] [38] [39]
Semantic web/The main objective of semantic web technique is to merge the data from distributed data stores and apply ontologies and certain reasoning techniques to combine it.	Friend of a friend	[40]
	The author uses the FOAF semantic web technique for cross network linkage analysis to merge the user profiles of same person from 11 different social networking websites using the semantics of Owl language on the basis of inverse functional property.	
	VoyeurServer	[41]
	Based on the open-source java-based Web Harvest Framework, the author designed the client-server Voyeur Server tool to allow developers to customize their data mining solutions for scraping data from online social networks.	
Opinion analysis/It can be considered a process of discovering and recognizing the positive or negative expression in comments, posts or blogs that can influence the decision or choices of online users.	Aspect-based	[42]
	Considering as basis and extending the work of the author suggested the use of NLP rules for sentiment and subjectivity classification at aspect level. Their research also includes development of various opinion visualization and summarization methods to understand the preferences of customers for various reviewed products.	[43] [44]
Opinion formation/Opinion formation basically deals with forming an opinion about any product, person or place that is highly affected by opinion of other influencers.	Homophily clustering	[45]
	Based on agent-based modeling approach, a model was proposed for investigating the coevolution of opinion and location	[46]

(Continued)

TABLE 15.1 (Continued)
Data Mining Techniques for Social Network Analysis

Approach/Definition	Tool/Technique/Experiment	Author/Year
	modifying the DW model allowing interactions between agents close in opinion and location and updating the same accordingly. The outcomes of random and homophilous mobility model were compared.	[47] [48]
Opinion definition and opinion summarization/An opinion in a document can be discovered and located in a text, sentence or topic, which needs summarization to sum up the various opinions stated by analyzing the degree and polarities of sentiments.	Support vector machine The author proposed a support vector-based classification model to perform feature and polarity classification on Amazon dataset having 535 sentences containing the ungrammatical customer reviews.	[49]
Sentiment orientation/A natural language processing-based technique to inspect the polarity of sentiments expressed for a product or thing on social networks in blogs, reviews, comments or surveys.	Naïve Bayes and Linear SVM A comparative analysis is performed on a movie dataset from IMDb containing 1000 positive and negative reviews using Naïve Bayes and Linear SVM algorithms to process the sentiments using the RapidMiner tool.	[50]
Product ratings and reviews/Studying the impact of customer reviews and ratings expressed online for a product for improving the performance of businesses.	Regression Following the mediation and moderation analysis from the study demonstrates the mediation effect of trust between hotel consideration and numerical rating.	[51] [52]
Aspect rating analysis/Evaluating the opinion at aspect level and analyzing the rating by each individual for every aspect of a product.	Latent aspect rating analysis The author proposed a latent rating regression (LRR) model to find an effective solution for LARA problem with the intention of analyzing the online expressed opinions at topical aspect level and discovering the rating given by every individual reviewer on all aspects of a product and weight factor of different aspects signifying its importance.	[53] [54]
Unsupervised classification/A classification somehow similar to clustering where exact number of classes is not known in advance.	Part of speech (POS) tagging A huge amount of unlabeled, tokenized monolingual text data is fed as input to the system where Chinese Whisper,	[55] [56]

(Continued)

TABLE 15.1 (Continued)
Data Mining Techniques for Social Network Analysis

Approach/Definition	Tool/Technique/Experiment	Author/Year
	a graph clustering algorithm is applied to distributional similarity data and neighboring co-occurrence profiles to generate two tagsets of high-medium and medium-low frequency words having hundreds of clusters. The weighted average cluster purity comes out to be 88% over 53% in 282 clusters with 26 having size more than 100. The efficiency of the constructed unsupervised POS tagger is measured using cluster-conditional tag perplexity measure PP.	[57]
Semi-supervised classification/An ML approach that forms cluster using unsupervised learning and then label large volume of unlabeled data using small volume of labeled data.	Document word co-regularization for semi-supervised sentiment analysis	[58]
	The author proposes a unique semi-supervised algorithm for sentiment analysis that uses combination of lexical prior knowledge and unlabeled examples. The suggested approach uses bipartite graph representation of data for carrying out combined analysis of sentiments at documents and words level.	
Supervised classification/The problem of supervised classification deals with task of finding suitable class for unknown data using a classifier trained using labeled dataset having samples with known classes.	Logistic regression, SGD, Naïve Bayes, Multimonial	[59]
	To classify critical patient's post and divert the attention of medical personnel to it, the authors extended their previous work and compared the accuracy of six different classifiers: logistic regression, SGD, Bernoulli Naïve Bayes, Multimonial Naïve Bayes, SVM and linear support vector on Twitter healthcare chat CSAQT.	[60]
Topic detection and tracking/According to a report, it is a sponsored initiative consisting of three tasks that is dividing speech into different stories, identifying stories or news regarding any new event and finding all stories related to the same topic in the stream.	Probabilistic models, classical topic detection and tracking	[61]
	They studied and observed that the quality of detected topics is highly influenced by the type of detection method used, sampling procedure, pre-processing of data, volume of activity and nature of event concluding the combination of n-gram and df-idft outperforms every other technique.	

(Continued)

TABLE 15.1 (Continued)
Data Mining Techniques for Social Network Analysis

Approach/Definition	Tool/Technique/Experiment	Author/Year
	First story detection	[62]
	Using the approach author presented their work to detect first story on Twitter and in parallel compared it with Wikipedia stream pages with abnormal large page views.	[63]
	Hotstream	[64]
	The proposed methodology is carried out in two stages that is story finding and story development stage where facts are focused on. In the first stage, sampling, indexing and grouping of similar messages from Twitter timeline was performed following by ranking in second stage.	[65]
	Incremental online clustering along with Naïve Bayes Classifier	[66]
	An incremental online clustering approach is proposed to address event identification problem and is evaluated over 2.6 million Twitter messages to differentiate between the event and non-event messages. Cosine similarity function as defined in is used as clustering similarity function where each cluster is represented by a centroid.	[67] [68]

15.5   RESEARCH ISSUES OF SNA

The online social networks are highly rich in data, which can be structured, semi-structured and unstructured in format. They provide unprecedented opportunities and challenges for DM and knowledge discovery process [28]. Few of the research issues that researchers face or come across while analyzing social networks are identified as follows.

15.5.1   LINKAGE BASED AND STRUCTURAL ANALYSIS

This type of analysis involves studying the evolving structure of the online social networks and examining the linkage behavior of network to determine and understand the communities, important nodes, links and regions of the network [6, 28].

15.5.2   DYNAMIC AND STATIC NATURE OF NETWORKS

Apart from studying the linkage behavior of a network, the study of its content is equally important and can provide better results in certain applications. For example, community detection that is generally content-based and richer in some topical expertise.

Static networks like bibliographic networks change slowly and are thus easier to analyze and process as related to dynamic networks like streaming networks—Facebook and YouTube—and mobile applications like Google Latitude where interactions among entities in motion led the structural changes at a very high pace [28].

15.6 CHALLENGES IN SOCIAL NETWORK ANALYSIS

Global network for sharing data and information is increased with the rise and development of internet and WWW. The easy use and accessibility features of internet affect the lives of users to an extent where users can access or share information globally from anywhere and anytime. Social networks are changing by joining of new members in the network; some existing members may leave the network or join the other groups in the networks. So, the social networks have dynamic nature that changes with time. Many new interesting areas of research have emerged because involvement of social networks in our life has increased day by day. Yet there are certain objections and issues related with social networks, some of which are listed as follows.

15.6.1 DYNAMIC DATA

Researchers need the dynamic data for their research work in SNA. However, the process of gathering dynamic data and analyzing it is actually a difficult task. Access to live data from social networking sites like Facebook is not available due to restrictions on the sites and some of the datasets shared by researchers on online web are static in nature [69].

15.6.2 IDENTIFICATION OF COMMUNITY

Identification of community is vital problem in SNA where the main motive is to identify the related groups of the members.

15.6.3 SPAM AND ADVERTISEMENT DETECTION

Due to exponential rise in count of members on SNS, the production of data has also increased in which detection of irrelevant data or information and advertisement has become very difficult for the researchers [69].

15.6.4 SECURITY

Members on SNS want to interact in the secure platform where their privacy can be controlled and ensured. Some social networking sites are providing the privacy on the data and the content shared by the member on the sites. So, it makes access of online data difficult.

15.6.5 DESIGN

The designing of SNA tools to access the data from the social sites is become very difficult or challenging process due to continuously changing nature of data on social sites.

15.6.6 PERSONALIZATION

Sometime members of same community on social sites have different tastes and at that time SNA faces the challenge to recommend the products, friends and other types of data to the members.

15.6.7 HETEROGENEITY

The structure of data on social networking sites is heterogeneous in nature. The analysis of this diversified data becomes very challenging for the researchers. SNA needs the structured data for the performance. So, the researchers first arrange the heterogeneous form of data for the analysis, which becomes time-consuming task.

15.6.8 MISSING DATA

Sometimes on SNS some data is missing, which creates the problem for the researchers to analyze the data. So, missing of data on sites becomes the big challenges for SNA.

15.6.9 INCOMPLETE

Incomplete data on SNS is also the big problem faced by the researchers in SNA.

15.7 CONCLUSION

The paper discussed a vast variety of DM techniques applicable for analysis of online social networks. Best possible efforts have been put to cover maximum crucial related work done in this area ranging from supervised, semi-supervised and unsupervised techniques. The aspiration behind writing this paper is to shed some light over the cruciality of the analysis of the massive data that is generated every second. The in-depth analysis also helps in gaining insight about the market and business trends, customer response to a product, improving business strategies and facilitating improved decision-making by the organizations. The paper presents various applications of SNA like community detection, sentiment analysis, recommender system, topic detection and tracking. It is finally concluded with the research concerns and problems involved in examination of online social networks and detailed discussion over them will be a part of our future study.

REFERENCES

1. X. Li, F. Elasha, S. Shanbr, and D. Mba, "Remaining useful life prediction of rolling element bearings using supervised machine learning," *Energies*, vol. 12, no. 14, pp. 1–18, 2019. doi: 10.3390/en12142706.
2. F. Schneider, A. Feldmann, B. Krishnamurthy, and W. Willinger, "Understanding online social network usage from a network perspective," *Proc. ACM SIGCOMM Internet Meas. Conf. IMC*, pp. 35–48, 2009, doi: 10.1145/1644893.1644899.
3. N. A. R. Abd Al-Azim, T. F. Gharib, M. Hamdy, and Y. Afify, "Influence propagation in social networks: Interest-based community ranking model," *J. King Saud Univ. – Comput. Inf. Sci.*, vol. 34, no. 5, pp. 2231–2243, 2022, doi: 10.1016/j.jksuci.2020.08.004.

4. M. Adedoyin-Olowe, M. M. Gaber, and F. Stahl, "A survey of data mining techniques for social media analysis," 2013, doi: 10.46298/jdmdh.5.
5. R. Kaur, and S. Singh, "A survey of data mining and social network analysis based anomaly detection techniques," *Egypt. Inform. J.*, vol. 17, no. 2, pp. 199–216, 2016. doi: 10.1016/j.eij.2015.11.004.
6. F. Ghareh, and M. Saniee, "A survey of data mining techniques for steganalysis," *Recent Adv. Steganography*, 2012, doi: 10.5772/53989.
7. H. Tankovska, "• Most used social media 2021 | Statista," Jan. 2021. https://www. statista.com/statistics/272014/global-social-networks-ranked-by-number-of-users/ (accessed Jun. 23, 2021).
8. H. Tankovska, "• Most used social media 2021 | Statista," Jan. 2021.
9. D. Elangovan, V. Subedha, R. Sathishkumar, and V. D. Ambeth kumar, "A survey: Data mining techniques for social media analysis," In International Conference for Phoenixes on Emerging Current Trends in Engineering and Management (PECTEAM 2018), pp. 109–115. Atlantis Press, 2018, vol. 142, no. Pecteam, 2018, doi: 10.2991/pecteam-18.2018.19.
10. J. Kim, and M. Hastak, "Social network analysis: Characteristics of online social networks after a disaster," *Int. J. Inf. Manage*, vol. 38, no. 1, pp. 86–96, 2018. doi: 10.1016/j.ijinfomgt.2017.08.003.
11. M. Mincer, and E. Niewiadomska-Szynkiewicz, "Application of social network analysis to the investigation of interpersonal connections," *J. Telecommun. Inf. Technol.*, vol. 2012, no. 2, pp. 83–91, 2012.
12. C. Palazuelos, D. García-Saiz, and M. Zorrilla, "Social network analysis and data mining: An application to the e-learning context," *Lect. Notes Comput. Sci. (Including Subser. Lect. Notes Artif. Intell. Lect. Notes Bioinformatics)*, vol. 8083, pp. 651–660, 2013. doi: 10.1007/978-3-642-40495-5_65.
13. E. Otte, and R. Rousseau, "Social network analysis: A powerful strategy, also for the information sciences," *J. Inf. Sci*, vol. 28, no. 6, pp. 441–453, 2002. doi: 10.1177/016555150202800601.
14. U. Can, and B. Alatas, "A new direction in social network analysis: Online social network analysis problems and applications," *Phys. A Stat. Mech. Its Appl.*, vol. 535, p. 122372, 2019. doi: 10.1016/j.physa.2019.122372.
15. A. Bermingham, M. Conway, L. McInerney, N. O'Hare, and A. F. Smeaton, "Combining social network analysis and sentiment analysis to explore the potential for online radicalisation," *Proc. 2009 Int. Conf. Adv. Soc. Netw. Anal. Mining, ASONAM 2009*, no. August 2014, pp. 231–236, 2009, doi: 10.1109/ASONAM.2009.31.
16. S. Tabassum, F. S. F. Pereira, S. Fernandes, and J. Gama, "Social network analysis: An overview," *Wiley Interdiscip. Rev. Data Min. Knowl. Discov.*, vol. 8, no. 5, 2018. doi: 10.1002/widm.1256.
17. H. A. Khanday, R. Hashmy, and M. April, "Exploring different aspects of social network," *IJETTCS*, vol. 4, no. 2, pp. 121–125, 2015.
18. M. S. Granovetter, "The strength of weak ties," *Inequal. Read*, vol. 78, no. 6, pp. 589–593, 2019. doi: 10.4324/9780429494468-61.
19. D. Liben-nowell, and A. C. Smith, "An Algorithmic Approach to Social Networks," *Language (Baltimore)*, 2005.
20. C. Faloutsos, "Social network data analytics," *Soc. Netw. Data Anal.*, no. March 2011, 2011, doi: 10.1007/978-1-4419-8462-3.
21. D. J. Watts', and S. H. Strogatz, "Collective dynamics of 'small-world' networks," *Nature*, vol. 393, p. 143, 1998. doi: 10.34277/1458-000-012-010.
22. S. Pandit, D. H. Chau, S. Wang, and C. Faloutsos, "NetProbe: A fast and scalable system for fraud detection in online auction networks," *Int. World Wide Web Conf. Comm.*, vol. 50, no. 3, 2007.

23. D. J. Watts, P. S. Dodds, and M. E. J. Newman, "Identity and search in social networks," *Science (80-.)*, vol. 296, no. 5571, pp. 1302–1305, 2002. doi: 10.1126/science. 1070120.

24. D. L. Hansen, B. Shneiderman, and M. A. Smith, "Calculating and visualizing network metrics," *Anal. Soc. Media Networks with NodeXL*, pp. 69–78. 2011. doi: 10.1016/ b978-0-12-382229-1.00005-9.

25. G. Plickert, R. R. Côté, and B. Wellman, "It's not who you know, it's how you know them: Who exchanges what with whom?" *Soc. Netw.*, vol. 29, no. 3, pp. 405–429, 2007. doi: 10.1016/j.socnet.2007.01.007.

26. J. H. Ward, "Hierarchical grouping to optimize an objective function," *J. Am. Stat. Assoc.*, vol. 58, no. 301, pp. 236–244, 1963. doi: 10.1080/01621459.1963.10500845.

27. J. M. Kleinberg, "LA Dalmatian islands," no. May 1997, 1997, [Online]. Available: www.harvard.edu

28. C. C. Aggarwal, "Social network data analytics," *Soc. Netw. Data Anal.*, pp. 1–15. 2011. doi: 10.1007/978-1-4419-8462-3.

29. J. Fumanal-Idocin, A. Alonso-Betanzos, O. Cordón, H. Bustince, and M. Minárová, "Community detection and social network analysis based on the Italian wars of the 15th century," *Futur. Gener. Comput. Syst.*, vol. 113, pp. 25–40, 2020. doi: 10.1016/ j.future.2020.06.030.

30. V. D. Blondel, J. L. Guillaume, R. Lambiotte, and E. Lefebvre, "Fast unfolding of communities in large networks," *J. Stat. Mech. Theory Exp.*, vol. 2008, no. 10, 2008. doi: 10.1088/1742-5468/2008/10/P10008.

31. Y. Zhang, E. Levina, and J. Zhu, "Community detection in networks with node features," *Electron. J. Stat*, vol. 10, no. 2, pp. 3153–3178, 2016. doi: 10.1214/16-EJS1206.

32. J. Yang, and J. Leskovec, "Overlapping community detection at scale: A nonnegative matrix factorization approach," *WSDM 2013 - Proc. 6th ACM Int. Conf. Web Search Data Min.*, pp. 587–596, 2013, doi: 10.1145/2433396.2433471.

33. D. Parthasarathy, D. Shah, and T. Zaman, "Leaders, Followers, and Community Detection," 2010, [Online]. Available: http://arxiv.org/abs/1011.0774

34. F. O. Isinkaye, Y. O. Folajimi, and B. A. Ojokoh, "Recommendation systems: Principles, methods and evaluation," *Egypt. Inf. J.*, vol. 16, no. 3, pp. 261–273, 2015. doi: 10.1016/ j.eij.2015.06.005.

35. M. V. Murali, T. G. Vishnu, and N. Victor, "A Collaborative Filtering based Recommender System for Suggesting New Trends in Any Domain of Research," *2019 5th Int. Conf. Adv. Comput. Commun. Syst. ICACCS 2019*, pp. 550–553, 2019, doi: 10.1109/ICACCS.2019.8728409.

36. K. Seyerlehner, G. Widmer, M. Schedl, and P. Knees, "Automatic music tag classification based on block-level features," *Proc. 7th Sound Music Comput. Conf. SMC 2010*, no. May, p. 13, 2010.

37. N. Dehak, P. J. Kenny, R. Dehak, P. Dumouchel, and P. Ouellet, "Dehak, kenny_front-end factor analysis for speaker verification.pdf," *IEEE Trans. Audio Speech Lang. Process.*, vol. 19, no. 4, pp. 788–798, 2011.

38. T. F. Gonzalez, *Handbook of Approximation Algorithms and Metaheuristics* (pp. 1–1432), 2007. doi: 10.1201/9781420010749.

39. Y. Deldjoo, M. Schedl, and M. Elahi, "Movie genome recommender: A novel recommender system based on multimedia content," *Proc. – Int. Work. Content-Based Multimed. Index.*, vol. 2019–Sept, pp. 1–4, 2019. doi: 10.1109/CBMI.2019.8877452.

40. J. Golbeck, and M. Rothstein, "Linking social networks on the web with FOAF: A semantic web case study," *Proc. Natl. Conf. Artif. Intell.*, vol. 2, pp. 1138–1143, 2008.

41. D. Murthy, A. Gross, A. Takata, and S. Bond, "Evaluation and development of data mining tools for social network analysis," *Mining Social Networks and Security Informatics* (pp. 183–202), 2013. doi: 10.1007/978-94-007-6359-3_10.

42. R. Gopikaramanan, T. Rameshkumar, B. Senthil Kumaran, and G. Ilangovan, "Novel control methodology for H-bridge cascaded multi-level converter using predictive control methodology," *Glob. J. Pure Appl.* Math, vol. 11, no. 5. 2015.

43. E. Marrese-Taylor, J. D. Velásquez, F. Bravo-Marquez, and Y. Matsuo, "Identifying customer preferences about tourism products using an aspect-based opinion mining approach," *Procedia Comput. Sci.*, vol. 22, pp. 182–191, 2013. doi: 10.1016/j.procs.2013.09.094.

44. E. Marrese-Taylor, J. D. Velásquez, and F. Bravo-Marquez, "A novel deterministic approach for aspect-based opinion mining in tourism products reviews," *Expert Syst. Appl*, vol. 41, no. 17, pp. 7764–7775, 2014. doi: 10.1016/j.eswa.2014.05.045.

45. M. Miller, S.-L. Lynn, and M. C. James, "Birds of a feather: Homophily in social networks," *Annu. Rev. Sociol.*, vol. 27, pp. 415–444, 2001.

46. G. Deffuant, D. Neau, F. Amblard, and G. Weisbuch, "Mixing beliefs among interacting agents," *Adv. Complex Syst.*, vol. 03, no. 01n04, pp. 87–98, 2000. doi: 10.1142/s0219525900000078.

47. M. Daszykowski, and B. Walczak, "Density-based clustering methods," *Compr. Chemom*, vol. 2, pp. 635–654, 2009. doi: 10.1016/B978-044452701-1.00067-3.

48. E. E. Alraddadi, S. M. Allen, G. B. Colombo, and R. M. Whitaker, "The role of homophily in opinion formation among mobile agents," *J. Inf. Telecommun*, vol. 4, no. 4, pp. 504–523, 2020. doi: 10.1080/24751839.2020.1772614.

49. T. H. A. Soliman, M. A. Elmasry, A. R. Hedar, and M. M. Doss, "Utilizing support vector machines in mining online customer reviews," *2012 22nd Int. Conf. Comput. Theory Appl. ICCTA 2012*, no. October, pp. 192–196, 2012, doi: 10.1109/ICCTA.2012.6523568.

50. S. Rana, and A. Singh, "Comparative analysis of sentiment orientation using SVM and Naive Bayes techniques," *Proc. 2016 2nd Int. Conf. Next Gener. Comput. Technol. NGCT 2016*, no. October, pp. 106–111, 2017, doi: 10.1109/NGCT.2016.7877399.

51. A. F. Hayes, "Introduction to Mediation, Moderation, and Conditional Process Analysis." https://books.google.co.in/books?hl=en&lr=&id=8ZM6DwAAQBAJ&oi=fnd&pg=PP1&ots=21AaoP_lZG&sig=cgiZwFllHbzVPrR06hcl2gKImcU&redir_esc=y#v=onepage&q&f=false (accessed Jun. 23, 2021).

52. D. Gavilan, M. Avello, and G. Martinez-Navarro, "The influence of online ratings and reviews on hotel booking consideration," *Tour. Manage.*, vol. 66, pp. 53–61, 2018. doi: 10.1016/j.tourman.2017.10.018.

53. Y. Lu, C. X. Zhai, and N. Sundaresan, "Rated aspect summarization of short comments," *WWW'09 - Proc. 18th Int. World Wide Web Conf.*, pp. 131–140, 2009, doi: 10.1145/1526709.1526728.

54. H. Wang, Y. Lu, and C. Zhai, "Latent aspect rating analysis on review text data: A rating regression approach," *Proc. ACM SIGKDD Int. Conf. Knowl. Discov. Data Min.*, pp. 783–792, 2010, doi: 10.1145/1835804.1835903.

55. C. Biemann, "Chinese whispers – An efficient graph clustering algorithm and its application to natural language processing problems," *Proc. TextGraphs 1st Work. Graph-Based Methods Nat. Lang. Process.*, no. June, pp. 73–80, 2020.

56. A. W. Castleman and Kh. Bowen, "Clusters: Structure, energetics, and dynamics of intermediate states of matter," *J. Phys. Chem.*, vol. 100, no. 31, pp. 12911–12944, 1996.

57. D. Freitag, "Towards unsupervised whole-corus tagging," *ACL Anthol.*, pp. 357–363, 2004.

58. C. Biemann, "Unsupervised part-of-speech tagging in the large," *Res. Lang. Comput.*, vol. 7, no. 2, pp. 101–135, 2009. doi: 10.1007/s11168-010-9067-9.

59. G. Fiumara, A. Celesti, A. Galletta, L. Carnevale, and M. Villari, "Applying artificial intelligence in healthcare social networks to identity critical issues in patients' posts," *Heal. 2018 - 11th Int. Conf. Heal. Informatics, Proceedings; Part 11th Int. Jt. Conf. Biomed. Eng. Syst. Technol. BIOSTEC 2018*, vol. 5, no. Healthinf, pp. 680–687, 2018, doi: 10.5220/0006750606800687.

60. L. Carnevale, A. Celesti, G. Fiumara, A. Galletta, and M. Villari, "Investigating classification supervised learning approaches for the identification of critical patients' posts in a healthcare social network," *Appl. Soft Comput. J.*, vol. 90, p. 106155, 2020. doi: 10.1016/j.asoc.2020.106155.

61. J. Allan, J. Carbonell, G. Doddington, J. Yamron, Y. Yang, and D. Systems, "Topic detection and tracking pilot study final report," *DARPA Broadcast News Transcr. Understanding. Workshop*, 1998.

62. S. Petrović, M. Osborne, and V. Lavrenko, "Streaming first story detection with application to twitter," *NAACL HLT 2010 - Hum. Lang. Technol. 2010 Annu. Conf. North Am. Chapter Assoc. Comput. Linguist. Proc. Main Conf.*, no. June, pp. 181–189, 2010.

63. M. Osborne, S. Petrovic, and R. McCreadie, "Bieber no more: First story detection using twitter and wikipedia," *Redirect. Subscribe. Ru.*, pp. 16–76, 2012.

64. A. Shiri, "Introduction to modern information retrieval (2nd edition)," *Libr. Rev*, vol. 53, no. 9, pp. 462–463, 2004. doi: 10.1108/00242530410565256.

65. S. Phuvipadawat, and T. Murata, "Breaking news detection and tracking in Twitter," *Proc. - 2010 IEEE/WIC/ACM Int. Conf. Web Intell. Intell. Agent Technol. - Work. WI-IAT 2010*, pp. 120–123, 2010, doi: 10.1109/WI-IAT.2010.205.

66 A. Mansour, C. Jutten, and I. Lis, "Kurtosis: definition and properties," *FUSION'98 International Conference*, vol. 17, no. August, pp. 40–46, 1998.

67. G. Kumaran, and J. Allan, "Text classification and named entities for new event detection," *Proc. Sheff. SIGIR – Twenty-Seventh Annu. Int. ACM SIGIR Conf. Res. Dev. Inf. Retr.*, pp. 297–304, 2004, doi: 10.1145/1008992.1009044.

68. H. Becker, M. Naaman, and L. Gravano, "Beyond trending topics: Real-world event identification on twitter," *ICWSM*, pp. 1–17, 2011, [Online].

69. P. Wadhwa, and M. P. S. Bhatia, "Social networks analysis: Trends, techniques and future prospects," *IET Conf. Publ.*, vol. 2012, no. CP652, pp. 1–6, 2012, doi: 10.1049/cp.2012.2481.

Index